America and the Arab States:
An ...

AMERICA AND THE WORLD

EDITOR: Robert A. Divine

The United States and Russia

JOHN GADDIS

From Revolution to Rapprochement:
The United States and Great Britain, 1783–1900

CHARLES S. CAMPBELL

America's Response to China:
An Interpretative History of Sino-American Relations

WARREN I. COHEN

The Cuban Policy of the United States:
A Brief History

LESTER LANGLEY

The Troubled Encounter:
The United States and Japan

CHARLES E. NEU

America and the Arab States:
An Uneasy Encounter

ROBERT W. STOOKEY

Mexico and the United States, 1821–1973:
Conflict and Coexistence

KARL M. SCHMITT

The United States and England in
The Twentieth Century

THEODORE WILSON

The Uncertain Friendship:
American-French Diplomatic Relations Through the Cold War

MARVIN ZAHNISER

America and the Arab States:
An Uneasy Encounter

ROBERT W. STOOKEY

Center for Middle Eastern Studies
The University of Texas at Austin

John Wiley & Sons, Inc.
New York • London • Sydney • Toronto

Cover design by Angie Lee

Library of Congress Cataloging in Publication Data:

Stookey, Robert W   1917–
  America and the Arab States.

  (America and the world)
  Bibliography: p.
  Includes index.
    1.   United States—Foreign relations—Arab
countries.   2.   Arab countries—Foreign relations—
United States.   I.   Title.

DS63.2.U5S76   327.73'017'4927   75-25874
ISBN 0-471-82975-7
ISBN 0-471-82976-5 pbk.

Printed in the United States of America
10 9 8 7 6 5 4 3 2 1

Foreword

Events in the fall of 1973 made the American people suddenly aware of the importance of the Arab world to their well-being. The October War led to a brief but intense crisis with the Soviet Union, highlighted by a worldwide alert of American military forces, and a longer and more agonizing energy crunch created by the five-month oil embargo imposed by the Arab producers. People who had viewed the Middle East as a remote corner of the globe now realized how important this volatile area could be to American security and prosperity. Yet the United States had experienced diplomatic and commercial contact with the Arab world for nearly two centuries, engaging in an inconclusive war with the Barbary pirates, sending out a dedicated band of missionaries and educators to Arab lands, and entering a little belatedly into the scramble for Middle Eastern petroleum. The historic American ties with the Arab peoples, however, conflicted with the anti-imperialist cast of the independent states that emerged after World War II. The prevailing American sympathy for the Jews who survived Hitler's holocaust created an even greater strain with the Arab nations as the United States aligned itself with the new country of Israel in 1948 and gradually became her chief external supporter.

Robert Stookey brings both diplomatic and scholarly experience to bear on his analysis of America's troubled relations with the Arab states. His years as a foreign service officer have imbued him with an awareness of the distorting impact of American sympathy for Israel on Middle Eastern policy; his study of the cultural and political behavior of the Arab peoples has conditioned him to see world events through their eyes. As a result, he writes critically of modern United States policy in the Middle East, regretting both the Cold War mentality that mistook legitimate Arab nationalism for Communist manipulation and the enduring commitment to Israel that inevitably antagonized the Arab states. His informed, analytical approach provides an effective counterweight to the prevailing national biases and offers the reader an opportunity to see the Middle East and its foreign policy dilemmas from a fresh perspective.

This book is one in a series of volumes tracing the history of American foreign policy toward the nations with which the United States has had significant relations over a long period of time. By stressing the continuity of diplomatic themes through the decades, each author seeks to identify the distinctive character of America's international relationships. I hope that this approach not only will enable readers to understand more deeply the diplomatic history of their nation but will make them aware that past events and patterns of behavior exert a continuous influence on American foreign *policy.*

ROBERT A. DIVINE

Preface

Before October 1973 the notion that small, militarily feeble, underdeveloped countries could choose and pursue courses of action seriously affecting the economic well-being and the safety of all Americans would have appeared bizarre. In that month the conservative rulers of several Arab states, in reprisal for United States actions they considered hostile to vital Arab interests, suspended the shipment of petroleum that had, gradually and imperceptibly, become necessary to the smooth functioning of the American economy. A local war concurrently undertaken by other Arab countries of strikingly different political orientation, in defense of those same Arab interests, engaged the prestige and moral commitments of the United States and the Soviet Union and brought the two superpowers into a confrontation fraught with the danger of nuclear war. America's European allies, with a few exceptions, hastened to disassociate themselves from, and even to condemn, the United States actions, and severe strain was placed on the solidarity of the Atlantic alliance. United States policy, it would seem, had not accurately assessed the nature and importance of American interests in the Arab states or made adequate provision to safeguard them. Major aspects of American relations with the Arab countries had been subsumed under broad principles assumed to be universally applicable. Relatively small groups of specialists within the bureaucracy, the press, and the American academic community had raised and studied the question what, in political terms, it means to be Arab and what, if any, unique considerations must enter into effective policy toward the Arab states specifically because they are Arab. The 1973 crisis left no doubt of the importance of the question.

I believe that many of the answers are deeply rooted in the Arab national experience and in a relatively long historical interaction on various planes between Arab and American, which has seldom been without some degree of tension. An awareness of this background helps to show how the present uneasiness in Arab-American relations arose. The relationship, whether cordial or contentious, will be of inescapable moment to the well-being of the United States during the coming decade or two. Such insights as the past can provide are certainly pertinent to the effort to ensure that the encounter develops toward mutual confidence and constructive cooperation.

The Arab world as considered here consists of lands whose peoples speak Arabic as their native tongue, share a common historical heritage, and live under sovereign governments symbolically united by membership in the League of Arab States.[1] Such a definition can be made without qualification only since December 1972, when Great Britain relinquished her tutelage of the Arab shaikhdoms in the Persian Gulf, which thereupon became independent entities; no territory where Arabs form a majority now remains under foreign control.

The Arab world is remarkably diverse. It includes countries with the highest per capita income known, and one that ranks among the five most poverty-stricken and undeveloped countries on earth. Its land varies between vast deserts inhospitable to settled human life and fertile, well-watered regions with bright promise of future expansion in production of food and fiber. Some Arabs are unlettered nomads; others are as highly educated, as sophisticated in commerce, industry, administration, and science as men anywhere. Arab political institutions are no less heterogeneous, ranging from traditional, patriarchal forms, to limited monarchy and liberal democracy, to regimes in which the state closely directs the major social, economic, and political processes. The broad spectrum of sociopolitical outlook, which breeds inter-Arab animosity and strife, is a complicating factor for an outside power, such as the United States, in dealing with the Arab countries. No

---

1. Current membership is: Algeria, Bahrain, Egypt, Jordan, Iraq, Kuwait, Lebanon, Libya, Morocco, Oman, Qatar, Saudi Arabia, Sudan, Syria, Tunisia, United Arab Emirates, Yemem Arab Republic, and People's Democratic Republic of Yemen.

single coordinated policy can be formulated and applied across the board to them all. Conversely, no successful policy toward an individual Arab state can disregard the sentiments and interests of the others. Disunited as the Arabs often appear, they hold in common certain attitudes that determine political behavior, among them the aversion to outside pressure or impingement on any part of the Arab territorial homeland.

The Arab homeland forms a broad region extending from the Atlantic to Iran, discontinuous only by the presence of the Israeli enclave. No Arab country is landlocked, and all except Lebanon extend into the vast arid region comprising the Sahara, Arabian, and Syrian deserts. Four subregions can be conveniently distinguished.

1. The Arabian Peninsula, a major portion of which is occupied by the Kingdom of Saudi Arabia, formed by the unification in the 1930s of the Asir and Hijaz provinces on the Red Sea coast, the central plateau of Nejd, and the Eastern Province of al-Hasa, on the Persian Gulf (which the Arabs call the Arabian Gulf). The state of Kuwait lies in the northeastern corner of the Peninsula; Bahrain is an archipelago to the southeast, and Qatar a peninsula jutting northward into the Gulf. Further east, the Trucial Coast states (Abu Dhabi, Sharjah, Dubai, 'Ajman, Ras al-Khaimah, Umm al-Qaywain, and Fujairah) have combined as the United Arab Emirates. The Sultanate of Oman occupies the northern segment of the Indian Ocean coastal plain and the adjacent range of mountains shielded from Saudi Arabia by the barren sands of the Empty Quarter. The Sultanate's southern province of Dhofar adjoins the People's Democratic Republic of Yemen, formerly the Aden Colony and Protectorates, extending almost to the strait of Bab al-Mandeb, the gateway to the Red Sea. The Yemen Arab Republic occupies the Red Sea coastal plain and the mountains inland, north to the Saudi Arabian border.

2. The Fertile Crescent forms an arc of productive lands skirting the northern reaches of the Syrian Desert. Iraq, its eastern segment, was formerly known as Mesopotamia—the "land between the rivers"—as the rivers Tigris and Euphrates flow into it from Turkey, combine as the Shatt al-'Arab, and discharge into the Persian Gulf. To the west, geographic Syria continues the arc westward to the Mediterranean and south to the Sinai Peninsula. Politically, the region is currently distributed among the republics of Syria and Lebanon, the Hashemite Kingdom of Jordan, and Palestine, including Israel.

3. The lower reaches of the Nile Valley and the great river's delta support the settled population of Egypt. Southward, upstream, the Sudan forms

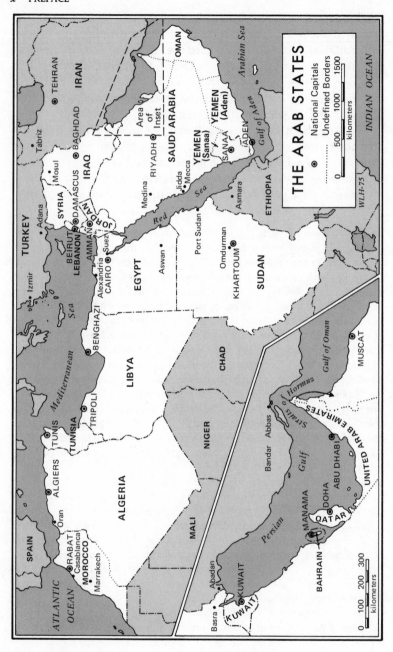

THE ARAB STATES

National Capitals
Undefined Borders

kilometers
0   500   1000   1500

WLH-75

a transition zone, both climatic and demographic, between the desert and sub-Saharan Africa. Egypt's Western Desert continues westward through the broad, thinly peopled, arid expanse of Libya.

4. The Maghreb—the "land of the setting sun"—is the North African region composed of the modern republics of Tunisia and Algeria and the Kingdom of Morocco. All share a legacy of French tutelage and a mixed Arab-Berber culture.

The term "Arab" refers, of course, to language and culture, not to race. Present-day Arabs are the descendents of numerous peoples whose ancient cultures contributed significantly to the development of Western civilization, among them Sumerians, Akkadians, Babylonians, Assyrians, Aramaeans, Phoenicians, Canaanites and Egyptians. Their Arabization resulted from the rise of Islam in the seventh century and the rapid conquest, under the proselytizing leadership of ethnic Arabs from the Hijaz and Yemen, of a vast empire that briefly touched the Loire in France to the west and China to the east. Islam and Arab culture were related but distinct things. The Arabs' religion outreached their language and customs. Persia (modern Iran), with its proud and already ancient civilization, embraced Islam but remained Persian in language and tradition, a permanent barrier to the eastward extension of Arabism. Christendom long held Anatolia (Asia Minor) against Islam; when, at length, it was conquered and converted, it received Turkish, not Arab, culture. For several centuries southern Spain shared a luminous Islamic civilization with North Africa, but a resurgent Christendom completed the reconquest of Iberia in the same year that its mariners landed in the New World. The Saharan wilderness and the swamps of the White Nile set natural barriers to the southward movement of Islam and its missionaries. Even within these confines Arabization was by no means total. Some populations adopted Islam but preserved their own folkways and separate ethnic identity; the Berbers of the Maghreb and the Kurds of Iraq remain to this day imperfectly assimilated to Arab culture. Other communities adopted Arabic as their native language but resisted conversion to the new religion; the Copts of Egypt and the communicants of Uniate, Orthodox, and other Christian churches in geographic Syria are important components of the population. Finally, Islam itself bred heterodoxies, and the Alawites of Syria, the Shi'a of Iraq, and the Druze of Lebanon and Syria are elements distinct from the Sunni, or orthodox, Muslim majority.

Islam addressed itself to all aspects of society, including the political and, in theory, the body of Muslims comprised a single state as well as a religious community. Historical reality conformed only briefly to the ideal, however, and the Arab Empire began to break up. Morocco became independent at the end of the Umayyad century. Under the Abbasids, ruling from Baghdad, South Arabia passed beyond effective central control, and a rival, heterodox caliphate, the Fatimids, arose in Egypt. During the Crusades, rule over the state passed from Arab hands into those of the Kurdish Ayyubids and later of the Ottoman Turks who, at the time of the European Renaissance, revivified Islam as a world power.

By the late eighteenth century, when some Americans began to concern themselves with the Middle East and North Africa, the Ottoman state had begun to decay. As caliph, its sovereign nevertheless claimed spiritual authority over all Muslims; as sultan, he asserted political sovereignty over a still extensive territory in Europe, Africa, and Asia, including all the Arab lands except Morocco. His bureaucracy, however, no longer ruled the remoter territories directly. The Barbary states of North Africa—Algiers, Tunis, and Tripoli—and the Mamelukes in Egypt recognized the suzerainty of Constantinople and paid tribute to the sultan, but otherwise acted as independent states. The Arabian Peninsula was left largely to its own devices except for the Hijaz, where the caliphs had responsibility for safeguarding the pilgrimage to the holy cities of Mecca and Medina, and later for Yemen, which the Turks occupied and defended against British encroachment from Aden. Only the Fertile Crescent was under close Ottoman administration. Iraq was distributed among the vilayets (provinces) of Baghdad, Basra, and Mosul. Syria, although possessing a general cultural unity, was similarly divided into three vilayets; furthermore, certain of its administrative districts—sanjaks—had specially tailored regimes and were to play individual historical roles: the Sanjak of Mount Lebanon, whose Christian inhabitants had long-standing ties with France and the Roman Catholic Church; the Sanjak of Jerusalem, sacred to Judaism and Christianity as well as Islam; and the Sanjak of Alexandretta (Turkish Iskenderun), which contained a sizable Turkish minority.

European colonial powers, during the century and one half of their ascendancy, attained varying degrees of control over most of the Arab world. American cultural and commercial interests developed largely on private initiative; affairs relating to Arab territories presented themselves to American officials as issues between the United States and the European powers or (until World War I) Turkey, not usually as United States-Arab matters. Only after World War II was the principle established that the United States had distinct geopolitical and economic interests of its own in the—now fully independent—Arab states. American policy toward the Arab countries, strictly speaking, thus has a relatively brief history. That it has fallen short of some of its aims will be apparent to readers of this book. If the work contributes to a wider appreciation of the gravity, complexity, intractability, and uniqueness of the problems confronting those responsible for the conduct of United States relations with the Arab states, and thus to informed discussion of our policies, my purpose will have been well served.

I am indebted to Robert A. Divine, editor of the series in which this book appears, for many constructive comments and suggestions. The general concept of the work owes much to Dr. Carl Leiden of the University of Texas, whose perceptive reading of the manuscript furthermore pointed the way to numerous improvements. In a work addressing itself to the many facets of American relations with eighteen countries over two centuries of time, some errors no doubt have gone undetected, and its judgments may not convince every reader; these are my responsibility.

Robert W. Stookey

Contents

CHAPTER I

The Origin and Growth of American Interests

During the first century and a half of its independence, the United States developed from a precarious and disunited association of communities fringing the western shore of the Atlantic to unquestioned status as a great power that had possessed and occupied a continent, built an unmatched industrial economy, and demonstrated its prowess in global war. The same span of time witnessed the inception and growth among the Arabic-speaking peoples of the Islamic world of a sentiment of common and distinct identity, based primarily on language, secondarily on religion. Within boundaries established by Ottoman administrative convenience, by the outcome of local strife, and later by accommodation among competing European imperialisms, territories were demarcated that were to become, after varying periods of foreign tutelage, Arab national states. United States government action and presence followed cautiously, even reluctantly, into these and other remote lands, in the wake of bolder American commercial and cultural enterprise. The substantial network of relationships between the Arab peoples and the United States that had come into being by the end of World War I was constructed almost exclusively on private initiative, although the latter gradually came to expect and demand government intervention in behalf of its freedom of operation and protection of its material assets abroad.

EARLY CONTACTS WITH NORTH AFRICA AND THE ARAB EAST

The restriction of the thirteen Colonies' maritime trade by Britain's mercantilist policy had contributed greatly to their revolt.

1

The well-being, even the survival, of the newly independent United States appeared to depend on the revival of foreign commerce, which the war for independence had brought nearly to a halt. Alexander Hamilton, arguing for a strong central government, contended that a weak nation is exposed to depredations on its property and forfeits even the privilege of neutrality in wars among other states. The strength of governments derives from their revenues which, in the American situation, could not be raised domestically in adequate volume. The genius of the American people would ill brook the "inquisitive and peremptory spirit" of excise taxes; taxes on farm land and dwellings were unproductive as well as unwelcome, while personal property was too "precarious and invisible" to be assessed directly.[1] Imposts on foreign trade were the alternative, and a cardinal principle of American policy in the early decades was the stimulation of external commerce. There were grave obstacles. The exclusivist policies of the European monarchies closed off access to their West Indies colonies and, across the Atlantic, a hostile Britain had to be bypassed either to the north through the Baltic or to the south into the Mediterranean. In the latter case, American trade with southern Europe, North Africa, the Levant, and Turkey depended on the sufferance of the Barbary states, which held the power to permit or deny passage of merchant shipping through the Gates of Hercules.

Although the four Barbary powers had already entered the period of decline from their seventeenth-century heyday that was to lead to European colonization, they still constituted a serious threat to the commerce of the smaller trading nations. Morocco alone of them was fully independent of the Ottoman Empire. The reign of Sīdī Muḥammad ibn 'Abdullah (1757–1790) restored some domestic order and tranquility following three decades of dynastic strife, anarchy, and territorial encroachment by Portugal and Spain; nevertheless, the area under the monarch's effective control was being progressively diminished by the movement of Berber tribesmen from the mountains onto the plain and by the pressure of nomads against the settled lands. The three regencies to the east had been founded in the sixteenth century by Turkish

---

[1] *The Federalist,* Nos. 11 and 12.

seafarers who played the role both of Ottoman naval forces and of corsairs preying on Christian shipping in the Mediterranean. Tunis, with its relatively strong cultural traditions, had absorbed the Turkish immigrants, as well as perhaps 80,000 Moors fleeing the Spanish inquisition, and its rulers had become a well-naturalized hereditary royal house. Algiers and Tripoli, by contrast, remained under the rule of Turkish sailors and janissaries, who elevated one of their number to absolute power as, respectively, Dey or Pasha, subject to confirmation by the Sublime Porte. Despite the latter's suzerainty, the three regencies dealt directly and independently with the European powers.

As self-conscious Muslim societies, the Barbary states regarded the condition of war as the normal one between themselves and the Christian nations, except where specific treaties provided a provisional basis for peaceful intercourse. In the absence of treaties European shipping was a legitimate object of seizure by force of arms; the proceeds of ships and cargo taken as prizes and the ransoming of crews taken captive and enslaved had become the primary economic base of Algiers and Tripoli, important to Tunis, and of some significance to Morocco, although more conventional commercial exchanges proceeded as well. Preoccupied by their ambitions and mutual rivalries in Europe and elsewhere, the Western powers took no combined action against piracy. They treated individually with the Barbary states, agreeing to treaties of which usual features were the payment of tribute (peace, after all, was an economic disadvantage to the North Africans), substantial gifts on the accreditation of consuls, and regularizing the ransom of captives. As such treaties might occasionally be violated or denounced, a seafaring nation was well advised to supplement the diplomatic effort to protect its shipping with naval convoying and patrolling.

Under cover of the mother country's treaties, and provided with British Admiralty passes, the American colonies had conducted a lucrative trade with Barbary and with the southern European ports to which the corsairs controlled access. Thomas Jefferson estimated that North Africa received one sixth by value of American wheat and flour exports and a fourth of its dried or pickled fish; lumber, rum, beeswax, and onions were shipped to various Mediterranean destinations. Returning cargoes, valued in 1769 at £228,

682, included wines, salt, oil, and Morocco leather. The commerce engaged from 80 to 100 colonial vessels amounting to 20,000 tons and employing 1200 seamen. Within two weeks of the Declaration of Independence the Continental Congress faced a situation in which the termination of British protection left American shipping exposed to the mercies of the pirates. An *ad hoc* committee recommended that a provision be included in the treaty with France, then under preparation, to ensure French protection for American vessels. Commissioners John Adams and Benjamin Franklin proved unable to obtain such an undertaking, and an appeal to the Netherlands was equally fruitless. Beginning in 1779 the Congress commissioned its senior diplomatic representatives in Europe to negotiate treaties of amity and commerce with various European countries, the Ottoman Porte, and all the Barbary states. Franklin, Adams, Thomas Jefferson, John Jay, and David Humphreys were at various times responsible for the ensuing negotiations. Results were long delayed. Transatlantic communications were slow and uncertain; the Commissioners were not agreed on policy; the Congress was inexperienced, dilatory, impecunious, and of divided counsel.

The necessity for developing an effective policy to protect the Mediterranean trade threw into relief two currents of opinion regarding American foreign relations. While the goal of liberal trade arrangements and the principle of most-favored-nation treatment established by Congress as early as 1778 were not in dispute, the means to these ends were. As commissioner to treat with Barbary, Jefferson, who was later to lead a party profoundly suspicious of a naval force as an instrument likely to result in tyranny at home and political entanglement abroad, advocated determined war against the pirate states until treaties on equal terms were achieved. Payment of tribute he regarded as expensive, of doubtful efficacy, and inconsistent with the national honor. Adams, by contrast, considered the Mediterranean trade worth preserving at any cost short of war, and pressed for acceptance of terms analogous to those agreed to by the European states as a matter of convenience. He opposed any heroic but ill-advised unilateral use of force, which even the great maritime powers were not prepared to undertake. In the event, American policy utilized both approaches, alternatively or in combination, as empirical circumstances, instead of as doctrine, required.

The Commissioners' deliberate labors bore their first fruits in Morocco, as a result of the accommodating and enlightened attitude of that country's ruler. On February 20, 1778 Sīdī Muhammad specifically included the United States in a declaration of his intention to ensure free entry of the ships of certain countries into designated Moroccan ports and most-favored-nation treatment of their trade; he followed this up with an expression of interest in concluding a treaty with the American government. The latter had not yet managed to make positive response by October 1783 when, his patience overtaxed, the Sultan ordered the seizure of the United States ship *Betsey* and interned her at Tangier. Through the intervention of Spain, whose good offices were inspired by the unrealistic hope of persuading the United States to renounce navigation of the Mississippi, the ship was released in July 1785. Another year elapsed before Thomas Barclay, American Consul General at Paris, arrived as the Commissioners' agent to negotiate a treaty. The agreement, concluded with little difficulty, included provisions of a liberality that surprised the European consuls on the spot: partial extraterritorial status for American citizens, a shipwreck convention, no tribute, no holding of American seamen for ransom, and most-favored-nation treatment of United States trade. In addition the Sultan provided Barclay with mediatory letters to the rulers of the Barbary states to the east.

These gratifying arrangements were called into question upon the Sultan's demise in April 1790. His son, Yazīd, denounced Morocco's treaties with all Christian states except Britain. At the urgent recommendation of President Washington and of Jefferson, now Secretary of State, Congress appropriated $20,000 for the "repurchase" of the treaty. Yazīd and the American envoy selected for the negotiation both died before discussions could begin. The ensuing struggle for succession to the Moroccan throne culminated in 1795 with the accession of Suleimān II, with whom the 1786 treaty was reinstated, at the bargain price of $13,000, after a moment of tension resulting from the supply by American merchants of arms to Suleimān's rivals.

Algiers was at once the most powerful and the most aggressive of the Barbary states and, with British encouragement, concentrated particular effort against American shipping. In July 1785 the Algerians captured two American-flag vessels and enslaved their crews, totaling twenty-one men. John Lamb, American agent to negotiate peace with Algiers, then on the point of leaving for that capital, was authorized to treat for the release of the captives at $200 apiece. The Dey, however, fixed the per capita ransom at the exorbitant rate of $3000, and Lamb was obliged to leave Algiers empty-handed. Official and private efforts over the next several years to free the prisoners came to naught and, in 1790, Jefferson laid the Algerian problem before Congress, offering the alternatives of provision of sufficient funds to meet the Algerian demands or of the construction of a navy to enforce the United States will. Congress responded by authorizing $40,000 for the "purchase" of a treaty, $25,000 in annual tribute, and $40,000 for ransom of the captives. John Paul Jones and Thomas Barclay, successively commissioned to conduct the negotiations, both died before they could fulfill the mission, which at length devolved on David Humphreys, United States Minister to Portugal. His mission proved abortive. Meanwhile, a state of war between Algiers and Portugal, which had kept Algerian ships bottled up in the Mediterranean, was terminated in 1793, and Algerian armed vessels could extend their attacks on American shipping into the Atlantic. Eleven American ships were captured during October and November of 1793, and the number of prisoners reached 119. Congress was stirred to action and, after heated debate, authorized the construction of six frigates and ten smaller armed vessels, which were to become the nucleus of the United States Navy. At the same time, diplomatic efforts were continued and a second mission of Humphreys to Algiers resulted in a treaty costing the United States a total of $642,500, providing for an annual tribute of $21,600 in naval stores, a shipwreck convention, but no extraterritorial rights. The Senate's approval was so long in coming that the United States was forced to add the gift of a frigate in order to secure the Dey's ratification, which was given on November 28, 1795. This less than satisfactory arrangement at least permitted American trade some access to the Mediterranean and gave proof of the taxing power of the federal government under the Constitution.

Somewhat more favorable treaties, at more modest cost and without formal tribute, were negotiated with Tripoli and Tunis and ratified respectively in 1797 and 1799. At the turn of the nineteenth century, the United States thus had treaty relations with all four North African states. Mutual jealousies among the latter and renewed dynastic quarrels in Morocco unfortunately rendered these arrangements fragile at a time when the European wars, following on the French Revolution, were encouraging a recrudescence of corsair operations. Treaties with the United States were denounced and depredations made on American shipping in violation of those that remained in effect. The developing American navy, however, was a new and ultimately decisive factor. Its first venture into the Mediterranean was, admittedly, embarrassing. When, in 1800, Captain William Bainbridge in the frigate *George Washington* was sent to deliver the annual tribute to Algiers, his ship was commandeered to transport the Dey's tribute and his ambassador to the Ottoman Sultan. A larger American force was despatched the following year, and a Mediterranean squadron was maintained thereafter until 1818, except for the period of the 1812 War. Without recounting the events of the Barbary wars in detail we may recall that the commodores of the American squadron, in addition to their conventional naval functions of the convoy of merchant shipping, the display of American might, and operations against the territory and shipping of the enemy of the moment, were entrusted with broad powers to treat with the North African rulers, supplementing the labors of civilian diplomats in the area. The burning of the captured frigate *Philadelphia* in the harbor of Tripoli in February 1804 contributed to the growth of American patriotic legend, and the bizarre expedition of "General" William Eaton from Egypt to Derna was one early attempt to further United States objectives by political action to overthrow a foreign regime. The lasting significance of United States intercourse with the Barbary states, however, lies in the dogged and eventually successful endeavor to vindicate policies laid down by the Continental Congress as soon as it addressed itself to external affairs: untrammeled, peaceful trade for American citizens on the terms available to the most-favored nation; the treating with other nations on a basis of strict equality and reciprocity; forbearance from the enslavement of captured personnel, even in wartime; and the principle of assistance to, instead of the pillage of, distressed merchant ships. The principles acted on by the first six administrations under the Constitution pointed toward the policy later elaborated as the Open Door and contributed to the development of international law in the field of belligerent and neutral rights. After the Congress of Vienna the nations of Europe followed the American lead in dealing with North Africa on a basis more of rational order than expediency. If the abolition of its chief industry by Algiers, proclaimed on December 23, 1816, did not mark the final end of piracy in the Mediterranean, it nevertheless symbolized the decline to which America had contributed.

The quest for trading partners led American merchantmen to the opposite extremity of the Arab world. A Salem ship called at Mocha at least as early as 1798. The trade with Yemen in coffee, gum, and hides developed rapidly and, by outbidding British and other European traders previously established, Americans managed to capture the lion's share of the market. The federal government left the merchants largely to their own devices in this remote land and, aside from sending gifts to the Imam in 1805, made no effort to enter into official relations with Yemen's ruler. With the spread of disorder in the country and the decline of the port of Mocha the Red Sea trade lasted barely a half-century.

Somewhat closer relations were established with Sayyed Sa'īd ibn Sulṭān, ruler of Muscat and its extensive dependencies including Zanzibar and territories on the East African mainland. Although New England vessels had frequently traded for copal at Zanzibar, they did so at a disadvantage in the absence of treaty relations between Muscat and the United States. In 1827 an enterprising merchant, Edmund Roberts, after a disappointing call at Zanzibar in his ship *Mary Ann,* proceeded to Muscat and appealed directly to the Sultan. The latter received him cordially and suggested that his business would be facilitated by closer official relations between the two countries. Upon completing his voyage Roberts obtained, through the intermediary of his friend New Hampshire Senator Levi Woodbury, who fortuitously had been named President Jackson's Secretary of the Navy, appointment as agent to negotiate treaties of commerce and friendship with Muscat as well as Siam and Cochin-China. Traveling in the United States Navy sloop *Peacock* he reached Muscat in October 1833 and soon agreed with the Sultan on a satisfactory treaty including a shipwreck provision both liberal and prospectively opportune. Roberts returned the following year with the ratified treaty in the *Peacock,* which ran aground off the Oman coast and sustained an attack by Muscati pirates. Although the United States soon stationed a consul at Muscat, trade prospered only modestly. Muscat shortly entered a period of economic decline and domestic unrest. Between 1855 and 1913 only one American ship called at port of Muscat; Muscati dates were shipped to the United States in vessels of other flags. The consulate was finally closed in 1915.

In the eastern Mediterranean, to which the United States achieved secure access by virtue of its policy and action in Barbary, the commerce that flourished throughout the nineteenth century was primarily with Turkey, not with the Arab territories of Egypt and Syria. Here, stimulated in the first instance by the impulses of the pilgrim and the evangelist, American activity before World War I was channeled into educational, scientific, humanitarian, and technical enterprises, sometimes of considerable scale. The federal government played a minimal role in these activities, confined largely to ensuring to its citizens personal safety, security of their property, and the enjoyment of such rights as the nationals of the European countries possessed. Insofar as there can be said to have been an American policy in the area, it was, in our national fashion, subsumed under general moral principles universally applicable. There was no occasion to formulate an "Arab" policy. A major part of the skewed knowledge that the American public gleaned concerning the Arab peoples was disseminated by Protestant missionaries working among them and by the institutions in the United States that sponsored their labors.

THE PROTESTANT MISSIONS

The first generations of American colonists—stern, literal Calvinists believing firmly in predestination, reckoning as few the number of saved souls but confident of their own salvation—contemplated with some equanimity the fate of the doomed multitudes in the outer darkness. Jonathan Edwards and his successors, notably Samuel Hopkins, arrived at the gentler belief that God's saving grace through Christ's sacrifice was sufficient to encompass the whole of mankind, provided only that men accepted it of their free will. But to accept it men must know of it, and God manifestly demanded of the Christian that he take the gospel to the millions not only of heathen and pagans but of merely "nominal" Christians denied access to the scriptures by the barrier of sterile ritual. At the dawn of the nineteenth century the evangelization of the nations was furthermore perceived to be a matter of urgency. Study of the prophetic texts showed that the millenium of peace would precede, not follow on, Christ's second coming, and properly informed calculation demonstrated that the new era would begin in the year 1866. It would be ushered in by the fall of Antichrist, who was either the Pope, the Ottoman Sultan, or both. For God's will to be done the crumbling edifices of Islam and Catholicism had to be destroyed by conversion to evangelical Christianity and the dispersed Jews had to be repatriated to the Holy Land and brought to Christ. The conviction of personal responsibility for the salvation of one's fellow men produces Christian martyrs; it did so among the New Englanders of the earlier American Bible Belt, as one aspect of the nineteenth-century American mission endeavor.

The Congregationalists and Presbyterians who founded the American Board of Commissioners for Foreign Missions and elicited its charter from the General Association of Massachusetts in 1810 were no aberrant group of zealots: they were proven, successful leaders of education, politics, and business as well as of religion in the northern states. Of the Board's twenty-six members in 1813 no less than eighteen were college graduates. While eleven were ministers of the gospel, it may be recalled that the clergy were the educators of the day, and five were, in fact, college presidents: of Yale, Bowdoin, Middlebury, Union, and New Jersey. Included were the governors of Connecticut and Rhode Island, the elder statesman John Jay, and three of the nation's wealthiest merchants.[2] The propriety of American effort to evangelize the nations was thus impeccable before responsible opinion. It was no coincidence that the missionaries carried with them an ideological baggage in which civic forms and virtue as defined in New England, austere social comportment, sound accounting practice, and reformed Calvinism formed an indivisible whole of which the excellence was felt to be manifest. Political dogma precluded government encouragement of missionary activities. The nation's

---

[2]James A. Field, Jr., *America and the Mediterranean World* (Princeton: Princeton University Press, 1969), p. 88.

leaders nevertheless considered evangelical and commercial enterprise as equally legitimate, and the principle of protecting the rights, property, and security of American citizens abroad was extended to the support of proselytizing efforts.

The American Board's first missionaries, ordained in 1812, were destined for India. Inevitably, however, its attention was drawn to the Bible lands, where it soon established three distinct missions: one at the Ottoman capital, Constantinople, one in Persia, and the Syrian mission based at Beirut, which is of concern here. In 1819 the Board sent two young ministers, Levi Parsons and Pliny Fisk, to explore the Levant field. Within three and six years, respectively, Providence made them martyrs to the cause through the nameless Syrian fevers to which many of their successors were to succumb, but not before they had begun to educate their sponsors in the realities of preaching the gospel under Turkish rule.

These realities did not make the missionaries' task an easy one. The Empire, extending from the Danube and the Caucasus to Algeria on the west, and to the Persian Gulf and Indian Ocean to the south and east, embraced peoples of many different tongues and ethnic origins. Instead of a single nation, it was a group of communities—*millets*—under an Ottoman sultan who was also spiritual leader of the orthodox Muslims. The social, religious, and political systems according to which the Ottoman institutions of government were conceived and administered were fully applicable only to Sunni Muslims. Shī'a Muslims and other heterodox Muslim sects (Druze, Nuṣairīs, Ismā'īlīs, etc.) were dealt with through their traditional feudal or religious leaders. Jews and Christians, being "peoples of the Book," were subject to the Koranic injunction of toleration, but liable to tribute. From the Turkish capture of Constantinople onward this relationship was formalized in the recognition of the Grand Rabbi of the capital and the patriarchs of the various Uniate and other Eastern churches as political, as well as religious, heads of their respective congregations, over whom they came to wield formidable power.

Convinced by faith and introspection that this edifice was about to collapse, the American Board initially contemplated moving on a broad front within the Empire toward universal conversion of Muslims, Jews, and "nominal" Christians to Protestantism. The Ottoman Jews, it soon became obvious, were totally unresponsive to the preaching of the gospel. A similarly negative attitude on the part of Muslims was reinforced by the inferior status accorded Christians in Ottoman society, and more particularly by the death penalty specified in Ottoman law for apostasy from Islam. Missionary attention perforce focused on the Eastern churches and the possibility of reforming them from within. The dignitaries of these, however, failed to appreciate the superiority of the Calvinist system over their own. Their hierarchies remained impervious to evangelization and bitterly hostile to the final resort of the missionaries: the winning of converts from the existing churches and the organization among them of new, Protestant, congregations. Such converts sacrificed the very real civil protection and the advantages of communal solidarity that they enjoyed under the *millet* system; it is thus not surprising that their numbers grew but slowly or that they were largely mission employees and their families. Orthodox and Druze communities occasionally expressed interest in wholesale conversion. Their motivation always proved to be not genuine conviction but an unrealistic aspiration to exemption from Ottoman law under American protection, or the hope of mitigating, by a sort of blackmail, the tax exactions of their own traditional religious authorities.

The establishment of the Syrian Mission coincided with the inception of a century of unrest, change, and decline in the Empire. Its personnel were obliged to withdraw for a time to Malta during the 1920s as a result of disturbances induced by the Greek war of independence. The following decade of Egyptian occupation in Syria was one of relative civil tranquility under the rule of Ibrāhīm Pasha, son of the Sultan's rebellious vassal Muhammed 'Alī of Egypt. The mission was again forced to evacuate its base when, during the restoration of the Sultan's authority in Syria, Beirut was bombarded and occupied by the British. Civil war between Druze and Maronites erupted sporadically on Mount Lebanon during the next quarter-century. Meanwhile, the Empire embarked on its intermittent effort at defensive modernization under the various programs termed collectively *tanzīmāt*. These included attempts to centralize administration and to introduce uniformity in fields such as education and the press, which inevitably affected mission activities and relations with Ottoman authorities.

These relations were of some delicacy, partly because the legal status of the mission's operations was ambiguous. Proselytization among Muslims was clearly illegal under Ottoman law—a prohibition to which the American missionaries submitted with far better grace and good faith than their British colleagues. Existing treaties acknowledged special relationships between Russia and the Orthodox *millet* in the Empire, and between France and the Uniate churches. The United States, in negotiating the 1830 treaty with Turkey, did not seek recognition of its interest in the handful of Ottoman subjects who were Protestants, and the latter became a *millet*, through British diplomatic intervention, only in 1850. Turkish law provided no guidelines regarding conversion among the Christian sects, and Ottoman officials concerned themselves with the matter only when the public peace was involved. It was, in fact, involved from the first, with the distribution by the Americans of the Bible in an Arabic translation supplied by the British. This version was scandalous to the Eastern churches in its omission of the Apocrypha, which they regarded as an integral element of God's word. When the mission's press came into operation at Beirut, it was used for the publication not only of politically innocuous, morally elevating material but also of tracts denouncing the "pagan," "idolatrous" ritualism of the Orthodox and Catholic churches. Conversions to Protestantism threatened both the revenues and the power of the native patriarchs, who complained bitterly to the Porte. Converts were subjected to reprisal; the Maronite Patriarch used his secular power on one occasion to have a convert imprisoned and put to death. The converts could look only to the missionaries for protection; the latter, in turn, expected the diplomatic, consular and, if need be, the naval officials of their government to protect their work from interference, whatever its source.

The United States government met problems arising from this situation according to a pattern, not unfamiliar in other settings, whereby Washington officials, under domestic pressures, adopted a substantially broader view of the rights and privileges of American citizens abroad than United States diplomats on the spot, more sensitive to local conditions and to the letter of agreements defining American rights. A case in point arose in 1841, when the mission staff moved from Beirut for the summer to Deir al-Qamar, a mountain locality with a mixed population of Maronites and Druze, between whom tension was already growing, and acquired property for a school for the Druze, who had evinced some interest in Protestantism. The Maronite Patriarch demanded that the Ottoman officials remove the missionaries, insisting that they had come in order to make "their usual attacks on the other faiths and thus to excite religious controversy, sedition and strife among the subjects of our lord, the Sultan." Commodore David Porter, the American Minister at the Porte, advised the missionaries not to resist expulsion from the mountain, pointing out that "no article of the treaty of commerce and navigation between the United States and Turkey gives [American citizens] the right to interfere in any way with the rites and religion of any person living under the authority of Turkey." The indignant missionaries, sharply reminding Porter that American property was in question, promptly reported the affair to their Board in Boston. The chairman of its Prudential Committee, who was moreover a recent governor of Massachusetts, complained to Washington. Secretary of State Daniel Webster administered a stinging rebuke to the Minister.

It has been represented to this Department, that the American Missionaries, and other citizens of the United States not engaged in commercial pursuits, residing and traveling in the Ottoman Dominions, do not receive from your Legation that aid and protection to which, as citizens of the United States, they feel themselves entitled, and I have been directed by the President, who is profoundly interested in the matter, to call your immediate attention to the subject, and to instruct you to omit no occasion, where your interference in behalf of such persons may become necessary or useful, to extend to them all proper succor and attentions of which they may stand in need, in the same manner that you would to other citizens of the United States, who as merchants visit or dwell in Turkey.[3]

To its diplomatic support of the missionaries Washington added the protection of its naval vessels. On his cruise in the eastern

---

[3]David H. Finnie, *Pioneers East* (Cambridge: Harvard University Press, 1967), pp. 128–129. Abdul Latif Tibawi, *American Interests in Syria* (Oxford: Clarendon Press, 1966), pp. 94–95.

Mediterranean in 1850 the captain of a United States frigate carried a letter addressed to the American missions in which the Mediterranean Squadron's commander informed them that the ship's presence was

for the general purpose of giving protection to our commerce and citizens, and particularly to inquire into the safety and prosperity of the Missions along the coasts, and to extend to them such care and assistance as they may require, and as he may deem reasonable and just.[4]

On the other hand, the tendency toward close construction reasserted itself at the Legation in Constantinople. In instructions to the American consul at Beirut in 1873 Minister Baldwin Hay observed,

As to what degree of religious toleration the Ottoman government may think fit to accord within the limits of the Empire, that is an affair of its own. No foreigner who objects to Ottoman law need live under it, and those who in spite of full knowledge still insist upon making this land their domicile must also take the peril of their position, being able to claim such rights only as are guaranteed to them by treaty.[5]

From the first, the Syrian Mission considered education as an essential adjunct to spreading the gospel. During the first two decades, its personnel endeavored to promote the formation of a well-educated native Protestant clergy that would serve and expand the nascent congregations. To this end school texts were imported or printed on the mission press, and "philosophical" apparatus for natural science experiments was brought from America; instruction was in English. The results were disappointing. With the revival of Syria's economy and the increase in its external trade during the Egyptian occupation, basic education and the knowledge of a European language became highly marketable assets. Pupils tended to seek the betterment of their economic condition by taking commercial or administrative employment instead of returning to their villages to propagate God's word under the guidance of their missionary mentors. The Mission was able to report to its sponsors only meager results from its conversion effort.

---

[4]Tibawi, op. cit., p. 128.
[5]Ibid., p. 221.

In 1844 the vigorous, able, and stiff-necked Rufus Anderson, who served the American Board as Secretary for a half-century, toured its Middle Eastern missions to determine which of them ought to be closed down. The Greek mission was, in fact, terminated. A rigid new policy was laid down for a geographically diminished Syrian Mission. Henceforth, no Board funds were to be devoted to purposes not directly pertinent to propagating the gospel. No native schools were to be supported except those in charge of converts. Schools were to be considered as places for preaching. The Beirut seminary, which had been permitted to lapse, was to be revived and transferred to the mountain station of Abeih, where its students would be remote from secular temptations. The mission's press was to undertake the printing of nonreligious materials only on a commercial basis. Anderson, over the following decades, held the mission strictly to this policy, which remained in effect a further quarter-century after 1870, when the Presbyterians withdrew from the American Board and, under a division of territory, assumed responsibility for the Syrian Mission. At a century's remove one may comprehend, if not sympathize with, the logic behind this narrowing of the mission's activity; in the light of historical perspective it appears at best unfortunately timed.

In interpreting the impressive figures reported at various periods for the number of schools supervised by the mission and the number of pupils served, it must be borne in mind that, except for the urban schools staffed primarily by American personnel, most of the schools were one-room Bible schools with a pitifully inadequate mission subsidy (typically, $50 a year), taught by instructors selected for their religious beliefs rather than for their ability or qualifications as teachers. The village Protestant schools were thus placed on a level with the local communal schools, Islamic as well as Eastern Christian, which long predated the missionary effort. Furthermore, partly as a reaction to the advent of the Americans, the Jesuits had returned to Syria beginning in 1831; astute educators liberally subsidized by the French government, they began the building of a school system with a far broader curriculum and more competent instruction than the Protestant mission schools, either American or British, could soon match.

The mission schools became a thorny political issue with the promulgation in 1869, under the Empire's modernization program, of a comprehensive education law providing for the establishment of state schools and for the regulation of privately run institutions attended by Ottoman subjects. The latter were to be licensed, their teachers were required to possess acceptable qualifications, and their curricula and textbooks were subject to review and approval by local education officials. The French Ambassador was among the first envoys at the Porte to accept these provisions, on behalf of the Catholic schools. The Protestant missions, by contrast, totally ignored the legislation, and the measure of Ottoman forbearance is that fifteen years elapsed before officials began to press for compliance. British and American missionary societies brought intense pressures to bear on their respective diplomatic missions in Constantinople to secure exemption of their schools from the law. The American Minister nevertheless felt obliged to accept its applicability; a factor in his attitude may well have been the fact that a diplomatic survey of the Protestant schools in all of Syria (including Lebanon and Palestine) revealed that of a total of 345 native teachers, only one held a diploma or certificate of any kind.[6]

Two consequences of the licensing altercation are worth noting. The Board of Foreign Missions of the Presbyterian Church was constrained to set about raising the standards of the schools it desired to keep in operation; its thinking moreover progressed so far by 1894 as to approve and assist the long-term efforts of a retired missionary, George A. Ford, to found an industrial training school at Sidon. On the other hand, the negative missionary attitude toward the Ottoman attempt to modernize and rationalize education set off a campaign of vilification of Islam and of Turks that, although less strident and less open in the United States than in England, had lasting effects on American public opinion. It reinforced prejudices already current and contributed to a climate in which the American Board, as late as 1915, could apply to the Rockefeller Foundation for support with the argument that "Islam has, in all history, been the foe of intellectual advance on the part of the people it governed, and unprogressive in all modern measures for the preservation and promoting of health."[7]

Firmly fixed as were the eyes of the Syrian Mission on the

---

[6]Ibid., p. 258 ff.
[7]John A. DeNovo, *American Interests and Policies in the Middle East, 1900–1939* (Minneapolis: University of Minnesota Press, 1963), p. 32. Cf. Tibawi, op. cit., p. 171 ff.

salvation of men's souls, it was nevertheless not indifferent to their physical and secular welfare and uplift. The first medical missionary was appointed to Syria in 1832; medical treatment gradually became an accepted adjunct of mission activity generally, and its principal focus in communities where there was no proximate hope of achieving conversions. Some mission personnel were furthermore restive at the contrast between the narrow scope of the established educational objectives and those of the Catholic missions. This sentiment was acted on by Daniel Bliss, a member of the mission, with the approval of his colleagues. In 1862, while the Civil War raged, he performed the remarkable feat of raising an endowment of $100,000 and effected the incorporation in New York of the Syrian Protestant College. Prudently, these depreciated American funds were kept intact until their value should recuperate, and a supplementary campaign was conducted in England to raise enough money to inaugurate the institution. The College opened in 1866 with sixteen students, thirteen teachers (including three missionaries), and a curriculum comprising the Arabic, English, French, Turkish, and Latin languages, mathematics, Arab history, religious history, and Bible study. On this modest foundation was gradually built the prestigious center of learning known after 1920 as the American University of Beirut. As its subject matter grew in sophistication—a medical college was added in the early years—English replaced Arabic as the primary language of instruction, over the objection, which proved unfounded, of those who feared that graduates would emigrate rather than remain in the Middle East to contribute to the area's progress. Although originally conceived to serve the religious purpose of training a native clergy, the College's liberal orientation from the outset was stated in an address by Daniel Bliss in 1871.

This College is for all conditions and classes of men without regard to colour, nationality, race or religion. A man, white, black or yellow, Christian, Jew, Mohammedan or heathen, may enter and enjoy all the advantages of this institution for three, four or eight years; and go out believing in one God, in many Gods, or in no God. But, it will be impossible for anyone to continue with us long without knowing what we believe to be the truth and our reasons for that belief.[8]

---

[8] *The Reminiscences of Daniel Bliss* (New York, 1920), p. 198; quoted in Zeine N. Zeine, *The Emergence of Arab Nationalism* (Beirut: Khayat's, 1966), p. 52, fn. 1.

Over time, a system of preparatory schools was created to fit students for the increasingly advanced work at the College.

A major achievement of the Syrian Mission and its press was the production of a new Arabic translation of the Bible, replacing the seventeenth-century Paris polyglot version. Begun in 1848 by Eli Smith and completed in 1867 by Cornelius van Dyck, the new version has been in use in the Middle East for a full century. Among the missionaries' collaborators on the project were Buṭrus al-Bustānī and Nāṣīf al-Yāzijī, who later became prominent in the Arab literary movement that marked the origin of contemporary Arab nationalism. As this circumstance has lent plausibility to the suggestion that the revival of Arabic language and literature was in large part due to the education and press activity of the missions,[9] it may be well to note that the renewal of this interest among the Maronites was already two centuries old, and that it was cultivated in their seminary at 'Ain Warqa, of which Bustānī and Yāzijī were both graduates. Aleppo had an Arabic press as early as 1702;[10] the Arabic classics were being printed in Constantinople and in Cairo well before the installation of the mission's Arabic press in 1836. The latter, preoccupied with the production of religious materials and a limited number of school texts, printed its first literary work only in 1887.[11]

In other Arab territories American missions prospered under different auspices. The United Presbyterian Church sent its first missionary to Egypt in 1854. The Coptic Church provided a source of recruits to Protestantism. Mission work was tolerated by Muhammad 'Alī's successors and, after 1882, encouraged by the British administration. By 1901 the Egyptian Mission claimed 220 stations and chruches, 50 native preachers, and 200 schools with 14,000 pupils.[12] In Iraq, an individual enterprise of James Cantine and Samuel M. Zwemer was, in 1894, taken under the sponsorship of the Reformed Church in America. Concentrating its effort in the fields of medicine and education, this mission's activity expanded

---

[9]E.g., George Antonius, *The Arab Awakening* (Beirut: Khayat's reprinted 1955; first published 1938), pp. 35–37.
[10]Phillip K. Hitti, *History of Syria* (New York: Macmillan, 1951), p. 677.
[11]Tibawi, op. cit., pp. 252–253; cf. Zeine, op. cit., p. 46 ff.
[12]DeNovo, op. cit., p. 10.

from its base at Basra to include, before World War I, Bahrain, Kuwait, and Muscat.

The endeavors of the major missionary boards were accompanied by more modest undertakings of smaller and less well-financed religious groups. Marginal to the missionary effort proper was a spate of projects around midcentury for the colonization of Palestine in anticipation of the impending millenium. The picturesque—and sometimes picaresque—adventures of the participants indicate the antiquity of American society's ability to produce unconventional personalities with off-beat objectives of which the pursuit abroad confronts American consular officials with novel and disconcerting problems.

THE GROWTH OF SECULAR INTERESTS

Relief and other philanthropic enterprise, such as educational endeavor, originated in and then diverged from strictly religious motivations. Missionaries took the lead in organizing American aid for communities uprooted or otherwise distressed from time to time in the Ottoman Empire. Their concern was, naturally, aroused in the first instance, and particularly poignant, where Christian minorities were concerned. United States emergency aid in the Middle East dates from the Greek revolt of the 1820s; the largest operations were undertaken on behalf of the Anatolian Armenians in the decade of the 1890s and during World War I. Muslim Arab communities, however, were at times in need and received aid, notably during the reassertion of Turkish rule in Syria in 1840, during the ensuing Druze-Maronite strife and, again, during World War I. Several aspects of these relief activities had lasting influences on American policy. The United States government was regularly involved, from the first, in making available naval transport for relief supplies. The principle that humanitarian acts were a legitimate call on official as well as private generosity became so firmly established that the Near East Relief organization formed during the War could be chartered by Congress and liberally supported with appropriated funds. Eligibility for American assistance came to be extended to all those in dire need irrespective of nationality or creed. Finally, an approach to aid was developed that went beyond providing immediate requirements for food,

shelter, and clothing, to embrace theoretical and technical education and the other services needed to rehabilitate the recipients
and enable them to stand on their own feet. The humanitarian
philosophy developed as a result of these mission-administered
operations has been seen as a precursor of the concept of continuing American aid to less-advantaged countries, and the practical
experience accumulated was, in fact, consciously drawn on in
formulating policies under President Truman's Point Four program.[13]

Touristic and other American secular interest in the Near East
was of surprisingly early date, particularly in Egypt, with its equa-
ble winter climate; in the decades preceding the Civil War American travelers were outnumbered only by the British. The
intellectual attention of the Western world as a whole was drawn
to Egypt by Napoleon's foray into that country in 1798 and by the
more permanent achievements of the large body of French scholars who accompanied his army and produced the monumental
Description de l'Égypte. The regime of Muhammad 'Alī, who massa-
cred the Mamelukes and assumed rule in 1805, made the land of
the Pharaohs far more hospitable to Western visitors than under
his predecessors. Many American tourists, typically well heeled
and well educated, contributed to the spread of American knowledge and interest by lecturing or by publishing accounts of their
journeys. *Incidents of Travel in Egypt, Arabia Petraea and the Holy
Land,* by the Tammany lawyer John Lloyd Stephens, appeared in
1837 and enjoyed spectacular success. George Gliddon, an En-
glishman who had served as American Consul at Cairo, toured the
United States from Boston to St. Louis from 1842 to 1844, lecturing to appreciative audiences on Egyptian antiquities.

This was the era of the plunder of Egyptian artifacts, as well as
of the birth of Egyptology with Champollion's decipherment of
the Rosetta Stone inscription, and Americans participated enthusiastically in the harvest. Colonel Mendes Cohen of Baltimore
returned from Egypt with 680 objects, eventually donated to Johns
Hopkins University. John Lowell, Jr., detained in Egypt by illness
in 1835, became a collector of antiquities, while sending instruc-

---

[13]Joseph L. Grabill, *Protestant Diplomacy and the Near East* (Minneapolis: University
of Minnesota Press, 1971), pp. 300–302.

tions to Boston for the founding of the Lowell Institute. The federal government was well disposed toward the effort, which continued throughout the century, to secure an American share of the past's curios to stock museum shelves and private attics. Space in naval ships was frequently made available to transport collections or bulky pieces. In 1880 Lieutenant Commander Henry H. Gorringe of the U.S. Navy was granted leave to organize the transport to America of an obelisk from Alexandria, deeded to the United States by the Khedive Ismā'īl. The 224-ton monolith was inserted into a hole opened in the bow of a chartered ship and, after an adventurous voyage, reached New York, where it stands in Central Park.[14]

Meanwhile, American scholars were following, at some remove, the European lead in expanding knowledge of the ancient Egyptian languages and scripts and in developing sound procedures for archaeological excavation. Students at the University of Pennsylvania in 1858 produced a creditable independent version of the Rosetta Stone text.[15] American institutions and individuals contributed to the British Egypt Exploration Fund, organized in 1882. The first American Egyptologist of major stature, Charles E. Wilbour, was a free lancer. As the Tweed Ring's press member, he acquired a reputation that precluded extended residence in the United States, but also a fortune that permitted him to pursue his literary interests abroad. Having studied with the great Maspero in Paris, he spent his winters after 1884 in Egypt, comfortably accommodated aboard his *dhahabiya*, devoting his time to the discovery, copying, and interpretation of ancient inscriptions.[16] The pleasures, which could be exceedingly luxurious, of houseboat life on the Nile attracted men of substantial wealth to Egypt, and some became sufficiently drawn to Egyptology to sponsor digs. Outstanding among Americans of this stamp was Theodore M. Davis of Rhode Island, who financed important excavations in the Valley of the Kings at Thebes beginning in 1903.[17] With the establishment of a chair of Egyptology at the University of Chicago in 1895,

---

[14]John A. Wilson, *Signs and Wonders upon Pharaoh* (Chicago: University of Chicago Press, 1964), pp. 58–60.
[15]Ibid., p. 58.
[16]Ibid., pp. 101–109.
[17]Ibid., pp. 115–123.

the discipline became a permanent feature of American scholarship, and the first incumbent, James H. Breasted, contributed substantially to public knowledge of Egyptian antiquity through his classic *History of Egypt,* and his more technical studies of the ancient texts. His work led directly to the founding of the University of Chicago's Oriental Institute, endowed in the first instance by the Rockefeller Foundation, which conducted investigations for many years at Medinet Habu and established a permanent epigraphic center at Luxor. George Andrew Reisner, a native of Indiana, had studied Semitics at Harvard, Assyriology and Egyptology at Berlin, and directed excavations in Upper Egypt financed by Mrs. Phoebe Hearst. When this support was terminated in 1905, Reisner occupied an Egyptology chair at Harvard and led expeditions during the following decades to Upper Egypt.[18] Harvard maintained a permanent installation near the Gizeh pyramids until after World War II. These solid bases of American scientific interest were decisive many years later in United States support of the UNESCO effort to salvage the ancient monuments of Nubia threatened with inundation and destruction above the Aswan High Dam.

In Asia early American interest inevitably concentrated on Palestine, the scene of the Bible stories most Americans learned in childhood. Many went as pilgrims or simply as curiosity-seekers. Some were drawn by the intellectual disciplines of the higher Biblical criticism and, as the science gradually developed, archaeology. The pioneer in objective study of the geography and topography of the Holy Land was Edward Robinson, an ordained minister and scholar trained in the meticulous German institutions of the day. In the company of the studious missionary Eli Smith he conducted searching geographical explorations in 1832 and 1852; the voluminous journal of his earlier sojourn won him the first gold medal of the British Royal Geographical Society awarded to an American.[19] The next notable American contribution to the objective knowledge of Palestine was made under the auspices of the U.S. Navy. In 1847 Lieutenant William Francis Lynch secured the permission of the Secretary of the Navy, and also of the Otto-

---

[18]Ibid., pp. 144–150.
[19]Finnie, op. cit., pp. 175–181.

man Porte, to descend the River Jordan and circumnavigate the Dead Sea, in newly designed metal boats, "in the interests of science and for the gratification of enlightened curiosity." The wide-ranging published account of the expedition, considerably predating Lynch's final report to the Navy Department, was a resounding public success, as were his public lectures. The latter were expanded and published with an appeal by the American Geographical Society for further exploration in Syria.[20] Geographic work was, in fact, carried forward by Americans, in cooperation with the Palestine Exploration Fund of Britain, on the east bank of the Jordan in a mapping expedition of 1873 conducted by a military officer with missionary advisors.[21]

American officials did nothing to obstruct, if little to promote, the employment abroad of America's technological talent and growing expertise. In the 1830s New England ship-builders Henry Eckford and Foster Rhodes were engaged by the Porte to apply their know-how to the reconstruction of the Ottoman navy, virtually destroyed at the Battle of Navarino. Among the Arab territories of the Empire only Egypt was at once disposed to enlist the services of American technicians and sufficiently independent of Constantinople to do so. As early as 1820 George Bethune English, graduate of Harvard, sometime student of the law and Christian theology, journalist, and protege of John Quincy Adams, who had him appointed Marine Lieutenant in the Mediterranean Squadron, resigned his commission, embraced Islam, and secured a position as artillery commander, with the rank of general, in the expedition that Muḥammad 'Alī was fitting out to conquer the Sudan. While English and two American colleagues made little positive contribution to the operation (his participation was cut short by illness), he published a widely read book on the expedition.[22]

A far more serious enlistment of American military talent was made by Muḥammad 'Alī's grandson, Ismā'īl. Disillusioned with French friendship as a result of an extremely costly arbitration award by the Emperor Napoleon III in a dispute between Egypt and the French firm constructing the Suez Canal, the Khedive

---

[20]Ibid., p. 262 ff.; Field, op. cit., pp. 262–284; Tibawi, op. cit., pp. 229–230.
[21]Tibawi, op. cit., pp. 230–232.
[22]Finnie, op. cit., pp. 143–149; Pierre Crabitès, *Americans in the Egyptian Army* (London: George Routledge & Sons, 1938), pp. 23–27.

dismissed the French officers advising his forces and, beginning in 1869, replaced them with Americans, mainly veterans of the Civil War recruited through private channels. Over a decade, a total of some fifty American officers, mostly highly competent, vigorous, and sincerely devoted to their employer, served Egypt under the orders of Major General Charles Pomeroy Stone, who held the title of the Khedive's Chief of Staff. Seldom in command of troops, the Americans acted chiefly in staff capacities. The general staff of which they formed the nucleus was never effectively integrated into the Egyptian army's command structure, which preserved its traditional inefficient pattern. It nevertheless made a major contribution to improving the Khedive's army by organizing education for the enlisted personnel, mostly illiterates. Solid technical achievements were recorded. The topographical survey of Egypt and the Sudan was much advanced. Fortifications were designed and constructed for Alexandria and the Delta. A hydrographic survey of the Horn of Africa determined precisely the location of the Cape Guardafui lighthouse. American officers played important roles in Egyptian expansion southward into Darfur and equatorial Africa. Lt. Col. Charles Chaillé-Long's explorations in Uganda and the Nile's sources, if not quite on the level he claimed for them, were nevertheless more substantial than conceded by the British, jealous of their priority in this field. France and Britain strongly resented the presence of American military advisors in Egypt and, with the establishment of their Dual Control of Ismā'īl's finances in 1876, were able to work effectively to dislodge them. The contracts of all the officers were terminated by mid-1878, save that of General Stone, who stood loyally beside Ismā'īl and his successor Tawfīq until well after the British occupation in 1882. The United States government adopted a tolerant attitude toward this activity without intervening in the arrangements. Chief of Staff General William T. Sherman assisted informally in locating qualified and available officers and granted leaves of absence to a few young officers on active duty to permit them the opportunity of gaining experience in Egypt—an act that stimulated questions on the floor of Congress.[23]

---

[23]William B. Hesseltine and Hazel C. Wolf, *The Blue and the Gray on the Nile* (Chicago: University of Chicago Press, 1961) passim; Crabitès, op. cit.; Field, op. cit., p. 389 ff.

TRANSITION

The American officers who served Khedive Ismā'īl sympathized with his aspiration to free Egypt from the restrictions of Ottoman suzerainty. They saw, perhaps more clearly than he, that Egypt's mounting debts to European banks would eventually result in the exchange of Turkish for European tutelage. The United States government viewed this prospect without alarm, however, and interposed no objection to the imposition of Anglo-French control over Egyptian finances. After the British occupation it cooperated in the foreign regime to the extent of naming judges to the Mixed Courts, which were a feature of the extraterritorial rights in which Americans shared.

American policy did not, in fact, seek to obstruct the building of the great colonial empires. As political institutions in the western European countries were gradually liberalized during the nineteenth century, American attitudes toward them mellowed. The idea that nations have a natural right to determine their own destiny was not lost sight of in America, and it was to be forcefully reasserted during World War I. United States policy nevertheless generally acquiesced in the principle, on which the colonizing powers acted, that the peoples of Asia and Africa were too ignorant and backward to make wise decisions for themselves and could become members of the community of civilized states only after extended periods of guardianship and education by an enlightened power. The United States itself, at the end of the century, took the occasion of unrest in Cuba to make war on Spain and to acquire a modest empire of its own in the Pacific. This was an uncharacteristic aberration, however, and America otherwise consistently avoided assuming responsibilities entailing the risk of dangerous encounters with the ambitions of the imperial powers.

Thus the United States firmly, if politely, rebuffed suggestions by both Tunisia and Morocco in 1871 that it take these countries under its protection, although the State Department went so far as to advise the Sultan of Morocco that the United States would use its good offices to prevent the dismemberment of his empire. The United States participated in the Madrid Conference of 1880, held to formalize international restrictions on the Sultan's sovereignty; the American delegation was primarily concerned with

guarantees of religious freedom in the country and, having failed
to have such provisions written into the resulting treaty, President
Hayes explained to Congress that the United States had "lost no
opportunity to urge upon the Emperor of Morocco the necessity
of putting an end to the persecutions so prevalent in that country
of persons of a faith other than the Moslem, and especially the
Hebrew residents of Morocco."[24] Shortly thereafter the State Department instructed its consul in Tangier to cooperate with an
agent assigned to that capital by the Union of American Hebrew
Congregations to monitor the treatment of Moroccan Jews.[25]

The rise of the colonial empires was attended by numerous
conflicts of interest and, under President Theodore Roosevelt, the
United States sought to use its growing strength and prestige to
ease friction among the major European powers. Encouraged by
his success in the mediation between Russia and Japan, which
culminated in the Treaty of Portsmouth, Roosevelt played a key,
if unobtrusive, role in 1905 in securing French and British agreement to the holding of the following year's conference at Algeciras, proposed by the Sultan of Morocco at the instigation of
the Kaiser—a role that did much to forestall the outbreak of war
between France and Germany. To the extent that the welfare of
Morocco itself entered at all into his concern, Roosevelt's aim was
the promotion of French tutelage over the country, which the
Conference, in fact, facilitated by according control over the
Moroccan police to France and her junior partner, Spain.[26] Roosevelt remarked to French Ambassador Jusserand, two years after
Algeciras, "As for the Moorish business, I wish to Heaven, not in
your interest but in the interest of all civilized mankind, that
France could take all Morocco under its exclusive charge."[27]

During its first several decades the United States had been constrained to devise policies for dealing with the Barbary states in
order to revive and protect its trade with North Africa and Turkey.
The trade had dwindled into relative insignificance by the early

---

[24]Luella J. Hall, *The United States and Morocco 1776–1956* (Metuchen, N.J.: The
Scarecrow Press, 1971), p. 224.
[25]Ibid., p. 229.
[26]Raymond A. Esthus, *Theodore Roosevelt and the International Rivalries* (Waltham,
Mass.: Ginn-Blaisdell, 1970), pp. 66–111.
[27]Ibid., p. 110.

twentieth century, and government action involving the Arab lands had gradually become confined to occasional support of the cultural and philanthropic enterprise of American citizens. Roosevelt's ventures into the politics of the great powers were sharply criticized in the American press and by influential Congressional leaders; his successor reverted to the traditional aloofness. International politics, however, forced itself on American attention during and after World War I. As participants in the making of peace, President Wilson and his advisors had to adopt some attitude toward disposition of the Arab and other non-Turkish territories of the Ottoman Empire. Balanced knowledge and experience on which to base a coherent American policy toward the Arabs and their political future were lacking. Their lands, certainly, were not unknown to the United States. During the previous century, many Americans had traveled and worked there and studied their geography and archaeology. Under direction of the mission boards close cultural links had been forged with some Arab communities. These, however, were primarily with religious minorities. The general American public remained largely unfamiliar, or frankly unsympathetic, with the culture, values, and aspirations of the Muslim majority. The American delegation at the Paris Conference undertook the first American analysis of the area's politics and its potential implications for United States interests. If no coherent policy resulted, and recourse was had to abstract principle, it was nevertheless a beginning.

CHAPTER II

The Elements of a Policy

WORLD WAR I

EXPLOITING OTTOMAN FEARS OF THE ANCIENT RUSSIAN ENEMY and apprehensions of further encroachment by the western European colonial powers, astute German diplomacy brought the Turks into World War I on the side of the Central Powers. Defeat of Turkey by the Allies, followed soon by their victory in Europe, placed before the Western statesmen meeting in Paris to design a new world order the question of how the far-flung and heterogeneous territories of the Ottoman state should be disposed. Self-determination of peoples was among the proclaimed war aims of the Allies, articulated with particular eloquence by President Woodrow Wilson. The inhabitants of the eastern Arab lands regarded themselves as a people who, by this principle, surely ought to be free and independent. The United States, however, shrank from the task of forcing reality to conform to the ideal and, in the event, the norms of imperialism took precedence over those of liberalism in the peace settlement.

Although the war was fought primarily in Europe, the Ottoman alliance with a Germany aspiring to a preponderant influence in the Turkish Straits and the Persian Gulf gravely threatened Britain's imperial communications; the Middle East, consequently, became the theater of important, if secondary, operations. Of these the largest in scale and the costliest in lives was the Gallipoli campaign of 1915 in which British, French, Australian, and New Zealand forces successfully stormed the entrance to the Dardanelles, but were forced to withdraw under the counterattack of Turkish forces commanded by Mustafa Kemal, whose shadow was presently to lengthen spectacularly. In November 1914 the British authorities in India sent an Anglo-Indian force to occupy Basra, the Shaṭṭ al-'Arab port that provided the Berlin-Baghdad Railway with its outlet to the Persian Gulf. Institution of colonial-style administration in Iraq went forward throughout the war, together with a military advance along the Tigris and Euphrates punctuated in 1916 by the Turks' capture of an entire British army. Upon the Ottoman collapse in October 1918, British troops were in possession of the three Mesopotamian vilayets of Basra, Baghdad, and Mosul.

To the west, Turkish troops moved, shortly after Ottoman entry into the war, from Palestine into the Sinai Peninsula in the hope of capturing the Suez Canal. British forces in Egypt succeeded in stemming this attack before it reached the vital waterway. An entire year passed before British and Commonwealth troops and supplies could be mobilized in adequate strength for a counteroffensive, prosecuted throughout 1916, by the end of which year British troops were at the borders of Palestine. Meanwhile, secret negotiations between the British Arab Bureau in Cairo and Hussein, Sherif of Mecca, culminated in June 1916 in the latter's abandonment of loyalty to his Ottoman suzerain, his assumption of the title King of the Arab Countries,[1] and the launching of the Arab Revolt with which the name of T. E. Lawrence is inseparably associated in history and legend. Persistent guerrilla attacks on the Hijaz Railway, essential to the supply and support of Turkish garrisons in the Hijaz, Asir, and Yemen, gradually weakened their hold on the western side of the Arabian Peninsula. The Arab capture of the village of Aqaba, at the head of the Gulf of Aqaba, facilitated close cooperation between British forces in Palestine and the Arab guerrillas under Hussein's son Faisal. In a coordinated campaign brilliantly conceived and executed by General Sir Edmund Allenby, the combined forces cleared the entire Sanjak of Jerusalem by the end of 1917 in the face of stiffened Turco-German resistance; Damascus was captured on October 1 of the following year, and all Syria was in Allied hands by the end of that month.

---

[1]George Antonius, *The Arab Awakening* (Beirut: Khayat's, reprinted 1955; first published 1938), p. 213. Britain and France recognized him merely as King of Hijaz.

THE ARABS AT THE PARIS CONFERENCE

Thus, when the heads of government of the major Allies convened in Paris in January 1919 to shape the structure of the postwar world, all the Arab lands were under some form of control by the Western powers, save for certain autonomous areas of the Arabian Peninsula. The prospect of dismemberment of the Ottoman Empire, which took definite shape when it embarked on war with Great Britain and France, had made it prudent for these powers to harmonize their respective aspirations to possession of its Arab components: Syria and Iraq (Mesopotamia). In the context of their attack on the Dardanelles, possession of which was a fundamental Russian war aim, the Entente Powers accepted Russia's claim to the region of the Straits following defeat of the Central Powers, British and French aspirations to be satisfied elsewhere in the Ottoman Empire.[2] Negotiations early in 1916 between Sir Mark Sykes and M. Georges Picot resulted in the agreement that bears their names. Insofar as it dealt with Arab lands, it provided that Great Britain was to exercise direct authority in the closely settled areas of southern Iraq and the ports of Acre and Haifa on the Mediterranean, while France was to have similar control of the Syrian coastal area south nearly to Acre. It was contemplated that one or more Arab principalities would be established in the interior region, in which British and French spheres of influence were delimited. A sector of Palestine comprising the areas sacred to Christianity, Islam, and Judaism was reserved for treatment as an international zone. The form that the latter's administration would assume was to be determined after consultation with the two Powers' Russian ally and with the Sherif of Mecca. Following Russia's acquiescence, the agreement was ratified in May. "Consultation" with Hussein was rather less than frank; several key aspects of the secret understanding were not disclosed to him, although he was persuaded to recognize Britain's obligation to support France's special interests along the Syrian coast.

---

[2]The various inter-Allied agreements and declarations regarding the Ottoman Empire are well summarized in Leonard Stein, *The Balfour Declaration* (New York: Simon and Schuster, 1961), Chapter XVI.

These arrangements were only one among a number of commitments and implied promises made by the Entente Powers regarding the future of Syria and Iraq, some glaringly inconsistent with others. In their negotiation with Hussein, the British permitted him to expect the future formation of an independent Arab kingdom in Syria and Iraq of which the possible extent was left equivocal. In the Balfour Declaration the British government undertook to work for the establishment of a Jewish national home in Palestine, a sanjak of the Syrian vilayet. Notwithstanding this pledge Great Britain declared repeatedly that future governments in Arab lands liberated from Turkish rule should be based on the consent of their inhabitants. Finally, Great Britain and France jointly declared their goal that the indigenous populations of such territories should establish governments through the free exercise of their own initiative and choice.[3]

THE KING-CRANE COMMISSION AND AMERICAN WITHDRAWAL

Insofar as these Anglo-French postures acknowledged the idea of self-determination of peoples, they departed from the long-accepted principle that territories conquered in war properly remain at the disposition of the victor, and deferred to revolutionary ideas advanced by the United States among its objectives in joining the hostilities. In Woodrow Wilson the Americans had raised up a man better able to conceive a world based on high moral principle than to force the world into the pattern. In his view, the causes of war lay in the self-seeking ambitions and rivalries of the great European powers, from which the United States could not always stand aloof. He envisaged an intergovernmental League in which such rivalries would be submerged and attenuated and that would assume responsibility for the disposition of the territories and peoples dependent on the Central Powers, which otherwise would become the object of further great-power friction. The twelfth of the Fourteen Points proposed "an absolutely unmo-

---

[3]British "Declaration to the Seven" issued to Arab leaders in Cairo June 16, 1918; Anglo-French Declaration issued in Iraq and Syria (including Palestine) November 7, 1918. Texts in Antonius, op. cit., Appendices D and E, pp. 433–436.

lested opportunity of autonomous development for the nationalities oppressed by Turkish rule." Being a man of the second decade of the century, not of the seventh when the assumption of un-trammeled sovereignty by peoples unskilled in the practice of Western democracy had come to be regarded normal and proper, Wilson interpreted his imprecise formula as compatible with a period of tutelage under an "advanced" nation. That the United States, which was not at war with Turkey and had heretofore abstained from any official discussion of the future disposition of the Ottoman dependencies, now asserted an interest in the matter was a significant departure in American policy. Its corollary was the repudiation of intergovernmental pacts concluded in secret, demonstrated in practice in Wilson's refusal at the Peace Conference to discuss the substance of Sykes-Picot and the other agreements existing among the European Allies. These certainly were not covenants openly arrived at; they had nevertheless become open covenants through the publication by the Bolsheviks of the Tsarist Foreign Ministry archives following the Russian Revolution.

The decisive American contribution to Allied victory endowed Wilson with enormous diplomatic weight when the Paris Conference convened, by virtue of which he was able to impose the establishment of the League of Nations as its first order of business and to ensure that detailed discussion of the liberated territories should take the form of allocation of mandates under the League's authority and supervision. When this phase was reached, Clémenceau and Lloyd George considered themselves bound, respecting the Arab lands in question, by their mutual understandings and their respective claims publicly advanced; the President, unable to discuss these without giving them status and having no better alternative plan of his own to propose, could only fall back on the principle of self-determination. The evidence laid formally before the Conference, together with events then transpiring on the ground in Syria and Iraq, brought into high relief the inconsistency between Arab aspirations and the proposed Anglo-French solutions, while raising doubts concerning the real preferences of the populations involved.

Amir Faisal attended the Paris Conference representing his father, the King of Hijaz. Hussein's decision to undertake hostilities against the Turks in cooperation with Great Britain followed discreet contacts between Faisal and the secret Arab nationalist societies that constituted the principal expression of Arab political opinion, notably al-Fatāt in Syria, and al-'Ahd, composed mainly of Iraqi officers in the Ottoman forces. Upon the entry of Turkey into the war these organizations hesitated to take the opportunity for revolt, fearing that they would merely exchange Turkish for European domination. In 1915, however, their combined leadership provided Faisal, who became a clandestine member of both organizations, with a statement of the conditions in which they would cooperate with Hussein and Great Britain against the Turks: recognition of the independence of the Arab countries of Syria, Iraq, and the Arabian Peninsula; abolition of foreign capitulatory privileges; the conclusion of a defensive alliance between the future Arab state and Great Britain; and a preferred economic status for the British.[4] Notwithstanding the failure of full agreement on these principles in the ensuing correspondence between Hussein and Sir Henry McMahon, British High Commissioner in Egypt, Hussein decided on revolt. Led throughout by Faisal, the Arab operations had important Iraqi and Syrian participation from the start, and north of Aqaba they were staffed overwhelmingly from those territories.

Faisal laid the case for Arab independence and unity before the Conference in a memorandum of January 29, 1919 and in person before the Council of Ten on February 6. While recognizing the need for advice and assistance, he asserted the linguistic and racial unity of the Arabs in Asia and their eligibility for independence under the principles laid down by President Wilson and accepted by the other Allies. The Arabs had fought beside the Allies in fulfillment of their promises, and the Allies must now fulfill theirs. Should there be any doubt, he suggested, regarding the wishes of the people concerned as to the choice of a mandatory, an international inquiry in the area might be conducted.[5] Faisal's case was ably supported before the Ten a week later and in numerous contacts with members of the American delegation by President

---

[4]Ibid., pp. 157–158.

[5]Lawrence Evans, *United States Policy and the Partition of Turkey 1914–1924* (Baltimore: Johns Hopkins, 1965), pp. 124–126.

Howard A. Bliss of the Syrian Protestant College, who specifically pressed the idea of an inquiry on the ground. Dissenting views were heard from a Syrian Christian delegation supporting a French mandate and rejecting control by "desert Arabs" under Faisal, as well as from Zionist spokesmen.[6]

President Wilson, meeting with his Council of Four colleagues on March 20, expressed the view that, as the mandate approach had been accepted, it would be wise to find out whether the French were actually desired in Syria and the British in Iraq, and perhaps to extend the investigation to Armenia and Cilicia. While not dismissing the evidence furnished by such experts as Dr. Bliss and General Allenby, he noted, these men had been involved with the population in educational or military pursuits. "If we were to send a Commission with no previous contact with Syria it would, at any rate, convince the world that the Conference had tried to do all it could to find the most scientific basis possible for a settlement."[7] The proposal was agreed to, and a committee was assigned to draft instructions for an inter-Allied Commission. In selecting the leaders of its American Section, Wilson appeared to act on an assumption not unknown before or since in presidential appointments but that "amazed" Secretary of State Lansing: that specialized, relevant knowledge is an impediment to objective judgment. Dr. Henry Churchill King, President of Oberlin College, and industrialist-philanthropist Charles R. Crane, named as Commissioners, were men of stature and repute but without previous experience in the Ottoman territories in question. They were, however, provided with able and informed assistants, including academicians and former Army Captain William Yale, familiar with Iraq and Palestine as a representative of the Standard Oil Company.

Clémenceau and Lloyd George soon had second thoughts concerning their hasty agreement to the enterprise. The Allied forces that had conquered Syria were for the most part British, and French units had only just begun to move into the Levant. The opposition of Muslim Syrians to any sort of French control was becoming more and more manifest and vocal. The necessary implication of the proposed inquiry was that the future of the territory

---

[6]Ibid., pp. 125–126; pp. 128–129.
[7]Harry N. Howard, *The King-Crane Commission* (Beirut: Khayat's, 1963), pp. 32–33.

remained in the balance and depended on the wishes of the population. Cooperation by British officers would inevitably appear to be intrigue directed toward depriving France of her agreed share in the Ottoman succession and thus introduce an intolerable irritant in already-deteriorating Franco-British relations. The Big Four became deadlocked, with Wilson insisting on early departure of the inter-Allied Commission, Clémenceau declining to name commissioners until French troops had replaced British forces in Syria, Lloyd George refusing to send his appointees until the French did, and Orlando unwilling to act except in concert with the British and French. The proposed mission had been well publicized in the Arab lands, where decisive results were expected from it. Following urgent warnings from Faisal and the Arab delegation in Paris that disturbances or even war would erupt if the Commission did not appear soon, Wilson decided to break the impasse by sending the American component to the area without further delay. The Commissioners arrived at Haifa on June 10 and devoted the next several weeks to a patient and thorough polling of the attitudes of the people in most parts of Syria, including Lebanon and Palestine.

Encouraged in the hope of genuine independence, the people of the area meanwhile moved to establish, within the reasonably permissive context of British occupation, a limited monarchical government with Faisal as king. The secret society al-Fatāt emerged openly as the Istiqlāl (Independence) Party and, with the newly formed Syrian Union Party, participated in elections in May to a National Congress, which convened at Damascus on June 20. Declaring itself to be legally representative of all Syria, the Congress adopted resolutions on July 2 destined to remain the stable basis of all orthodox Syrian nationalism: the repudiation of the provisions of the Sykes-Picot Agreement and the Balfour Declaration; full sovereignty for a united Syria, including Palestine; refusal of foreign political control of any nature, while accepting outside economic and technical help, preferably from the United States, or from Great Britain failing American aid, but not from France under any circumstances. Published widely throughout Syria, the Damascus Resolutions met with enthusiastic support from the majority, who were Sunni Muslims, and the more cautious approval of Shī'a, Alawites, Druze, and certain Christian

e the salt of the earth and who worked hard to have a clear
ven for America now look at me askance and say, What did
an by sending the Commission? Why are we put in such a
? Are Americans ruthless and cruel like the others?[9]

ss, alone among the Allies, the United States had acted
ciple of ascertaining and respecting the inclinations of
arding their destiny. The ideals of self-determination
ation of colonialism were American ideals, standing in
th the actions of the European powers that now gov-
and Iraq. The hopes and confidence that continued to
in America, together with the on-going cultural and
deavor of private American institutions, provided the
tes with a fund of good will among the Arabs that
y slowly during the interwar decades. The most power-
agent was American sympathy with, and effective sup-
e Zionist movement that, relating also to the Ottoman
asserted its claims for the attention of the world's
simultaneously with those of the emerging Arab na-

JCH-PROMISED LAND

eighteen centuries of dispersion and life in many cul-
Oriental and Western, the Jews preserved a core of
entity in religion and in the memory of the Late Bronze
ge Kingdoms of Israel and Judeah. As the nationalism
e a salient feature of European society in the latter half
teenth century intensified, the "otherness" of the Jews
hem to increasing pressures, notably in Russia, where
came to be virtually a policy of state. Alone among
peoples, the Jews possessed no territory distinctively
where they were in a majority and could build their
and cultural institutions. "Zion," certainly, figured
ly in Judaic ritual and, over the ages, small numbers of
raveled to Palestine to pray and study in the ancestral
he 1880s there was a trickle of Jewish immigrants,

abill, *Protestant Diplomacy and the Near East* (Minneapolis: University
Press, 1971), p. 237.

sects; they were roundly denounced by the Uniate Maronites of Mount Lebanon and a portion of the Greek Orthodox Community.

The findings of Commissioners King and Crane confirmed in detail these reactions from the Syrian population and formed the basis for their closely reasoned recommendations to President Wilson. Briefly, they advised that the desire of the overwhelming majority for Syrian unity be respected, while preserving the local autonomy of Lebanon that had existed under the Turks. Bound by their instructions to envisage a mandatory regime, they recommended a single mandate of limited term, during which the tutelary power would devote its effort to fostering education, national spirit and institutions, and economic independence. The preferable mandatory power was the United States, if the American people were willing to accept the responsibility; in view of popular apprehensions that Great Britain would simply colonize the territory, she was a poor second choice, while sentiment against French rule made her quite inadvisable except, in last resort, as a mandatory for Lebanon. Given the universal sentiment among the non-Jewish majority of nine tenths in Palestine, an "extreme" Zionist program would have to be imposed by overwhelming military force; the program should therefore be drastically scaled down and the aim of a distinctly Jewish commonwealth abandoned. Finally, the mandatory should secure the rights of all minorities and make provision for the proper administration of the sites sacred to the three great monotheist religions. On more tenuous evidence of popular desires, the Commissioners made analogous recommendations regarding Iraq, which they did not visit, endorsing Great Britain as mandatory.

The unilateral investigation had no sequel either in the deliberations of the Peace Conference or in the orientation of American policy toward the emerging Arab nations in Asia. While it was in progress Wilson realized belatedly that he had left the Congress and American opinion far behind him in his move toward expanded United States responsibilities in world affairs. The Covenant of the League of Nations, written into the Treaty of Versailles with Germany, constituted the firmest basis for an American voice in the Turkish settlement, and this treaty was in imminent danger of rejection by the Senate. When the commissioners returned to

Paris, the president had departed for the United States to mobilize public support for ratification. His strenuous efforts failed in their purpose and brought on the grave impairment of his health in the fall of 1919. The following spring he fulfilled a commitment to his Council of Four colleagues by testing his countrymen's willingness to assume a mandate for Asia Minor, based on the Harbord fact-finding mission to Armenia and the Caucasus; the proposal was turned down by the Senate after cursory, not to say contemptuous, consideration. The preponderance of such concern with the Middle East as existed in the American public was concentrated on Armenia, and involvement with Syria was never a serious possibility. The preoccupied Wilson took no action on a telegram in which King and Crane summarized their recommendations. Their full report was deposited with the United States delegation in Paris in August and was shown informally to British representatives but not placed before the Council. There is no evidence that the President himself ever read it, although he released it informally for publication in 1922.[8]

The American people thus refused to share responsibility for enforcing the principles for which they had spent enormously in lives and wealth. Their leadership was deprived of the decisive voice in international affairs with which their President spoke during the first half of 1919. Formal apportionment of the Ottoman spoils had to await the emergence through revolution of a revitalized Turkish nation and its assertion by force of arms that Anatolia and the Straits were its patrimony. Great Britain and France meanwhile agreed to proceed in the Arab territories as though a settlement existed. The Allied Supreme Council met on April 24, 1920 at San Remo and decided to offer mandates to France for Syria and Lebanon, and to Great Britain for Iraq and Palestine, including Transjordan. These being accepted, British forces withdrew from the Syrian interior, freeing the French to move on Damascus and to extinguish Faisal's precarious kingdom, now two years old, from which Lebanon had just seceded. Publication of the San Remo decisions touched off a violent revolt

[8]The Report was published officially only in 1947, in *Papers Relating to the Foreign Relations of the United States: The Paris Peace Conference, 1919*, Vol. XII.

against the British occupation in Ira[q] principle of direct administration was While the mandatory relationship was acknowledged that it should be regula Arab government was formed and, in tions, the deposed Faisal was chosen 1921.

Meanwhile, Faisal's elder brother A claimed at the Damascus Conference Iraq) had appeared in Ma'ān, in Trans retainers, evidently to seek revenge o destitution of Faisal. Sir Winston Chu for the Colonies, who was then (M conference in Cairo among British invited Abdullah to meet with him arrangement was made (that proved jordan region was detached from t Mandate and established as a separ Abdullah. Mandates corresponding were drafted by the interested powe approval in July 1922, and were pro 1923 following signature of the T Turkey renounced her rights to the United States had withdrawn its de ference in December 1919 and, League, played a minimal role in d dates. The succeeding Republican a ventions with Great Britain and Fra sought to protect the economic and in these territories.

While America thus shrank bacl Arab lands, the King-Crane miss lasting impact on the minds of th couraged to believe that it would first instance, United States reje signifying that the Commission's acted on, produced an angered sent ary William Jessup wrote to his k

Men wh expressi America predican

Neverth on the peoples and rep contrast erned S be repo welfare United eroded ful erosi port for settleme statesme tions.

THE

Throu tures bo common and Iron that beca of the ni subjected oppressi Europear their ow own civi prominer Jews had land. By

[9]Joseph L. of Minneso

mainly from Russia, who settled permanently in the land. Nevertheless, the concept that Palestine was necessarily the territorial site of a national home was only one among many currents of thought that composed the Jewish revival movement in its early phases. The first World Zionist Congress, held at Basle in 1897, stated the aim of Zionism as the colonization of Palestine, looking toward the establishment there of a Jewish state "secured by public law." The making of public law, however, was a function of the governments of the great powers. Theodor Herzl, founder of the World Zionist Organization, was rebuffed successively by the Ottoman Sultan and the German Kaiser in his effort to secure recognition of Palestine as the Jewish national home, and he investigated several alternatives, including Argentina, Cyprus, and East Africa. A remarkable concatenation of circumstances in the context of World War I, however, made it possible for Herzl's successors to succeed where he had failed.

Unilaterally, France had advanced prewar claims to integral Syria that Great Britain could not ignore. The Turkish attack across Sinai from Palestine, however, brought home to the British the critical importance of that territory to the defense of the Suez Canal. In the absence of strong Russian support for the French aspiration, Great Britain was able to establish in the Sykes-Picot negotiations the principle of some sort of international regime for Palestine. British hope for exclusive possession persisted, however, and the idea was born that the cooperation of world Jewry might contribute to the objective. Key British statesmen—Prime Minister Lloyd George, Foreign Secretary Balfour, and Lord Milner, an influential member of the War Cabinet—were Zionists by sentimental conviction. They moreover calculated that Zionism was the most powerful force in Jewish life and that Jewish communities in important countries were in a position to influence their governments toward sympathy with the Allies, given some expression of British support for Zionist aims. Concurrently, Jewish opinion would be stimulated in favor of British control of Palestine. The anti-Semitic Tsarist regime would never have countenanced such action; with the February 1917 revolution, however, this obstacle disappeared, and one could even speculate that Jews, believed to be influential in the new Russian regime, might deter it from making a separate peace with Germany. Meanwhile,

major figures within the world Zionist leadership had retreated
from their initial neutralism in the war and had come to pin their
hopes on Great Britain. The movement's senior representative in
England, Dr. Chaim Weizmann, was well connected in high official circles and had made important contributions to British military technology; the fact that he had in consequence become
persona gratissima with key government leaders greatly facilitated
the coordination of Zionist and official British policies.

The large American Jewish community could not fail to be a
matter of close concern both to the British government and to the
Zionist leadership, in view of the crucial importance of United
States attitudes for the outcome of the war. By no means monolithic in outlook, American Jewry had arrived from Europe with
a broad range of ideologies. Of its two major components, the
smaller, of German origin and earlier in point of time, was approaching full acculturation in the new environment; many had
attained wealth and social standing. Leading members of this segment were sensitive to potential embarrassment by identification
with a "nation" other than the American,[10] and broke with the
Federation of American Zionists when, following Herzl's death,
the World Zionist Organization repudiated the notion of founding
a Jewish national home elsewhere than in Palestine. The later, and
larger, component of American Jewry came from Eastern Europe.
While some socialists among them envisaged the ultimate extinction of Jewish and other ethnic identities, the great majority arrived with a keen sense of separate nationhood as yet unaffected
by their new cultural surroundings. They empathized fully with
the writings of Louis Lipsky and his colleagues in the Federation
of American Zionists, fervent proselytizers quite prepared to acknowledge an incompatibility between their aspirations and
American citizenship.[11] In order to mobilize material resources,
however, or to exert influence in the broader American community, the Zionists could not dispense with the leadership of Jews
already successfully established. In the distinguished jurist and

---

[10]The point is made in Yonathan Shapiro, *Leadership of the American Zionist Organization 1897–1930* (Urbana: University of Illinois Press, 1971), p. 23. Shapiro
notes that "nation" and "state" are distinct concepts in German, whereas they
approach synonymity in American usage.
[11]Ibid., p. 43.

Supreme Court Justice Louis D. Brandeis, a convert to a moderate mode of Zionism, the movement found a leader with powers of persuasion over the most prominent American Jews as well as access to the country's highest political authorities.

Sympathy for Zionism in the United States was not the exclusive creation of the Jewish community. Many Protestant Christians arrived at such a concept by their own route. A Presbyterian minister, William E. Blackstone, at the head of a distinguished delegation, petitioned the State Department in 1891 for a Jewish homeland in Palestine and, in 1916, he procured the passage of such a resolution by the Presbyterian General Assembly.[12] President Wilson himself, who read the Scriptures daily, came to the conclusion that Armenians and Jews, both peoples of the Bible, would be reborn politically after the War.[13] Those like the missionaries with experience in the Holy Land, on the other hand, were in a position to foresee that strife was inherent in the basic incompatibility of Zionism with the interests of the existing population of Palestine, and held sharply contrasting views.

The British government was divided on the question of public support for Zionism. Following inconclusive discussion of the proposal in the War Cabinet on September 3, 1917, proponents of the idea sought to fortify their position by eliciting the views, presumed favorable, of President Wilson. The latter's response to a low-key enquiry from the Foreign Office was not encouraging; the President considered the time inopportune for any statement beyond an expression of general sympathy without real commitment. The frigidity of the President's response appears to have been based on several factors. His closest advisers on external affairs, Colonel House and Secretary Lansing, were cool toward Zionism; the proposed action tended to prejudge disposition of the territory of a country with which the United States was not at war, to the benefit of Great Britain and possible detriment to interests of other Allies; it would moreover finally extinguish hopes, which the United States had already acted on abortively, that Turkey might be wooed away from its alliance with the Central Powers.[14]

---

[12]Grabill, op. cit., p. 178.

[13]Ibid., p. 178.

[14]The complex story of the U.K.-U.S. consultation is set forth in Stein, op. cit., pp. 503–529.

A month later, under pressure of Zionist urgings and rumors of German courting of the movement, the British reopened the subject with Wilson who, after some hesitation, approved a draft statement that, with minor editing, was issued by the British Foreign Minister on November 2 in these terms.

His Majesty's Government view with favour the establishment in Palestine of a national home for the Jewish people and will use their best endeavours to facilitate the achievement of this object, it being clearly understood that nothing shall be done which may prejudice the civil and religious rights of existing non-Jewish communities in Palestine or the rights and political status enjoyed by Jews in any other country.

There was, in fact, no way in which a Jewish national home could be established without disturbing the existing non-Jewish communities in their possession of Palestine, to the prejudice of their civil rights. With some justification, given the circumstances of the declaration, the dominant Zionist faction equated "national home" with "state" or "commonwealth," and ignored the reference to non-Jewish communities as inconsequential and irrelevant. The Balfour Declaration was the assertion of an impossibility; its disingenuity was forthrightly acknowledged by its author in a memorandum written at the Paris Conference two years later.

So far as Palestine is concerned, the Powers have made no statement of fact which is not admittedly wrong and no declaration of policy which at least in the letter, they have not always intended to violate. . . . The four Great Powers are committed to Zionism. And Zionism, be it right or wrong, good or bad, is rooted in age-long traditions, in present needs, in future hopes, of far profounder import than the desires and prejudices of the 700,000 Arabs who now inhabit that ancient land. In my opinion, that is right. What I have never been able to understand is how it can be harmonised with the declaration,[15] the Covenant or the instructions to the Commission of Enquiry.[16]

The declaration, written into Britain's mandate for Palestine, held her to a program against which discerning men, Zionists and others, had long warned: that of the gradual building up of a Jewish community in a territory already populated until it was strong

---

[15]I.e., the Anglo-French Declaration of November 1918.
[16]Quoted in Stein, op. cit., pp. 649–650.

enough to assert statehood. Herzl contemplated the wholesale move of Jews into a territory without, or cleared of, other inhabitants, secured to the Jews as a state by the powers. "Infiltration," he wrote, "is bound to end badly. It continues until the inevitable moment when the native population feels itself threatened and forces the Government to stop a further influx of Jews."[17] Intercommunal riots erupted in the Mandate as early as May 1921. In the Churchill White Paper of the following year the British government made clear that, in its interpretation, the "national home" did not mean a predominantly Jewish state, rejected World Zionist Organization pretensions to participation in the governing of Palestine, and envisaged restrictions on immigration. Strife recurred with growing intensity until 1939 when the British, "having fought, flogged and hanged the Arabs to a standstill . . . conceded their viewpoint"[18] in a White Paper meeting the Arab demand that Jewish immigration be stemmed and eventually halted.

Although Balfour construed the United States to be among the powers committed to Zionism, America refused official support for the movement, as it refused to assume other obligations in the Near East. Wilson's acquiescence in the declaration was confirmed privately to leading American Zionists, but was not publicly and formally stated. In 1922 Congress passed a joint resolution endorsing the national home for the Jews in Palestine, and both major political parties thereafter regularly incorporated a Zionist plank in their platforms. Practical activity related to Palestine, however, remained in the hands of the Jewish community, within which strains persisted over the issue of orthodox Zionism—the specific pursuit of the goal of a Jewish state—and Palestinianism—building up the social and economic infrastructure of the Jewish community in Palestine. Brandeis' effort at the World Zionist Organization conference at London in 1920 to wrest control of the Organization from Weizmann on this issue was defeated, largely because of the Justice's unwillingness to leave the Supreme Court bench to devote full time to the cause. He lost control of the

---

[17] *The Jewish State* (1896), quoted in Stein, op. cit., p. 92.
[18] Desmond Stewart, *The Middle East: Temple of Janus* (Garden City, N.Y.: Doubleday & Co., 1971), p. 309.

movement even in the United States for a decade. Meanwhile, the community's wartime cooperation in relief operations in Palestine developed into up-building endeavors of such scale that in most years the resources made available to the Jews in the territory exceeded the Mandate's official budget. Gradually the ideological issue disappeared as the distinction between the principles of Zionism and Palestinianism became blurred in the minds of most Americans.

As in the other Arabian mandates, United States interests in Palestine were secured by separate negotiation with the mandatory power. A British-American Convention signed on December 3, 1924 confirmed existing economic and cultural interests and provided that they should remain unaffected by any modification of the mandate terms unless assented to by the United States. Under this provision American officials intervened from time to time to protect the predominantly Jewish investment in Palestine during the ensuing fifteen years, while steadfastly refusing to accept the Zionist contention that it obligated the United States to ensure the realization of the full Zionist program.

BETWEEN THE WARS

Elsewhere in the Arab world American policy between the two world wars accorded with the public distaste for entanglements and responsibilities abroad. The region was conceded to be one primarily of British and French concern. It was nevertheless a period of modest expansion of official contact with the emerging Arab states, of muted encouragement of their aspirations to self-determination, and of a support for the philanthropic, economic, cultural, and scientific enterprise of private Americans more notable for its benevolence than its vigor.

Early in the war famine conditions in the Levant, together with Turkish deportation and massacre of the Armenians, stimulated American missionary and lay organizations to form the Near East Relief Commission which, with government assistance in the form of finance, personnel, transport, and diplomatic support, did much to alleviate suffering and starvation. It remained in being after the war, becoming the Near East Foundation in 1930 and enlarging the scope of its activities to include the settlement of displaced persons, economic development, housing, health, education, and rural improvements based on systematic research.

Educational activities of the missions expanded, with a shift of emphasis reflected in 1920 in the redesignation of the Syrian Protestant College as the American University of Beirut. The quest for converts to Christianity (or Protestantism) was progressively subordinated to improvement of the quality of life through the provision of technical, scientific, and professional training. The mission schools attracted students from the Muslim majority in increasing numbers, since they were acknowledged to have no political axes to grind. In 1919 a new major institution of higher learning appeared with the founding of the American University at Cairo. In Lebanon, Syria, and Iraq the mission school systems were extended, with an increasing attention to the education of girls marked by the establishment in Beirut of a women's college. Considerable effort was devoted to medical facilities; in addition to the existing tuberculosis sanitarium on Mount Lebanon, the Presbyterians maintained the sole modern hospital in Tripoli and a medical center at Deir al-Zūr, while the Dutch Reformed Church opened hospitals at Amara, in Iraq, and at Matrah, adjacent to Muscat.

The interwar period was the golden age of Middle Eastern archaeology; Americans had developed a high competence in this science, and United States universities and museums conducted numerous excavations alone or in collaboration with British and French institutions. Among the more important of these undertakings were the Yale "dig" in association with the French Academy at Dura-Europas extending from 1928 to 1937; the Ur expedition of the University of Pennsylvania and the British Museum (1922 to 1933); the Oriental Institute of the University of Chicago at Megiddo in Palestine, Khorsabad in Iraq and various sites in Egypt; and Harvard University at Luxor and elsewhere in Egypt. In 1923 an American School of Oriental Research was founded at Baghdad, paralleling the similar institution in Jerusalem. American philanthropists contributed liberally to museum facilities in both locations. Popularized in Sunday press supplements and less sensationally in books and magazine articles, archaeological discoveries contributed to an intelligent awareness of the Arab lands within the American public, balancing somewhat the caricatured impressions derived from fictions such as *The Desert Song* of operetta and the silent film *The Sheik*. For the Arabs themselves, increasing knowledge of their ancient cultures heightened a sense of national pride and reinforced the burgeoning nationalist spirit.

The American government's firm insistence on an open door for its citizens' commerce in the Arab countries bore its most noteworthy fruit in the field of petroleum, which will be discussed in the next chapter. Conventional trade proceeded in fields such as the processing and export of dates and licorice root from Iraq to the United States. More imaginative were the development activities of Charles R. Crane, of the King-Crane Commission, in the Arabian Peninsula. Crane, who had already demonstrated an interest in the region by equipping the missionary hospital at Matrah with plumbing fixtures, visited Imam Yaḥyā of Yemen in 1926. Their discussions led to a varied program of technical assistance involving a minerals survey, the design and construction of roads and bridges, and the establishment of model farms. For this work Crane employed a young American engineer, Karl S. Twitchell, who made six trips to Yemen between 1927 and 1932. As news of these operations spread, King 'Abd al-'Azīz ibn 'Abd al-Raḥmān Āl Faisal Āl Sa'ūd (referred to hereinafter by his less formal title "Ibn Saud") invited Crane to visit him in Jidda, requesting his assistance in developing water resources in Hijaz. Assigned to this task, Twitchell made little progress in that field but discovered gold mines, exploited and abandoned in antiquity; Crane and Twitchell succeeded in organizing an American syndicate that reopened and worked the mines until the deposits were exhausted in the 1950s. At Ibn Saud's request, Twitchell played a part in the negotiations leading to the award of the Aramco oil concession in Saudi Arabia.

The gradual strengthening of American contact with the Arab world took place against a background of political and social change varying widely in quality from region to region, and in which United States official policy played a quite marginal role, content to leave responsibility in British and French hands so long as the essential interests of American citizens, narrowly construed, were respected.

A large part of the Arabian Peninsula was unified under the rule of Ibn Saud, secular leader of the Unitarian ("Wahhabi") movement, whose Islamic reform program constituted one aspect of nascent Arab nationalism. From his ancestral base in the inland region of Nejd, Ibn Saud seized the Persian Gulf province of al-Hasa on the eve of World War I, finally defeated the rival Rashīd dynasty in 1921 and, in 1924, moved against King Hussein's Hijaz domain, consolidating his conquest of that province and Asir, to the south, the following year. The Kingdom of Saudi Arabia in its present configuration was proclaimed in 1932. Four years before, Ibn Saud had requested United States recognition of his status as an independent monarch. The State Department regarded American interests in the Kingdom too minimal to justify formal relations, and responded unfavorably. Three years later the matter was reconsidered, recognition extended, and a basic treaty of friendship and navigation negotiated, signed in November 1933. A nonresident minister was named only in 1940, and resident diplomatic representation was not established at Jidda until 1942.

Yemen, under Ottoman occupation throughout the war, asserted its full independence on the evacuation of Turkish troops. President Wilson ignored Imam Yaḥyā's letter requesting recognition. United States relations with Yemen were not established until 1945, although intermittent informal contact was made by the American consul in the British Colony of Aden, the sole resident American official in the Peninsula between the Wars.

With one exception, the arc of quasiindependent territories, mostly quite small, extending along the Indian Ocean and the Persian Gulf between the Aden Protectorate and Kuwait had special arrangements with Great Britain by which the latter handled their external relations, and the United States found no reason to seek a change in this situation. The exception was the Sultanate of Muscat and Oman. Although American interests there were limited to a Reformed Church medical mission, formal relations remained in effect and, with a touch of nostalgia, the State Department instructed Paul Knabenshue, the American minister in Baghdad, to travel to Muscat in 1934 on a formal visit to Sultan Saʿīd bin Taymūr Āl Bū Saʿīd, commemorating the centenary of the United States treaty with Muscat. On his own initiative the Sultan reciprocated in March 1938, when he visited Washington as President Roosevelt's guest.

The rest of the Arab world remained during the interwar decades under varying degrees and forms of European occupation and administration, no more palatable to the peoples of the former Ottoman territories for being designated mandates rather than colonies or protectorates. Disappointed expectations of true independence fanned the flames of rising nationalism, exacerbated animosities against the imperial powers, and endowed the period with a distinctly violent stamp. Apportionment of the area served its purpose of containing inter-Allied rivalries and satisfying their major respective ambitions. At the same time, it established boundaries, both geographical and psychological, within the Arab East that promoted the accentuation of existing cultural and political differences. A wartime political unity of sorts had been achieved between the Fertile Crescent (Iraq and geographical Syria), the Peninsula and even, marginally, Egypt. Arabs remained united in the determination to fight for unrestricted freedom. In each occupied territory, however, the struggle posed its distinctive tactical problems as mandate officials adapted their methods to local circumstances. Mutual suspicion between British and French administrations further inhibited regional coordination. As a consequence, Syrians, Iraqis, or Egyptians pursued Syrian, Iraqi, or Egyptian independence, developing national leaderships, each with its own parochial outlook and aspiration to sovereign authority, thus storing up stumbling blocks in the path of future Arab unity.

In Iraq Great Britain sought, on the whole successfully, to minimize the financial burden of governing a territory heterogeneous both ethnically and confessionally, while preserving the essentials of economic advantage and empire defense by accelerating the transfer of administration to local hands. Acting through the pliant and subtle King Faisal, the British rapidly relinquished routine government functions to the Iraqis, while reserving ultimate control of finance, defense, and foreign relations. Within the outward trappings of elected, responsible government, effective power was reserved to a small, self-seeking oligarchy of politicians, landowners, merchants, and other notables. The Mandate was terminated by treaty in 1932, although Great Britain retained key defense installations and a significant measure of informal influence on the ruling clique. Achievement of independence, following closely on the demise of Faisal and the accession of his less stable son Ghazi, was marked by a massacre of the Assyrian community, a heterodox Christian community on which the British had mainly relied in recruiting forces to maintain public order; revolts in other segments of this violence-prone society were ruthlessly suppressed. In 1936 Iraq set a far-reaching precedent in the Arab world with the army *coup d'état* of Bakr Sidqī. Iraqi officers felt a deep emotional involvement in Syrian grievances against the French and in the rebellion of the Palestine Arabs; while the Sidqī regime endured only briefly, the army was thenceforth a basic factor in Iraqi politics.

By contrast the French, in the passionate conviction (not unknown to other imperialisms) that the expenditure of blood and treasure gives clear and enduring title to the lands of weaker peoples, sought to ensure the permanence of their presence in Syria by accentuating the social fragmentation of the territory. To the largely Maronite former Sanjak of Mount Lebanon were added the predominantly Sunni Muslim cities of Beirut and Tripoli, the mixed Biqā', and the Shī'a area south of Sidon, establishing the expanded region as the separate Mandate of Greater Lebanon, proclaimed the Republic of Lebanon in 1926. Elsewhere in Syria separate administrations were formed for Jabal Druze, the Alawite region of Latakia, the Sanjak of Alexandretta (with a sizeable Turkish minority), and the Jazira, with its large Kurdish population. The carefully selected but nonetheless fervently nationalistic politicians of the National Assembly were permitted to draw up a Syrian constitution in 1926, after the long and sanguine process of pacification was temporarily accomplished. The resulting draft, however, insisted on the political unity of Syria, including Lebanon and Palestine, on sharp restriction of French military facilities, and on early termination of the Mandate, all unacceptable to the French. In 1930 the High commissioner promulgated an inoffensive constitution by decree under which elections were held; no basis for accommodation could be found, however, and a wave of nationalist riots engulfed the country. In the more conciliatory climate of the Front Populaire, new Syrian elections were held, and negotiations opened on a treaty modeled after the Anglo-Iraqi agreement. Soon, however, the lowering prospect of a new European war led France to subordinate other concerns to her national defense. In order to meet the growing Fascist menace in the eastern Mediterranean, France concluded an agreement in 1938 with Turkey under which the latter was permitted to enter the Hatay (the Sanjak of Alexandretta, or Turkish Iskenderun) to "assist in maintaining order"; the following year the Sanjak was annexed to Turkey by French consent, over vehement Syrian protest. French public sentiment meanwhile intensified against relaxing the grip on Syria; France failed to ratify the proposed treaty; direct French administration was reinstituted, and all progress toward Syrian independence halted.

Great Britain had proclaimed its protection over Egypt at the outset of the war, extinguishing the shadowy remnant of Ottoman sovereignty, and governed the country under a none-too-gentle martial law until the armistice. The war had greatly sharpened Egyptian aspirations toward independence and, when the British endeavored to establish constitutional arrangements perpetuating the protectorate, they encountered dogged obstruction from a nationalist movement led by Sa'd Zaghlūl who, heading a nationalist delegation—*Wafd*—was rebuffed by the British High Commissioner, denied a hearing at the Paris Conference, denied concessions during negotiations in London, and finally exiled to Malta. On the initiative of Colonial Secretary Winston Churchill, Great Britain unilaterally declared Egypt an independent constitutional monarchy, reserving to herself, however, absolute discretion regarding the security of imperial communications, defense, the protection of foreigners and minorities, and the Sudan, which Great Britain and Egypt had, in theory, governed jointly since 1898. These sweeping restrictions on sovereignty infuriated the Wafd which, rapidly developing into a dynamic political party with mass appeal, won a majority in elections held early in 1924 and organized a government, meanwhile fomenting a campaign of agitation and assassination against the British occupation culminating in November in the murder of Sir Lee Stack, Commander-in-Chief of the Egyptian Army. The resulting crisis provided King Fuad the opportunity to strengthen the position of the royal palace and, for a decade, Egyptian politics was a turbulent three-cornered struggle among the Wafd, the King, and the British. In an Anglo-Egyptian Treaty of 1936 concessions were made on both sides, although major nationalist objectives remained unsatisfied.

The United States, concerned only with the safeguard of its citizens' cultural activities, formally recognized the British protectorate in 1919 and refused the Wafd a hearing both in Paris and in Washington. American diplomatic representation in Cairo was raised from agency to legation in 1922, and an American judge continued to sit on the Mixed Courts, which were a feature of the capitulatory regime. While the United States, having received British assurances regarding its interests in Egypt, reaped a modicum of Egyptian good will by supporting termination of the capitulations at the Montreux Conference of 1936, its role in Egyptian interwar politics was essentially that of spectator.

Further west, the United States had scant concern for Libya, now an Italian colony seized from the Ottomans in 1911, for Tunisia, under French protection since 1881, or for Algeria, which France asserted to be an integral part of her national territory. Only in Morocco did the United States seek to defend its quite modest interests by formulating and pursuing a specific and consistent policy, the object of which was to preserve the freedom of trade secured to Americans by a long series of international agreements since 1836. Under the French and Spanish protectorates imposed in 1912 (only the former recognized by the United States), this right could be defended against encroachment by the occupying powers only by upholding the principle of the Sultan's unimpaired sovereignty and the inviolability of the capitulatory privileges that his predecessors had accorded to Americans. By maintaining, alone among the powers, a diplomatic mission in Morocco, and by vigorous protest of French infringements of the capitulations, the United States preserved the essential framework of Moroccan independence in international law, thereby contributing to the restoration of full Moroccan sovereignty in 1956. American public imagination was captured by the Rif rebellion of the 1920s. Journalists Paul Scott Mowrer and Vincent Sheean wrote sympathetically of the Rif cause, and private citizens organized an "Americas' Commission for the Riff" to secure "justice and autonomy for an unconquerable people."[19] On the other hand, a group of American aviators volunteered for service with

---

[19]Luella J. Hall, *The United States and Morocco 1776–1956* (Metuchen, N.J.: The Scarecrow Press, 1971), pp. 758–759.

the Sherifian Air Guard and were warmly welcomed by the French for thus joining "the fight of Western civilization against the Islamic culture." Replying to a protest by the Women's League for Peace and Freedom, the State Department explained that its representative in Morocco had been asked to caution the airmen that their enlistment was contrary to United States law.[20] During the hostilities, a young American anthropologist-archaeologist, Carleton Coon, with his recent bride, passed back and forth unhindered between the Spanish and Rif lines taking precise measurements of Berber skulls.

With the great majority of Arab countries thus under foreign tutelage of some sort, problems calling for official intervention in behalf of American interests were usually matters for discussion with the European power concerned. The Arab territories were, however, moving with varying velocities toward control of their own destinies, and the growth of United States diplomatic contact kept general pace with the formation of local government institutions. America remained associated in the Arab mind with principles of self-determination and anticolonialism, which indeed corresponded with the attitudes of important segments of American opinion. American cultural and humanitarian enterprises continued to develop, with a new sophistication and adaptation to the needs and desires of the people served. Against this background of American benevolence without commitment, reciprocated by a vague sympathy, three interrelated sets of American interests gradually took shape. Through vigorous assertion of the Open Door axiom, American enterprise secured a stake in the petroleum resources of the Arab states that, over time, assumed increasing importance for American security and economic well-being. Second, the strategic geographic situation of the Arab lands endowed them with a significance for American national defense in a contracting world that, only dimly perceived before the outbreak of war in 1939, took on urgent clarity during the struggle against the Axis Powers and heightened poignancy in the ensuing cold war with the communist states. Finally, the dynamism and anti-Western elements of Arab nationalism, intensified in geometric proportion by the establishment and expansion of the state of Israel,

---

[20]Ibid., p. 759.

brought the United States face to face with irreconcilable Arab and Israeli demands on its sympathies and actions. The form in which these issues presented themselves to American policy and the manner of its response are the subject of the following chapters.

CHAPTER III

The American Interest in Arab Oil

MOST AMERICANS WERE SHOCKED to learn in October 1973 that imports of Arab oil represented the margin between opulent life and austerity. Few realized that the United States was then importing a million barrels per day of Arab crude and an additional million barrels of products refined from oil originating in Arab states; this represented 14% of the American oil supply and 7% of all energy consumed. The Arab embargo closed factories, increased unemployment, chilled homes, reduced the citizen's traditional easy mobility, lengthened lines at service stations, and raised a threat of rationing of fuel of all types. The notion that the United States needed Arab oil was a novel one. On principles largely unrelated to the needs of the American consumer, the government had abetted the effort of American enterprise to secure a share in the development of Arab oil wealth. It assisted the operations of the principal beneficiaries, the giant integrated international oil corporations, with liberal tax provisions and welcomed their contribution to the American balance of payments position, since their earnings were chiefly in European currencies. Specific oil policy, on the other hand, aimed primarily at protecting relatively high-cost domestic production against competition from inexpensive oil imports. Foreign policy statements consistently mentioned our interest in the continued availability of Middle East oil to Western Europe on reasonable terms. Since the question whether (and on what terms) Arab oil should also be available to the United States is now clearly relevant, some understanding of the origin and evolution of the Middle East petroleum industry is important to any account of relations between America and the Arab countries.

A DOOR RELUCTANTLY OPENED

In 1919 the American Commission to Negotiate Peace cogently stated the case for formulating a positive United States policy regarding the disposition of the Ottoman Empire. In addition to humanitarian and liberal considerations, the Commission's memorandum set forth the "selfish" argument that the United States had important commercial interests, actual and potential, in the Ottoman territories that would be impossible to defend without an effective voice in the settlement. The only way to vindicate the policy of the "open door" was to be on the spot and *hold* the door open.[1] Among the specific objects of the Commission's concern were the petroleum resources believed, although not yet proved, to be present in the area, notably in Iraq. Captain Yale, experienced in oil matters, kept the problem before his colleagues; in May he had expressed apprehension that Great Britain would endeavor to exclude the United States from a share of any oil that might be found in the territories under her control. "It is necessary", he wrote,

to point out the extreme importance to the American nation of maintaining a strong position in the petroleum trade of the world. It is a fact that the native petroleum resources of the United States are becoming exhausted and that the maximum production has already been nearly, if not quite, reached. It is proper to observe that, during the war, 80% of the petroleum products of the Allies were shipped from the United States. This was accomplished at a great sacrifice to the reserves above and under ground, and at prices which were fixed by the United States Government. . . . Our national safety, the maintenance and expansion of our foreign and domestic trade, must depend in large measure upon the assurance to the United States of continued supplies of petroleum. With our requirements constantly increasing, with our own supplies about to decline and with more than half of the potential production of the world located without our territorial limits, the necessity of guaranteeing now to American industry the right to have its part in the development of the petroleum resources about to pass under British control will be apparent.[2]

By October Yale learned with some agitation of a secret understanding by which France renounced her claim to the province of

[1]Harry N. Howard, *The King-Crane Commission* (Beirut: Khayat's, 1963), p. 284.
[2]Ibid., p. 59.

Mosul in favor of Great Britain; both would share in the exploitation of Iraq's oil, while France would ensure the right of way for a pipeline across Syria to the Mediterranean seaboard.[3] Although Yale's urging failed to push the United States into the peace settlements, his concern coincided with that of the American petroleum industry, of high federal officials, and of the Congress. Many major oil fields in the United States had yet to be discovered; the war had gravely depleted known reserves and, in view of the rapid expansion of the automotive and other energy-consuming industries, experts warned of the possible exhaustion of America's own petroleum within a decade or two. Institutions devised for close wartime cooperation between government and the oil industry were nevertheless terminated abruptly at the close of hostilities, and prices began to rise sharply. Secretary of the Navy Josephus Daniels authorized destroyers on the Pacific coast to seize fuel oil in the hands of suppliers but withheld from the Navy at what the crusty Secretary considered reasonable prices.[4] Daniels publicly proposed the nationalization of United States oil resources; Senator Phelan of California introduced a bill by which the government itself, through a public-sector corporation, would stimulate American oil development in foreign countries. Both government and industry thus sensed a necessity for vigorous development of foreign oil sources. In the postwar international political climate, a coordinated effort was, in fact, required to open the Near Eastern door to American petroleum enterprise.

Britain's intention to reserve economic opportunity for her own nationals in the regions that her troops occupied became apparent at the close of hostilities. British officials denied to Socony[5] representatives access to areas in Palestine to which it had valid exploration rights granted by the Ottoman government and rifled the files of the company's local agent. In Iraq, Socony geologists were denied permission to travel in the country, while British geologists were allowed unrestricted exploration privileges. Wilson's last Secretary of State, Bainbridge Colby, instituted an acrimonious and ultimately inconclusive correspondence with the British For-

---

[3]Ibid., p. 269.
[4]Gerald D. Nash, *United States Oil Policy 1890–1964* (Pittsburgh: University of Pittsburgh Press, 1968), pp. 44–45.
[5]Standard Oil of New York; later Socony-Vacuum, then Mobil.

eign Minister, Lord Curzon, continued under the following administration by Secretary Charles Evans Hughes. The salient points at issue were:

1. The United States insisted that, under the mandate principles agreed at Paris, its nationals were entitled to complete commercial and industrial equality. Great Britain maintained that such equality was assured only to members of the League of Nations, which moreover was the proper forum for discussion of mandate terms.
2. On the more general principle of the open door the British pointed out, not unjustly, that the United States discriminated against foreign oil exploration not only on its own territory but in the Philippines, Haiti, Costa Rica, and elsewhere.
3. To the asserted need for supplementing America's depleted oil reserves, Curzon retorted that the United States produced 70% of the world's petroleum, and its nationals another 12% in Mexico, whereas the British share of world production was a mere 4½%.
4. Great Britain maintained that petroleum rights in the vilayets of Baghdad and Mosul were accorded to the Turkish Petroleum Company (a conglomerate of European interests, including the Anglo-Persian Oil Company of which the British government was a major shareholder) by a letter of intent dated June 28, 1914 from the Ottoman Grand Vizier to the German ambassador in Constantinople.[6] The United States, on solid grounds, dismissed the letter as not constituting a concession.

At the suggestion of the director of research for the American Petroleum Institute, Van H. Manning, and with the active encouragement of the secretaries of State and Commerce, seven major American oil companies organized an informal consortium[7] to exploit promptly any success the government's diplomatic effort might achieve.

Anglo-American tensions reached a peak with the signing in April 1920 of the San Remo Agreement by which Great Britain and France made explicit their intention to develop Iraqi oil to the exclusion of other powers. The British, however, had reason to avoid final alienation of American opinion. By early 1922, when the Washington Conference was setting bounds to Anglo-Ameri-

---

[6]Benjamin Schwadran, *The Middle East, Oil and the Great Powers* (New York: Praeger, 1955), p. 196.
[7]The original American group was composed of Standard of New Jersey (later Esso, then Exxon), Socony (Mobil), Mexican, Gulf, Texaco, Sinclair, and Atlantic.

can naval rivalry, the British posture respecting Iraqi oil relaxed. Anglo-Persian officials anticipated that American capital and engineering experience would be needed for the Iraqi operations.[8] More particularly, the future of the vilayet of Mosul, then assumed to be an unusually promising area for oil exploration, remained in doubt. (Assigned over Turkish protest to the prospective Iraqi mandate by the Treaty of Sèvres, Mosul was reconsidered at the Lausanne Conference, convened in November 1922, which "bucked" it to the League of Nations Council; the latter awarded most of the vilayet to Iraq in December 1925, pursuant to an advisory opinion of the Permanent Court of International Justice.) Meanwhile a French national, Franklin-Bouillon, had concluded a treaty in October 1921 with the Turkish nationalist government in Ankara terminating the state of war between the two countries and promising France broad economic privileges that would presumably extend to Mosul if the area should revert to Turkey. Furthermore, the Turkish Grand National Assembly in April 1923 revalidated a prewar railway and petroleum concession granted to a firm organized by an American, Admiral Colby Chester, who soon proved better able to mobilize American diplomatic support than American capital in support of his claims. Discreet feelers put forth by the Turkish Petroleum Company (whose German share had become a French war prize) to the American oil industry in 1921, confirmed through diplomatic channels the following year, indicated that TPC was prepared to admit United States interests to participation in the development of Iraqi oil. Discussions were instituted in July between the newly constituted American group and TPC; not until July 1928 did the exceedingly complex negotiations end in agreement among all participants.

Secretary Hughes' diplomacy respecting the Iraqi oil issue has not been greatly admired. It is true that the abstract principles on which he insisted so rigidly were clearer to him than to the businessmen compelled to give them substance in negotiation with the British and French TPC officials to whom these principles were repugnant. It is equally true that the principles were ultimately defeated in practice. While steadfastly refusing to acknowledge

[8]John A. DeNovo, *American Interests and Policies in the Middle East 1900–1939* (Minneapolis: University of Minnesota Press, 1963), p. 187.

TPC's concessions claims as valid and opposing the grant in Iraq of a monopolistic oil concession that would close the door to any American company interested in the region's petroleum resources, Hughes countenanced negotiations between a handful of American firms and a putative concessionary dedicated to the idea of exclusive rights. In an effort to meet the open door principle, the American group persuaded the TPC to agree that, within a limited period after the award of a concession, the company would select a designated number of areas for its own development and open others to free and competitive bidding. Detailed provisions along this line, satisfactory to none of the parties, were written into the TPC concession awarded in 1925, but discarded in a modified agreement of 1931 that established the principle of integral development of Iraq's oil by the company, now renamed the Iraq Petroleum Company (IPC), and its subsidiaries.

The prewar concept of the TPC envisaged that its participants would act only in concert in undertaking petroleum development in the Ottoman Empire. The principle was reasserted in the secret Anglo-French accord at San Remo in the form of the "Red Line" Agreement by which the participants agreed to abstain from independent action in the former Ottoman territories including the entire Arabian Peninsula, Kuwait excepted. This "self-denying" clause, whether interpreted as orderly international cooperation or as aspiration to monopoly control, ran directly counter to open door philosophy. Hughes, while admitting that the American companies negotiating with TPC were free to bind themselves in this manner, asserted that their action would not bind the State Department, which would remain free to support other American concerns seeking a share in the region's oil resources.

Following protracted multilateral negotiations over the share of C. S. Gulbenkian, the middleman in the original TPC concession from the Ottoman government, all participants reached a working agreement in July 1928 establishing the familiar formula of 23 ¾ % each for Anglo-Persian (later Anglo-Iranian, then British Petroleum), Royal Dutch Shell, Compagnie française des pétroles, and the American group, and the remaining 5% for Gulbenkian. For purposes of its participation the American group (by then consisting of Standard of New Jersey, Gulf, Atlantic, Pan American, and Standard of New York) formed the Near East Development Corporation in February 1928. Subsequently Gulf withdrew; Standard of New Jersey (later Esso, then Exxon) and Socony (later Socony-Vacuum, then Mobil) acquired the interests of the remaining partners, becoming thenceforth equal owners of NEDC. With discovery of the major Kirkuk field in 1927 and completion of pipelines to the Mediterranean, one across Transjordan and Palestine terminating at Haifa, the other across Syria to Banias, with a branch to Tripoli, in Lebanon, IPC became a significant factor in the world's petroleum supply.

Therefore, far from opening the Iraqi door wide to American enterprise, United States diplomacy had contributed to the association of two major international companies controlling worldwide producing, refining, transport, and marketing facilities in a monopolistic operation with large corporations owned in significant proportion by the European governments—British and French—which at the same time exercised political control over much of the Arab world. The partners shared important basic concerns and attitudes: a need for assured access to reserves of petroleum, and a desire to minimize the uneconomic effects of exhuberant competition in production and marketing resulting from the rapid postwar expansion of the global oil industry. The Red Line Agreement of San Remo expressed the common intention to ensure that the development of Middle Eastern oil should not outrun the quantity that could be profitably sold. Similarly, the so-called "as-is" agreement of 1928 among New Jersey Standard, Anglo-Persian, and Royal Dutch Shell aimed at the elimination of wasteful and expensive duplication in competition for markets.[9] Whether these policies reflect the determination of an alleged international cartel to maximize its members' profits at the expense both of consumers and of the oil-producing countries or a sense of responsibility for the orderly and economic growth of a vital international industry has long been, and remains, the subject of impassioned debate. It is certain, on the other hand, that the terms of the concessions, from the pioneering D'Arcy agreement in Persia in 1901 forward, tended more to secure the companies' right to formulate and pursue their own policies than to reserve to the host governments

<hr>

[9]George W. Stocking, *Middle East Oil: A Study in Political and Economic Controversy* (Vanderbilt University Press, 1970), pp. 84–86.

effective management of their countries' oil resources. Following a rather uniform pattern, the agreements granted exclusive development rights over vast areas, often entire countries, for extended periods of time, during which the concessionary firm was excused from taxation. These features, together with royalty provisions, accounting procedures, arbitration arrangements, and the disposition of natural gas, all contained the germs of controversy. Disputes developed rapidly and intensified as the oil-producing states grew in sophisticated understanding of Western business methods, achieved full sovereignty, and acquired the ability to impose terms in harmony with their perceived national interests.

By virtue of its treaty arrangements with the Arab territories bordering the Persian Gulf, Great Britain was in a position—even, until 1927, in Saudi Arabia—to influence decisions of the rulers regarding concessions and terms. In practice, the British saw to it that, regardless of the source of capital, operating companies were of British registration and administered by British directors. American companies became interested in the area in large part through the labors of the New Zealander, Major Frank Holmes who, in the 1920s, acquired for his Eastern and General Syndicate an imposing portfolio of exploration licenses and concession options for sale to firms with larger capital resources. Turned down successively by Shell, Anglo-Persian, and Jersey Standard, his rights in the island shaikhdom of Bahrain were taken up in 1927 by the Gulf Oil Corporation, which promptly conducted encouraging geological work. Gulf, however, still a member of the American group contemplating participation in TPC, was bound by the Red Line Agreement, and its TPC colleagues refused either to participate jointly in a Bahrain concession or to permit Gulf to retain it alone. Accordingly, Gulf sold its option to Standard of California. The latter encountered the obstacle of British insistence on British registration and management. Following intervention by the State Department with the British government, arrangements were made for the charter in Canada of the Bahrain Petroleum Company (Bapco) under conditions ensuring that key personnel should be of British nationality and acceptable to the British government. Bapco's first producing well was completed in May 1932, and output soon exceeded the requirements of California Standard's markets. The Texas Company, being in the complementary situation of possessing insufficient crude to supply its established markets, exchanged a half interest in its marketing facilities east of Suez for a half share in Bapco, and the California-Texas Company (Caltex) was registered in the Bahamas for the handling of merchandising operations. As the markets involved were for refined products, as distinct from crude, Bapco undertook construction of a refinery on Bahrain, completed in 1937 and later greatly expanded to process crude piped from the Saudi mainland, an operation that increased in importance to Bapco as Bahrain's modest reserves of crude dwindled.

The defenses set up by the British government, Anglo-Persian, and IPC against encroachment by "outsiders" in the Middle East were breached in the 1930s. As Sultan of Najd early in World War I, Ibn Saud had concluded a treaty of protection with the British whereby, in consideration for an annual subsidy, he undertook to grant no economic concessions without British agreement and to refrain from attacking King Hussein's Hijaz dominions. The British High Commissioner in Iraq, Sir Percy Cox, in the context of negotiations in 1923 with Ibn Saud over border incursions by the Wahhabis, reluctantly acquiesced in the grant of an exploration permit and option in al-Hasa to Major Holmes' Eastern and General Syndicate. The latter carried out inconclusive geological work for a time, but soon defaulted on its annual rental obligations; Ibn Saud warned the firm that the agreement was liable to cancellation. Meanwhile the British, disillusioned with Hussein, terminated their subsidy to Ibn Saud, leaving him free to occupy the Hijaz. A new Anglo-Saudi treaty signed at Jidda in 1927 terminated British restraints on Ibn Saud's freedom to award concessions. The monarch was now without foreign subsidies, and revenues from the pilgrim traffic were declining both because of the deepening world economic depression and of Muslim apprehensions of the Wahhabi *Ikhwān.* Ibn Saud was consequently in desperate need of new revenues with which to administer his expanded realm. In 1932 he authorized the engineer Karl Twitchell to seek offers from American oil firms. Finding no interest at the Texas Company, Twitchell applied to Gulf which, as a signatory of the Red Line Agreement, loyally relayed the invitation to IPC and to Standard of California which, encouraged by its recent strike in Bahrain, became the sole independent contender in negotiations at Jidda in the spring of 1933.[10] California succeeded in winning a concession over IPC, largely because it was willing to offer more substantial initial payments than the IPC representatives and also to make them in gold. The concession of May 29, 1933, covering al-Hasa (later named the Eastern) Province with right of preference elsewhere in the country, was the prelude to one of the world's major petroleum operations. Initially exploited by a wholly owned subsidiary of California Standard—California Arabian Oil Company (Casoc)—the Texas Company was admitted to a half share in 1936. Shortly after the end of World War II, faced with enormous capital outlays in developing the concession and in constructing a pipeline to the Mediterranean ("Tapline"), Casoc recruited Socony (Mobil) and Standard of New Jersey (Exxon) to the venture which, in 1944, had been renamed the Arabian American Oil Company (Aramco). The new partners' IPC associates, Compagnie française des pétroles and Gulbenkian, objected to their independent action in violation of the Red Line Agreement; a revised arrangement with IPC leaving them free to participate in Aramco was reached only after two years litigation and negotiation.

The IPC consortium, abetted at the official level by the British government, endeavored to keep such intrusions into the Middle East within manageable bounds. The Political Resident at Bushire, responsible for British interests throughout the Persian Gulf, advised the Ruler of Qatar in 1933 to award an oil concession only to a British firm, thus frustrating an expression of interest by California Standard; an award was made to Anglo-Iranian as IPC agent in 1935; oil was discovered in important quantities in 1939, although materials shortages precluded commercial production until the postwar period. In 1935 IPC established Petroleum Concessions Limited as an instrument for securing exploration and development rights within the Red Line area. Subsidiaries were formed to manage the Qatar concession, areas granted by the Trucial Coast rulers, and parts of Syria, Lebanon, Palestine, and Cyprus.

---

[10]Major Holmes appeared briefly at the talks, but withdrew when the Saudi negotiators suggested that he would be expected to pay the arrears under his lapsed permit in order to enter the competition.

The Red Line had been drawn so as to exclude the state of Kuwait from the region in which the IPC partners were bound to act only in concert, and the Shaikhdom's oil prospects became the object of renewed Anglo-American rivalry. Major Holmes' Syndicate secured an option there in the 1920s and, having failed to dispose of it to Anglo-Persian, agreed to negotiate its transfer to Gulf Oil Corporation. The British government intervened with the Ruler, however, insisting that the concession should go to a British concern; Anglo-Persian geologists appeared in Kuwait with drilling equipment. Gulf appealed to the State Department for diplomatic assistance, which was forthcoming from Secretary Stimson and Andrew Mellon, the American Ambassador in London. Hesitating to confront the United States with an outright refusal to admit Gulf to Kuwait, the Foreign Office adopted delaying tactics. The ensuing two-year impasse was broken by direct negotiation between Gulf and Anglo-Persian; they applied jointly for rights in Kuwait to be shared equally under management of an *ad hoc* British-registered firm, the Kuwait Oil Company, Ltd. The Ruler awarded a concession on this basis in December 1934. While, as in Qatar, production had to be deferred until the mid-1940s, the immense Burgan field had already been discovered in 1938.

In Libya an exceedingly liberal general petroleum law enacted in 1955 immediately attracted numerous concessionaries, both major and independent and, by 1961, the country had joined the ranks of important producers. In Algeria major oilfields were discovered as early as 1956 by a joint Franco-Algerian public sector firm; participation by American oil and gas firms became feasible only after the country's independence in 1962.

EVOLUTION OF UNITED STATES PETROLEUM POLICY

The federal government has historically intervened in the United States oil industry reluctantly and only for compelling reasons of national security or intolerable disruption of the economy. Through antitrust action against the Standard Oil Company in 1911, a condition of monopoly in the industry was modified to one of oligopoly. During World War I, the United States Fuel Administration effectively coordinated the production and distribution operations of the oil companies, while efforts of the Navy

Department to effect direct entry of the government into these activities failed. With the hasty dismantling of wartime controls in 1919, the industry was left to its own devices, apart from diplomatic efforts to facilitate American participation in the discovery and development of oil resources abroad.

Apprehensions of the exhaustion of the country's own petroleum, which had preoccupied Josephus Daniels and William Yale, were of brief duration. By the end of the 1920s major oilfields had been discovered in Texas, Oklahoma, and California. Their rapid development produced a glut of oil that soon flooded the market; the surplus encouraged wasteful production practices, violent price fluctuations, and cutthroat competition. The Coolidge administration, unresponsive to the need expressed by industry leaders for stabilizing government supervision and unwilling to relax antitrust laws to permit cooperation among the companies to restrain production, did no more than to approve tax benefits in the form of 27½% depletion allowance enacted by Congress in 1926 and the study by the Federal Oil Conservation Board of possible approaches to coordination. Meanwhile, certain states, notably Texas and Oklahoma, established agencies to limit and prorate production. Herbert Hoover declined even to entertain the notion of federal controls and went no further than to encourage industry conservation practices and to withdraw some public lands from private prospecting. As the Great Depression deepened after 1929, the chaos was compounded by imports of low-cost crude resulting from the successful foreign operations of the large international corporations. Under the New Deal serious attempts at rationalization were made. The national government assisted individual and collective state efforts to restrict production, and voluntary agreements to the same end within the industry were legalized. Prices were stabilized under federal guidelines. By the eve of World War II cooperative action among the states, the industry, and the national government had become a usual and accepted process. Events during the conflict emphasized the government's role of supporting the foreign operations of American oil enterprise while demonstrating that its transfer from private to public hands was not a feasible policy.

At the outset of the war Casoc (later Aramco) development of Saudi Arabia's oil had progressed to a point where the royalties paid to Ibn Saud reached an annual rate of nearly $2 million. Wartime dislocations impeded operations and sharply cut the King's oil revenues while simultaneously bringing to a virtual halt the annual Muslim pilgrimage, his only significant alternative source of income. Not unnaturally he looked to Casoc for a solution to his fiscal problems and, in January 1941, demanded advance royalties of $6 million annually while the emergency lasted. The company responded in the first instance with a loan of half this amount, but appealed for longer-term help to the United States government on the ground that a private firm could not properly underwrite the solvency of a sovereign state. President Roosevelt, sympathetic to Casoc's problem but finding no legal basis for government aid to Saudi Arabia, adopted the position that support of Ibn Saud's regime was a British responsibility. He instructed Federal Loan Administrator Jesse Jones, who was then negotiating a substantial loan to Great Britain, to stipulate that a subsidy should be paid to Ibn Saud from its proceeds. By this device Casoc's advances to the King against future rents and royalties dropped from nearly $3 million in 1940 to $79,651 in 1943, while British payments rose during the same period from $403,000 to $16,618,280.[11] The arrangement afforded Britain an opportunity to enhance its influence in Saudi Arabia; alarmed that this might lead to the loss of its concession in whole or part, Casoc appealed once more to the United States government, proposing that the latter assume Ibn Saud's indebtedness to Britain, while Casoc would set aside reserves in Saudi Arabia from which future United States needs in petroleum would be met at well below world prices.[12] Roosevelt responded to Casoc's immediate concern by a decision, which proved adequate, finding Saudi Arabia eligible for lend-lease assistance.

The armed services, the Office of War Mobilization, and the State and Interior departments were meanwhile concerned more and more with the drawdown of domestic oil reserves under pressure of war requirements. Under the guidance of Harold Ickes, Secretary of Interior, long an advocate of nationalization of the American petroleum industry, an interdepartmental committee

---

[11]Stocking, op. cit., pp. 92–95.
[12]Ibid., p. 97.

drew up plans for a Petroleum Reserves Corporation through which the government would acquire and exploit overseas oil supplies. Formed by presidential order in June 1943, the PRC instituted negotiations with California Standard and the Texas Company first for the outright purchase of Casoc's entire assets, then for a substantial financial and management interest in them. The notion met with indignant refusal by the parent companies and vigorous protest throughout the domestic industry, reechoing on the floors of Congress.[13] Shifting ground, Ickes next took up a plan originating in the Navy Department, by which the PRC would build and own a pipeline from Saudi Arabia to the Mediterranean coast to carry crude, and products refined at Bahrain, in support of the Allied war effort. This plan stimulated equally heated debate; it was abandoned, both to retain the cooperation of the domestic industry and to avoid subjecting the Anglo-American alliance to political strain. In a last-ditch effort to create a direct government role in the petroleum industry Ickes persuaded Roosevelt to seek agreement with Britain on mutual cooperation in the exploitation of Middle East oil. A draft agreement defining respective interests and prospective modalities of collaboration in the area was negotiated during the spring and summer of 1944. It met with opposition from independent American producers apprehensive of competition from cheap crude imports, as well as the majors, whose executives had not been consulted and who saw in the proposed treaty a first step either toward nationalization or toward the formation of a cartel. Modified slightly in 1945, after it became evident that it stood no chance of approval in the Senate, the agreement was reported out favorably by the Foreign Relations Committee but never voted on by the whole Senate.

Thus, by the end of World War II, a stable pattern had been established for the relationship between the government and the industry. The latter was to remain primarily in private hands but under general public supervision. Government was expected to foster the industry by research, tax benefits, and even subsidy when circumstances justified, to assist by regulation in maintaining its economic stability, and to support by diplomatic action its interests abroad.[14]

---

[13]Ibid., pp. 98–99; Nash, op. cit., pp. 173–174.
[14]Nash, op. cit., pp. 249–250.

United States oil policy has moved within these narrow limits under recent administrations. The key issue of the 1950s was that of crude oil imports, on which the industry was clearly divided between the major international firms, whose interests were best served by free import of the inexpensive oil they produced abroad and the husbanding of their domestic reserves, and the independents, whose chiefly domestic production was vulnerable to low-cost competition. These conflicting interests were complicated at the national policy level by considerations of national security, of which the importance had been amply proved by the experience of two global wars, and of our relations with foreign countries, including the Arab states, where American companies held concessions and which resented the denial of free access to the American market for their oil. By the end of the 1950s, after repeated efforts of the Eisenhower administration to induce voluntary curbs on imports had failed, the Secretary of Interior was empowered to establish quotas and license petroleum imports.

THE REVOLUTION IN CONCESSION TERMS

The early Middle East oil concession agreements were concluded on terms that took full account of the companies' investment of substantial capital in highly speculative ventures. The host governments, whether because they were not entirely free agents (as in Iraq or Kuwait) or were in desperate need of revenue (as in Iran or Saudi Arabia), willingly surrendered their sovereign taxing powers and the management of their chief (if as yet undiscovered) economic resource in return for rents and other fixed but assured payments, and a specified royalty on each ton of oil produced and exported. The realization, after World War II, that the Persian Gulf region held the world's richest reserves of oil attracted companies smaller than the international giants that had pioneered the area. Meanwhile, it became apparent that only a relatively modest proportion of the industry's profits accrued to the governments of the producing countries. In the first instance governments and rulers, notably Ibn Saud, simply made generalized demands on the concessionaries for increased payments to cover their rapidly rising expenses. Meanwhile, a new generation of Arabs and Iranians was acquiring, through Western education and on-the-job experience, a sophisticated knowledge of the international oil industry's structure, and they were becoming competent to call effectively into question the terms of the existing concessions on grounds of equity, law, economics, and policy. Venezuela set a momentous example for the Middle Eastern producers in 1948, when she introduced a tax of 50% on the profits of the companies producing oil within her territory.

The original pattern of arrangements between the major international companies and the countries on the Persian Gulf was first significantly breached in the Kuwait-Saudi Neutral Zone (which remained politically undivided until the late 1960s). The respective concessions for the Saudi and Kuwaiti shares were noteworthy both for the liberality of the terms and for the fact that the recipients were independent American companies without established overseas markets. A consortium of nine (later ten) companies organized as the American Independent Oil Company (Aminoil) was awarded rights for Kuwait's share. The Ruler retained significant rights in the producing and refining companies to be formed and a one-eighth share of local profits; a bonus of $7.5 million was payable on signing of the agreement, annual rents of $625,000, and royalty of $2.50 a ton (about 33 cents a barrel) on oil produced and exported—by far the highest rate yet known in the Middle East.[15]

These terms obviously had to be matched with respect to the Saudi half of the zone. Aramco, which held preferential rights there, chose to relinquish them. Ibn Saud's ministers were thus free to award a concession for the Saudi share to J. Paul Getty's Pacific Western Oil Company (later the Getty Oil Company) in January 1949. Getty undertook to pay an initial bonus of $9.5 million, annual rent of $1 million, and royalties of 55 cents a barrel; he agreed to give Saudis preference in subscribing to publicly issued shares, to build a refinery, and to deliver products without cost to Riyad and Jidda; the Saudi government was to receive a one-eighth share in production profits and a one-fourth share in those from refining operations.[16]

---

[15]Stephen Hemsley Longrigg, *Oil in the Middle East: Its Discovery and Development* (London: Oxford University Press, 1954), pp. 214–215.
[16]Ibid., p. 215.

The profit-sharing principle being thus introduced into the Middle East, Aramco adapted it to the renegotiation of its concession terms in Saudi Arabia between 1949 and 1950. The King and his advisors were well aware that the Aramco venture was immensely lucrative. In the five years beginning in 1944 its profits rose from $2.8 million to $115,062,120. By 1950 the Company had paid more than $100 million in corporation taxes to the United States government—in 1949 alone about $43 million, or $5 million more than its payments to the Saudi government. By a new arrangement concluded in December 1950, Aramco agreed to pay the Saudi government, as an income tax, one half of its net profits after meeting its foreign tax obligations, all royalties, rentals, and other payments due the government being treated as credits toward the government's share in the earnings. Meanwhile, in negotiations with the United States Treasury and State departments, the Company secured permission to treat its payments to the Saudi government as operating costs in calculating its liability under the American tax laws. This nominal 50-50 profit-sharing formula was reflected immediately in vastly increased Saudi revenues, while Aramco's profitability remained substantially unaffected.[17]

While the other major concessionaries greeted Aramco's formula with consternation, they were obliged to follow the lead, and comparable amendments were introduced in Kuwait and by the IPC group in its various holdings.[18] Even in Iran, where negotiations begun in 1948 to improve the terms of Anglo-Iranian's concession failed of their purpose and the industry was nationalized, equal sharing of earnings was a feature of the eventual agreement between Iran and the international consortium, which fell heir to AIOC's producing function in 1954.

OIL PRICES AND COLLECTIVE ACTION

As long as a fixed royalty per unit of petroleum exported remained the principal basis of the producing countries' revenue from the industry, their interest lay primarily in maintaining a

[17]Stocking, op cit., pp. 145–150.
[18]Ibid., pp. 150–151.

high rate of production. With the shift of the basis to profit sharing, revenue was a function not only of volume but also of the price at which crude was billed for export, which thus became of vital concern to the governments of the producing states.

The Middle Eastern oil industry was, by and large, the creation of seven integrated international oil firms: Standard of New Jersey (Exxon), Socony (Mobil), the Texas Company, Standard of California, Gulf, Royal Dutch Shell, and the predecessors of British Petroleum. Through interlocking contractual arrangements and less formal understandings, the companies sought to ensure worldwide stability in the industry by means of uniform accounting and pricing practices and by setting limits to mutual competition. Development of the reserves in the Persian Gulf area, easily capable of supplying the needs of the entire eastern hemisphere at production costs spectacularly below those of other sources, threatened to disrupt the global operations of the industry. During World War II, a procedure was perfected whereby, in general terms, the competitive f.o.b. crude oil price in the Caribbean area adjacent to the United States, the world's largest producer and consumer of oil, formed the basis of announced—"posted"— prices in the Persian Gulf and at the pipeline terminals in the eastern Mediterranean, with adjustments for the differential in freight costs to Western Europe from the two regions. Operation of this device depended on a high concentration of control of the sources of oil entering international trade and on common pricing. At the same time, it provided the benefit of flexibility for the participating companies. The function of the concessionary firms was production only; their customers were their own parent firms. There was thus no conventional free market for Middle Eastern oil. Crude oil could be, and often was, shipped to the parents' refineries at substantial discounts from posted prices. While this practice could be viewed as a simple bookkeeping adjustment from the point of view of the large, integrated companies, it had grave implications for the interests of the countries where the oil originated, who furthermore had little or no voice in the arrangements.

The structure of the global petroleum industry meanwhile came under critical scrutiny in the United States. A searching study was submitted in 1952 by the Federal Trade Commission to the Senate

Select Sub-Committee on Small Business, of which the thrust was indicated by its title: *The International Petroleum Cartel.* Later published, the report contributed to the education of the growing community of Arab oil officials, nurturing their belief that a huge international combine was enriching itself at their countries' expense.

The basing-price system broke down during the decade of the 1950s under the impact both of an increase in the world supply of oil exceeding market requirements and of a pronounced diffusion of control over petroleum reserves, although the process was somewhat obscured and retarded first by the interruption of Iranian oil shipments between 1952 and 1954 and later by the dislocations resulting from the closure of the Suez Canal in 1956 to oil tankers and other shipping. The output of the Persian Gulf area expanded enormously. North Africa emerged as a major producing region, and Russia became a significant exporter, willing to undercut established prices and to offer unorthodox barter or credit terms. Finally, numerous independent firms entered the field together with Italian, French, and other government-sponsored agencies. Few of the independent concerns had refining or large retail marketing networks of their own, and the difficulty of disposing of their crude encouraged them to sell at considerable discounts from posted prices.

The Arab oil-producing states, in these conditions, competed in some degree with each other in the world petroleum market. At the same time their sense of common interest was intensified by the conviction that existing contractual arrangements with the concessionary companies were inequitable and inconsistent with national sovereignty. In the course of inter-Arab consultation and coordination procedures, the first Arab Petroleum Congress was held at Cairo in the spring of 1959, the first of a series at which the concerns both of the governments and of the companies were aired and bold new concepts floated in the presence of representatives of the world press. Shell and British Petroleum had, in February, announced reductions in the posted price of Middle East crude, which threatened the balance between Persian Gulf and Caribbean prices. Venezuela's interests were directly and adversely involved, and the Venezuelan minister of mines and hydrocarbons, present at the conference, gained a sympathetic hearing from representatives of Iran, Saudi Arabia, Kuwait, and Iraq for the idea of mutual coordination to protect their similar interests. Immediately after the announcement in August by Esso Export Corporation of reductions in its Middle East posted prices, representatives of these states met at Baghdad and founded the Organization of Petroleum Exporting Countries (OPEC). Its purpose was to serve as a collective bargaining agency to ensure stable prices and thus an adequate, predictable level of revenue for the producing countries, while allowing for a reasonable rate of profits for the concessionaries. Competently staffed and pursuing realistic objectives, OPEC has become a permanent feature of the world oil scene, including in its membership most of the noncommunist net exporters of oil. Despite the unwillingness at first of the major companies to acknowledge its broadly representative role and the frequently conflicting interests of the member states, it has survived as a research, information, and coordinating institution of increasing effectiveness. Its first goal, that of restoring world oil prices to the pre-1959 level, was not achieved for a decade. On the other hand, it contributed substantially to settlements advantageous to its members of the royalty-expensing and marketing costs issues.[19]

THE LION'S SHARE OF ARAB OIL

American firms first entered the Arab petroleum industry between World War I and World War II as junior, not very welcome, partners of government-sponsored European enterprises. The ability of the major American companies to mobilize large amounts of capital, materials, equipment, and technical skill permitted them eventually to dispose of more than two thirds of the Arab oil entering world markets.

Table 1 shows the approximate production of ten Arab states in 1967, the participating American firms, and the percentage of output they controlled—nearly 60%. The preponderant position of the integrated majors emerges clearly; they held, among themselves or in partnership with European concerns, the concessions

---

[19]Ibid., pp. 357 ff.

Table 1 United States Participation in Arab Oil Production (1967)*

Country	Production (million barrels per day)	Participating Companies	Percentage United States-Controlled
Libya	2.674	Texaco, Exxon, Standard of California, Nelson Bunker Hunt; Texas Gulf Producing Co., Mobil, Amerada, Continental, Marathon, Occidental, Standard of Indiana, Phillips	88.0
Saudi Arabia	2.598	Aramco (Standard of California, Texaco, Exxon, Mobil)	100.0
Kuwait	2.292	Gulf	50.0
Iraq	1.216	Exxon, Mobil	23.7
Algeria	0.822	Mobil, Phillips, Sinclair, El Paso	8.9
Abu Dhabi	0.532	Exxon, Mobil	14.3
Neutral Zone	0.415	Aminoil, Getty	33.2
Qatar	0.346	Exxon, Mobil	13.4
Egypt	0.190	Standard of Indiana, Phillips	50.0
Bahrain	0.70	Standard of California, Texaco	100.0

Total production: 11.785 barrels per day United States-controlled: 6.884 barrels per day or 58.4%

* Figures adapted from George Lenczowski, Ed., *United States Interests in the Middle East* (Washington: The American Enterprise Institute, 1968), Appendix B, pp. 127–129. Dubai, where Continental Oil, Sun Oil and Texaco jointly held a 50% share of the concession, began production in 1969.

in the largest producing countries except Libya (i.e., Saudi Arabia, Kuwait, Iraq, and Abu Dhabi). This was, of course, the year of the June War, which resulted in a sharp increase in Libyan production to compensate for the interruption of deliveries from the Gulf to Western Europe. The conflict furthermore resulted in the expropriation of the American concessions in Algeria and in intensified tax pressures on the companies.

The disruption of oil transport and supply accompanying the June War bore heavily on Western Europe, but had relatively minor impact in the United States. The preponderant position of American companies in the Arab petroleum industry appeared to be secure, under long-term contracts that might be modified by mutual agreement but not, it was assumed, terminated. Problems between the companies and the governments concerned appeared to bear on economic issues in which the United States government was not accustomed to intervene. If impetuous action by a producing country led to interruption of its exports, the shortfall could easily be made up from its competitors, and its own economy would be the principal victim of its poor judgment. United States policy makers saw little necessity for asserting a more direct government role in an international industry best left to regulation by market mechanisms, except for use of the import quota system to protect the position of domestic American producers, and to harmonize conflicting interests of the majors and independent companies operating abroad. As early as 1969, American officials sought to form a common front with the European Common Market countries to moderate the rise in petroleum prices. The EEC governments, however, resenting the disproportionate position of the seven Anglo-Saxon international majors and hoping to make advantageous arrangements between their own officially sponsored companies and the producing states, failed to respond to the American demarche.

The assumptions underlying the complacent hands-off policy toward the industry were eroded rapidly during the years following 1967. Contrary to expectation, the principal exporting countries, including the Arabs, were able to concert common policies and to maintain sufficient discipline and solidarity to make them effective. Tidy factors of supply and demand became less and less adequate to explain or predict oil prices and movements. Political factors already in gestation for several years were becoming essential parts of the equation.

Table 2, read in conjunction with Table 1, indicates in broad terms the evolution of the industry between 1967 and 1972 under impact of the revolution in concession terms for the seven largest Arab producers. Bearing in mind that further, very substantial, rises in prices were to occur in 1973, it may be noted that Libya had already reduced its rate of output somewhat during this period, while nearly doubling its revenue. Saudi Arabia doubled its output while tripling its oil income. Kuwait cut production by more than half while doubling revenue. Algeria, with a petroleum industry now fully nationalized, increased production by one fourth while expanding revenue by well over 400%. Purely economic considerations could not account for the modest increase of output by these countries—about 17%—while tripling their revenues, during a period when the surge in world consumption was just beginning to produce its full impact and proven reserve figures were rising rapidly. Governments of the producing states were assuming decision-making functions previously reserved to the concessionary companies, and they had begun to exercise their discretion according to political as well as economic criteria.

SOVEREIGNTY AND THE SANCTITY OF CONTRACT

Oil industry officials and some others attending the 1959 First Arab Petroleum Congress were profoundly shocked when Frank Hendryx, an American legal advisor to the Saudi Arabian government, asserted that the government of a petroleum-producing country has not simply the right but a clear duty to modify unilaterally the terms of a concession agreement, or even to cancel it, when such action is in the interest of its people. The principle had been invoked in Iran in 1951, when the oil industry was nationalized with results deeply, if temporarily, disruptive of the country's economic and political life. The Iranian experience served for a time as a caution for the Arab producing countries, which had reaped the benefit of increased revenues during the interruption of Iran's exports. During the 1950s, against a background of growing Arab knowledge of the intricacies of the international oil industry, amendments had been introduced in concession terms. These were

Table 2 Oil Revenues of Arab States

Country	1972 Production (million barrels per day)	Oil Revenues (Millions of United States $) 1967	1971	1972 (estimated)
Saudi Arabia*	5.80	852	2160	2779
Kuwait*	1.04	718	1395	1549
Libya	2.19	631	1766	1560
Iraq	1.47	361	840	780
Algeria	1.06	200	320	870
Qatar	.47	102	198	244
Abu Dhabi	1.04	105	431	575
Totals	13.07	2969	7110	8357

* Including Partitioned (former Neutral) Zone.

arrived at through negotiation with the companies, however reluctantly consented to. As the Arabs came to realize that fundamental decisions concerning the development, exploitation, and conservation of their principal resource were beyond their control and subject to considerations to which the interests of their people were at best secondary, they moved during the 1960s to place the industry within the purview of their own authority, whether by agreement with the companies or by the simple exercise of their sovereign power. By the end of the decade, the structure of the industry was changing significantly. While broad principles concerning objectives and means were held in common among the Arab states, the pace of change varied from country to country, and the resulting patterns were by no means homogeneous.

A systematic statement of the producing countries' aims and policies was embodied in an OPEC Resolution adopted at its Sixteenth Conference in June 1968.[20] The ultimate goal was defined as the direct development by the member governments themselves of their countries' hydrocarbon resources, with such outside capital, technical services, and marketing assistance as required to be obtained on a commercial basis. Where a government is not yet in a position to undertake the task itself, its contractual arrangements with concessionaries should provide for a maximum participation by the government and control over all aspects of operations. The area of existing concessions should be progressively and expeditiously reduced. The government itself should set a posted, or "tax reference" price, consistent with prices prevailing in other states members of OPEC, as a basis for calculating the operating company's income and its payments to the government, determined to compensate for increases in the prices of manufactured goods traded internationally. While a government may, in its discretion, extend a guarantee of fiscal stability to an operator for a limited period, its profits should be held to a reasonable level. All operators in a given country should be required to keep accounts according to the government's instructions and available at all times for its inspection. Under government supervision the operators

---

[20]No. XVI 90. Text in Sam H. Schurr, Paul T. Homan et. al., *Middle Eastern Oil and the Western World: Prospects and Problems* (New York: American Elsevier, 1971), pp. 124–126.

should be required to follow sound, long-term conservation practices. All disputes arising between governments and operators are exclusively within the jurisdiction of the competent national courts, unless and until specialized regional courts are established. The statement, as has been observed,[21] comes close to asserting the rights of governments to alter the terms of concessions according to changing circumstances. Arab governments had already acted on these general principles, with varying degrees of vigor and of violence to existing contracts.

The early concession agreements reserved to the companies discretion in the rate of off-take, transport, refining, and marketing; typically, the concessionaries moreover held a monopoly of refining and marketing of products within the host country. The role of the latter was thus somewhat analogous to that of an absentee landlord. Following Iran's lead of the mid-1950s, the major Arab producers moved to participate directly in their domestic oil industry and to develop a position in the world market independent of the large, integrated companies.

One by one the producing countries formed national oil companies to manage their domestic refining and product merchandising, to engage in prospecting and development in areas not covered by concessions, to dispose of crude oil received as royalties in kind from the operators, to enter downstream operations such as transport and refining, to undertake joint ventures with foreign firms both private and state owned, and to establish petrochemical and other industries. The Kuwait National Petroleum Company (KNPC) was formed in 1960, Saudi Arabia's Petromin (General Petroleum and Minerals Organization) in 1962, the Iraq National Oil Company (INOC) in 1963, Algeria's SONATRACH shortly thereafter, and the Libyan General Petroleum Corporation (later Libyan National Oil Company—LINOCO) in 1968. Except in Algeria, where petroleum development had been largely a state enterprise from the first, the operations of the national companies had little impact on the structure of the world market. Tanker fleets, refining capacity, and distribution networks in the consuming countries remained, for the most part, under the control of the international firms. Until the late 1960s government action was directed mainly toward maximizing revenues and securing a voice

---

[21]Ibid., pp. 126–127.

in the management and conservation of oil resources instead of toward fundamental change in the world industry.

Although the operating companies were under steady pressure in all the producing countries, national aspirations were pursued with particular vigor in Iraq, where popular sentiment against IPC as a symbol of imperialism, strictly economic factors, and a rather inflexible attitude on the part of the consortium produced a bitter, protracted dispute persisting, with some intermissions, throughout the decade, aggravated by disagreements with Syria over pipeline transit fees. The full range of objectives set forth in the OPEC resolution summarized above was pressed: relinquishment of territory, government-supervised accounting, government-established tax reference prices, conservation, and government participation in ownership and management. Conciliation proved ultimately beyond reach. The company's assets were nationalized, and the dispute afforded opportunity for the Soviet Union to gain a significant foothold in the Arab oil industry.[22]

MIDDLE EAST OIL AND THE AMERICAN NATIONAL INTEREST

It emerges clearly from the foregoing discussion that American officials have consistently seen close links between the security of the United States and the operation of the Middle East petroleum industry. Before the 1973 crisis issues stemming from this relationship were debated primarily within the executive branch of the government, and the decisions reached were implemented through cooperation of the major American oil firms. A particularly momentous problem of this nature arose following the nationalization of Iran's oil operations in April 1951 by the nationalist government of Dr. Muhammad Mossadeq. The expropriated concessionary, Anglo-Iranian, owned in part by the British government, at first refused to accept the Iranian decision, and a protracted impasse ensued during which the British endeavored, successfully, to obstruct the sale of Iranian crude and refined products in world markets. The major American companies, in view of

---

[22]The controversy is admirably recounted in Stocking, op. cit., pp. 230–269; 300–315.

their close operating arrangements with Anglo-Iranian, cooperated in these efforts, increasing their off-take of Arab oil to replace the shortfall resulting from the halt in Iranian production. It soon became apparent that no compromise was possible whereby Britain could regain exclusive control of Iran's oil. Within a year the Department of State became convinced that resumption of Iranian oil exports to Western markets was necessary in order to prevent Iran's slipping behind the Iron Curtain and to forestall disruption of the industry in the Arab states, also. The Department concluded, moreover, that the problem could be resolved only through participation in the Iranian oil industry by American firms already well established in the Middle East. This objective, however, conflicted sharply with the intentions of the Anti-Trust Division of the Justice Department toward these same companies.

Following submission of the Federal Trade Commission's *International Petroleum Cartel* report previously mentioned, the Department of Justice instituted, in July 1952, a grand jury investigation looking toward criminal indictment of the five American majors for conspiring illegally to combine in restraint of the international oil trade. Secretary of State Dean Acheson sought, on foreign policy grounds, to have the proceedings dropped. Regardless of the eventual court decision, he informed the Assistant Attorney General, the public accusation against the oil companies would be interpreted by the peoples of the Middle East "as a statement that, were it not for such conspiracy, they would be getting a higher return from their oil resources. This will, of course, strengthen the movement for renegotiation of the present concession agreements and may give encouragement to those groups urging nationalization.... The net effect will probably be to cause a decrease in political stability in the region." Furthermore, the Secretary added, the instability already existing was such as to discourage investment by new American enterprises in the development of Middle Eastern oil; only the majors, that is, were capable of doing the necessary job.[23]

---

[23]The relevant government documents have recently been declassified, compiled and published for the United States Senate Committee on Foreign Relations, Sub-Committee on Multinational Corporations, under the title *The International Petroleum Cartel, the Iranian Consortium and U.S. National Security* (Washington: USGPO, 1974).

In the context of National Security Council consideration of the Iranian problem, the Justice Department vigorously, but unsuccessfully, contested the State Department thesis that an "American" solution could be achieved only with the participation of the major companies. In the closing months of his administration President Truman directed Secretary Acheson to institute the multilateral consultations which eventually culminated in the Iranian Consortium formed in 1954, including the five American majors. Invoking reasons of national security, the President furthermore instructed the Attorney General to abandon criminal action against the companies and to institute a civil complaint instead, on condition that the firms cooperate by voluntarily providing the documentation that a grand jury would have demanded by subpoena.

The Eisenhower Administration proceeded with the Iranian issue according to its predecessor's assumptions. The new President appointed Herbert Hoover, Jr. to carry forward the negotiations, according to the concept of an international consortium including the firms against which the Justice Department had now brought civil suit. On the recommendation of the National Security Council, the President requested the Attorney General to take full account of United States foreign relations in prosecuting its case (which, indeed, was already somewhat compromised by the government's need for the defendants' cooperation in rehabilitating the Iranian oil industry). When the probable composition of the consortium became clear, Eisenhower sought and obtained from the Attorney General (over the objection of the Anti-Trust Division) an opinion that the companies' participation would not in itself constitute violation of antitrust legislation. This action drew the teeth of Justice Department efforts to dissolve the interlocking structure of the international oil industry and compel it to operate on the basis of free commercial competition in all its stages: exploration, production, refining, transport, and marketing.

The Iranian dispute had obvious implications for United States concerns in the neighboring Arab states. Both presidents, together with their defense, security, and foreign policy advisors, were alarmed at the prospect that the passing of Iranian oil from Western control into that of an Iranian government animated by xenophobic nationalist sentiment would encourage similar nationalist aspirations in the Arab oil-producing countries and jeopardize both Western access to Arab oil and the terms of its availability. Having, through diplomatic action in 1946, assisted Iran in restricting Soviet influence in its internal affairs and, through the 1954 oil settlement, helped to minimize British control of its major industry, the United States could come to generally congenial terms with Iranian nationalism consistent with American political and security aims. Arab nationalism, on the other hand, had orientations and aspirations which American policy makers, in a quest now three decades old, have not fully reconciled with their concept of the political, strategic, and economic security of the United States and its allies.

CHAPTER IV

American Security Encounters Arab Nationalism

WORLD WAR II ADDED NEW MILITARY AND POLITICAL DIMEN-
SIONS to Arab-American relations, arising from Allied strategy
against the Axis Powers. Among their proclaimed war aims, the
Western allies evoked a vision of a new world order in which all
nations would prosper in freedom and peace under liberal democratic institutions, which quickened Arab aspirations toward full
independence. The conflict moreover sapped the sources of
strength that had enabled the British and French to hold and
expand their empires after World War I. America's wartime hopes
were, unfortunately, not realized. War did not end. The world
seemed as unsafe as before for democracy. The self-determination
of one nation often preempted assets other peoples regarded as
their inalienable heritage.

In the war's aftermath the United States sought at first to leave
responsibility for the stability and security of the emerging nations of Africa and the Middle East to the former imperial powers.
The latter proved unequal to the task. Communism, in the view
of the more articulate segments of American public opinion and
of the national leadership, replaced Nazism as the clear and
present danger to American democracy and security; as communist regimes appeared in one country after another in Eastern
Europe and Asia, the United States felt called on to assert an
unprecedented, sustained world leadership to stem and repulse the
tide. The role was one in which the American apprenticeship was
limited. Some of the problems involved were furthermore novel
on the world scene. The proliferation of sovereignties obliged the
United States to treat with governments pursuing aims inconsistent with their countries' true interests as Americans saw them,

diverging from the paths in which the United States, unilaterally or in consultation with its allies, endeavored to lead the "free" world, and often incompatible with America's own goals. Where the Arab world was concerned, the relatively few Americans who were familiar with the ancient roots, contemporary vitality, and orientation of Arab national feeling and were thus in a position to evaluate the practicality of some aims the American leadership pursued in the Middle East, were rarely in a position to sway major policy decisions. The inevitable failure of some American policies is perhaps of less lasting importance than the fact that, in the absence of general awareness of the motives underlying Arab attitudes and actions, Americans tended to explain the obstruction of their own aims in terms of perversity, irresponsibility, ignorance, or wickedness on the part of the Arabs and their leaders.

FROM WORLD WAR TO COLD WAR

The nature and scope of American wartime activities in the various Arab countries were largely a function of allied strategy against the Axis. In the east, American military engineers shared with British colleagues the operations of the Persian Gulf Command, organized to maintain a channel of supply to the Soviet Union across Iranian territory. In Saudi Arabia, as we saw in the preceding chapter, mutual Anglo-American suspicions and rivalry for influence with Ibn Saud's regime became a minor irritant in relations between the two allies. When legislation permitted, President Franklin Roosevelt adjudged Saudi Arabia eligible for lend-lease assistance; American aid could thereafter be provided directly to the King without passing through British hands. A small military training mission instituted a durable American association with the Saudi armed forces. During the final year of the war United States Army engineers constructed a military airfield at Dhahran, destined to become a major international airport after serving as an important link in postwar American global logistics. Roosevelt invited Ibn Saud to meet with him in February 1945, following the Yalta Conference, aboard a United States Navy warship at Suez. The King took the occasion to express Arab apprehensions at Jewish immigration into Palestine. The President, who had reassured him on this score a few years before, repeated, and shortly afterward confirmed in writing, that the United States would make no basic change in its basic policy in Palestine without full and prior consultation with both Jews and Arabs.

Egypt and the vital Suez Canal were an unquestioned politicomilitary responsibility of Great Britain, which felt obliged to take harsh measures to ensure that Egypt remained a secure base of wartime operations. The country was heavily penetrated by Axis propaganda and espionage that, during the nadir of Allied fortunes early in the war, extended into the Egyptian royal palace. In 1940 British pressure obliged King Farūq to dismiss 'Alī Māher, his Axis-sympathizing Prime Minister. His successor, Hussein Sirrī, more pliant but also weak, could not contain the anti-British agitation, fomented by the Muslim Brotherhood and other nationalist groups, which intensified with the British setbacks in the Western Desert during 1941. In January 1942, in a humiliating show of force against the palace, the British forced Farūq to accept his principal domestic political enemy, Wafd leader Muṣṭafā al-Naḥḥās, as head of government. The Wafd cooperated loyally with the Allies during the remaining years of the war without, however, becoming reconciled to the 1936 treaty's restrictions on Egypt's sovereignty and her influence in the Sudan.

After the defeat of France in June 1940, the Levant and Maghreb territories became a threat to the British position in the Mediterranean and eastward communications. The feeble Vichy regime was unable to interpose effective obstacles to the activities of German and Italian agents in Syria and Lebanon, or to the passage through Syria of German air support (which in the event proved inadequate) for the anti-British regime of Rashīd 'Alī al-Kaylānī in Iraq in May 1941. The British reacted by occupying the Levant states in June 1941 in cooperation with small Free French contingents. The Free French endeavored to persuade the indigenous leaders that treaty arrangements with France were essential to protect their countries against Turkish, Zionist, and British designs and to ensure them of a leading position within the Arab world. This effort, however, was resisted by burgeoning nationalist movements led in Lebanon by the Maronite Beshāra al-Khourī and the Muslim Riyāḍ al-Ṣulḥ, in Syria by Shukrī al-Quwaṭlī's Nationalist Bloc. Through respect for the long-standing Entente Cordiale by which Great Britain and France avoided interference with each other's colonial policies, the British at first hesitated to intervene otherwise than by exhorting all sides to moderation. After three years of mounting tension marked by insurrection, French arrest of the Lebanese government's entire top echelon, bombardment of Damascus, and substantial reinforcement of the French occupation forces, the British demanded the withdrawal of French troops from the major cities and the relinquishment of responsibility for public order to the Lebanese and Syrian governments.[1] The latter, having qualified themselves for charter membership in the United Nations by belated declarations of war against the Axis, brought their case against France before the General Assembly's inaugural meeting in London in January 1946; portentously, their cause was vigorously championed by the Soviet Union. Shortly thereafter, Charles de Gaulle having stepped down as French Prime Minister, the French and British agreed on a simultaneous troop withdrawal; the Lebanese and Syrians thus were left masters in their own houses for the first time.

Only in the Maghreb territories were United States ground forces engaged in large-scale operations against the Axis. While American military and civil officials necessarily had to concern themselves with local politics, the objective of ensuring a stable situation in which tactical and logistical operations could proceed unhindered took precedence over the pursuit of longer-range ideological objectives. In practice, American authorities accommodated themselves to the French administrations that remained in charge of the territories throughout successive shifts of posture among the Allies, the two French factions, and the Axis powers. President Roosevelt, certainly, had a rosy vision, unencumbered by prosaic data, of a free, happy, postwar North Africa made prosperous with American assistance. During the wartime American presence, leaflets publicizing the Atlantic Charter and the Four Freedoms distributed by the United States propaganda services gave heart to more and more assertive independence movements. When the American landings of November 1942 in Morocco had been consolidated, Roosevelt met with Prime Minister Churchill

---

[1]George Kirk, *The Middle East in the War* (London: Oxford University Press, second impression, 1953), p. 272.

at Casablanca the following January. He took the occasion to invite the young Sultan, Sīdī Muḥammad bin Yūsef, to dinner, and expatiated glowingly on the social and economic progress Morocco might achieve through American cooperation after the war. In correspondence thereafter with the Sultan the President promised to act "personally" after the hostilities to promote Moroccan independence. Optimistically mistaking this sympathy for settled American policy[2] the Moroccans endeavored to loosen the imperial powers' restrictions on their country's integrity and sovereignty. In January 1944 the Istiqlal ("Independence") Party, organized under the leadership of Ahmad Balafraj with the discreet encouragement of the Sultan, issued a manifesto asserting Morocco's claim to territorial unity and untrammeled sovereignty under Sīdī Muḥammad's rule. The United States abstained from interfering with French and Spanish repression of the ensuing popular agitation, while insisting on the continuing validity of its treaties with the Sultan's predecessors.

Upon the entry of American forces into North Africa, President Roosevelt wrote to Muḥammad al-Munṣif, Bey of Tunis, requesting his cooperation in repelling Axis forces from his territory. The Bey, having no army other than an ill-equipped bodyguard and no control over the Vichy French occupation troops, was in no position to oblige, and his domain was soon overrun by Axis armies that invaded Tunisia in January 1943. Munṣif was forced to submit to certain Axis exactions (discrimination against Jews, recruitment of laborers for service in Europe, decorations for Italian and German officers, etc.) but, with the authority of the French Resident-General weakened, he was emboldened to reassert a modicum of Tunisian self-rule. He organized a broadly representative government, incorporating representatives of the two nationalist Destour ("Constitution") parties. This trend was reversed within six months when, after defeat of the Axis forces in North Africa, the Free French asserted direct control, deposed the Bey, executed numerous Tunisians charged with collaboration with the Axis, and imprisoned thousands more. In 1944 the French authorities requested the removal of the American Consul in Tunis, Hooker

---

[2]Luella J. Hall, *The United States and Morocco 1776–1956* (Metuchen, N.J.: The Scarecrow Press, 1971), p. 1002.

A. Doolittle, who had sought to intervene in behalf of certain nationalist leaders.[3]

Of special concern to the United States in Algeria, occupied by American and British forces after delicate negotiations with the local French authorities and the Free French, was the status of the territory's Jews, against whom the Vichy regime had introduced discriminatory measures. Among these was the abrogation of the Crémieux Decree of 1870, which had conferred full French citizenship on Algerian Jews. General Giraud, the new Resident General, lifted the discriminations promptly after the Allied landings without, however, restoring the decree, which remained in abeyance despite agitation by French, American, and international Jewish organizations.[4] Robert Murphy, the senior American diplomatic representative in North Africa, discreetly encouraged the efforts of the nationalist leader Ferḥat 'Abbās toward social, economic, and political reforms on behalf of the Algerian Muslims. The Algerian "manifesto" of February 1943, expressing aspirations for self-government and civil equality, became an early milestone on the long path toward Algerian independence.

The global conflict thus brought the United States into somewhat closer contact with the Arab peoples in several spheres of activity. In harmony with the general principles in the name of which the war was being waged, American officials from the President down gave sympathetic, if usually muted, encouragement to Arab aspirations toward unrestrained independence. Participation in repelling the Axis' southward and eastward thrust educated American strategists in the importance of the Mediterranean's southern and eastern shores. For a brief period at the end of hostilities, however, it appeared that the American politico-military role had been played to its end, and that the persisting Franco-British links with the Arab lands would provide a sufficient bulwark against the Soviet expansionist ambitions apparently implied in the Greek civil war, Soviet territorial demands on Turkey, and Soviet support of the leftist dissident regime in Azerbaijan. Acknowledgment by the British that their capabilities were

---

[3]Kirk, op. cit., p. 412, fn.
[4]Robert Murphy, *Diplomat among Warriors* (Garden City, N.Y.: Doubleday & Co., 1964), pp. 160–161.

inadequate to defend Turkey and Greece produced the Truman Doctrine of 1947, embodying formally the principle of direct American action in countering communist advances in the Middle East. As the United States moved to organize a defense in depth for the countries immediately adjoining the communist bloc and to forestall any possible threat to Western access to the region's petroleum, it was obliged to seek the cooperation of Arab countries where a nationalist movement with deep historical roots was approaching a peak of intensity and demanding of political leaders the pursuit of aims not readily reconcilable with American objectives. Some understanding of the background and preoccupations of Arab nationalism is essential in explaining the frustrations of American postwar policy in the Arab world and the emergence of an adversary relationship instead of the partnership that the United States sought to establish.

ARAB NATIONALISM

Nationalism has been broadly construed to mean the belief among a large group of people that they comprise a political community entitled to independent statehood and a willingness of this group to grant their community a primary and the terminal loyalty.[5] One anomaly of the contemporary Arab world is the persistence of numerous states commanding the loyalty of citizens who at the same time regard themselves as members of a single Arab nation. This dualism is a source of complex psychological tensions. Whether or not the terminal loyalty will in time be granted to the several Arab states, an Arab nationalism transcending them all is now a political force that must be defined and understood. Peoples commonly seek in their antecedents evidence of the enduring excellences that set them above and apart from others and, where these are not adequately described in history and legend, imagination readily fills the gap. Definition of the Arab nation has assumed several forms over time. During Islam's first millennium, need was seldom felt to distinguish the Arabs within the general Muslim community. In the nineteenth century sustained intellec-

---

[5]Richard W. Cottam, *Nationalism in Iran* (Pittsburgh: University of Pittsburgh Press, 1967), p. 3.

tual contact between Arabs and Western Europe coincided with the rise of European nationalisms and with the encroachment of Western culture and power on the Islamic world. In the quest for a valid redefinition of the Arab nation in the altered circumstances and a remedy for its manifest weaknesses, some Arab thinkers adopted Western concepts and modes of thought. Only partial consensus among Arabs emerged on the attributes, aims, and destiny of their nation. Traditional Islamic ideas and intrusive notions of Western origin both contribute to contemporary nationalist thought among Arab theorists and leaders.

Although it would be an anachronism to speak of Arab nationalism before the nineteenth century—*qawmiya,* the Arab term for the concept, is a neologism of the 1920s—some of its aspects have ancient roots. The Arab cultural strain that achieved lasting salience was that of the Arabian Peninsula's nomadic tribes. In this harsh environment the individual depended utterly for survival on solidarity and cooperation with his immediate fellows; his identity was submerged in and defined by his membership, primarily of his extended family, then of clan, sept, and tribe, in diminishing force. Water and pasturage, necessary to sustain life, were scarce, dispersed, and inevitable objects of competition. First and terminal loyalty extended only to small communities, bound by kinship, seldom transcending the individual's firsthand acquaintance, each in a chronic state of enmity or actual conflict with its neighbors. In such a hostile world traits of manliness, courage, and solidarity were prized; so was honor, seen as vengeance for the shed blood of a kinsman or the violation of a woman, both threats to the community's integrity. On the other hand were institutionalized virtues tending to mitigate the basic aggressive outlook. Intertribal raiding was conducted by acknowledged, if not universally observed, rules that limited bloodshed. The role of an unbiased mediator between warring factions was a highly honored one. Hospitality and the granting of asylum, even to one recognized as an enemy, were binding obligations. Finally, aggressiveness was verbalized. Language was the bedouin's only fine art and, while the poet's rhymed insults leveled against a rival tribe could provoke physical conflict, at other times the exchange of oral abuse served as a surrogate for actual warfare. The social orientation thus briefly outlined became a permanent part of Arabic literature. It accompanied the Arabs on their world conquest and became fully naturalized in environments more generous and gentle than the one that gave it birth. Contemporary Arab political behavior constantly echoes the tradition in its internal divisiveness, its hostility toward outsiders, its reliance on mediation (not adjudication), and the frequent use of the word as substitute for the sword.

Among the elements of pre-Islamic Arab character that, suitably adapted, took permanent root in the new religion were the dualism between the in-group and the rest of mankind, and the revered status of the Arabic language. From the outset the community of believers—*dār al-Islām*—was set in contrast with and opposition to *dār al-ḥarb*, the "abode of war" embracing all infidels. The feeling of unity and solidarity expressed in the folk saying *lā umam bil-Islām* ("there are no separate nations within Islam") had its corollary in the maxim *al-kufru millatun wāḥida:* "the infidels are a single nation." However, some peoples incorporated in Islam, notably the Persians, possessed vigorous and distinguished cultures to which they remained attached, and they clove to their own languages and traditions. Arabs reacted to the assertion of the merits of these extraneous cultures by insisting on their own superior worth as the people to whom, and in whose tongue, God's ultimate revelation was given to man. The *shu'ūbiya* controversy of Abbassid times reflected the dispute on the plane of literary polemic. The term has been revived lately, with its pejorative connotation, to attack the tendency in Arab countries to give pride of place to parochial patriotisms over the universal Arab community.

As the vitality of the Arab imperial dynasties waned, the Arabs adapted without murmur to the passing of rule into the hands of the Kurdish Ayyubids and ultimately the Turks. Misgivings arose only when it became apparent that the Ottoman sultans were no longer able to defend Islam against encroachment from *dār al-ḥarb.* Intermittent efforts of the central government to strengthen the empire through military modernization and political liberalization went forward simultaneously with the emergence of national sentiment among its various peoples, under the stimulus of European thought and example. In the ferment of ideas during the last quarter of the nineteenth century and the first few decades of the twentieth century, the Arab literary revival was translated gradually into a sentiment of separate political identity. Ideological development proceeded along conflicting lines of secularism and of the revitalization of Islam, a dichotomy that remains unresolved in the Arab nationalist movement.

Within the Ottoman empire the despotism and oppression of the later sultans, Abdül 'Azīz (1861–1976) and Abdül Ḥamīd II (1876–1909), weighed scarcely more heavily on their Arab subjects than on the Turks and other Muslims. Possessing the language of the Faith as their mother tongue, the Arabs were peculiarly qualified to interpret the sharī'a. They could aspire not only to religion-related functions but to high administrative position and to senior rank in the armed forces. Arabs, along with Jews, Armenians, and other minorities, joined with Turks in the Committee of Union and Progress, seeking to place Abdül Hamīd's absolute power within constitutional bounds. The movement briefly achieved this aim in 1908, when a constitution of 1876, curbing the Sultan's prerogatives and ostensibly placing all peoples of the empire on an equal footing, was reintroduced. In the ensuing blush of brotherly enthusiasm the Ottoman Arab Fraternity (al-Ikhā al-'Arabī al-'Uthmānī) was founded with the aims of protecting the constitution, uniting all races in loyalty to the Sultan and promoting their equality, and of fostering education in Arabic language and customs in the Arab provinces. These hopes were frustrated by the rise of Turkish nationalism. The Young Turks thwarted Abdül Hamīd's attempt of 1909 to regain absolute power and deposed him in favor of his weak brother Muhammad V. The move toward regional autonomy was reversed. Elections were managed to give the Turks, or their obedient clients, highly disproportionate representation. Turkish was declared the sole official language of the state, and measures were instituted to make it the primary vehicle of instruction throughout the empire. The high-handed assertion of Turkish supremacy stimulated emerging Arab national feeling. While the Ottoman Arab Fraternity was ordered dissolved, other overt associations were formed among responsible, respected, loyal Arabs—al-Muntadā al-Adabī (Literary Club) in 1909 and Ḥizb al-Lāmarkaziya al-'Uthmānī (Ottoman Decentralization Party) in 1912—that sought to reverse the repressive policies and served as clearinghouses for the exchange of political and cultural ideas among Arabs from various parts of the empire. A significant part of the movement was forced underground and abroad, where organization and agitation for reform and decentralization proceeded among Arab students and exiles, particularly those from geographical Syria and Iraq.

Even within the secularizing wing of the movement, aims and ideas were not uniform, as may be seen in the resolutions of successive Arab nationalist conferences held in Paris during this early period. The League of the Arab Fatherland in 1905 called for full independence and unity of the Asian Arab territories. It demanded the separation of civil and religious powers, the concentration of which in a single hand was asserted to be an important cause of the Islamic empire's decline. Members of all sects should be equal before the law. The crown of a constitutionally limited monarchical state would be offered to a prince of the Egyptian ruling house. The caliphate, which had become "contemptible and ridiculous" in Turkish hands, would be entrusted to an Arab sherīf —a descendent of the Prophet—of blameless life and unsullied honor. Interestingly, the League excluded Egypt from the envisioned state. Recalling that the early Arab caliphs had never managed to consolidate hold over Egypt and the Asian regions simultaneously, the League stated that the Isthmus of Suez is a natural boundary dividing Egypt that is "Berber" in race and whose pre-Islamic language had no resemblance to Arabic, from the truly Arab homeland.[6]

In 1913, before hopes for collaboration with the Young Turks had been finally extinguished, a Syrian-Arab Congress demanded sweeping reforms within the Ottoman state. Arab political rights were to be assured by effective participation in the central administration. At the same time, the Arab vilayets were to be selfgoverning, with Arabic as an official language. Peacetime military obligations were to be discharged locally. Similar aspirations of other ethnic groups were viewed sympathetically.

The entry of Turkey into World War I confronted the nationalist movement, particularly the segment inspired by British and French liberal principles, with difficult ideological choices. As we

---

[6]Matthew Smith Anderson, *The Great Powers and the Near East 1774–1923* (New York: St. Martin's Press, 1970), pp. 148–149 (quoting Negib Azoury, *Le Réveil arabe dans l'Asie turque*).

have seen, the temporal ambitions of the Hashemite sherifs of Mecca and the hopes of certain Syrian and Iraqi separatist organizations appeared for a time to coincide with British imperial interests and led to the Arab Revolt. At the same time, the war tended to deepen the incipient xenophobia 'of other nationalist currents. 'Azīz 'Alī al-Maṣrī, a former Egyptian officer in the Ottoman army whose secret *Qaḥṭāniya* organization had been discovered and banned by the Turkish authorities, was living in retirement in Egypt. He cautioned his followers against cooperation either with the Ottoman government or with the Allies who, he feared, sought merely to replace the Turks as rulers over the Arabs. Early in the war a broadside was addressed from Cairo to the descendents of Qaḥṭān and 'Adnān, the two legendary progenitors of the Arabs. Couched in the ferocious rhetoric characteristic of much subsequent nationalist expression, it called on the Arabs to arise both against Turkish tyranny and against the economic imperialism of the European powers.

... See how your natural resources have been alienated from you and have come into the possession of England, France and Germany. Have you no right to these resources? You have become humiliated slaves in the hands of the usurping tyrant; the foreigner unjustly dispossesses you of the fruit of your work and labor and leaves you to suffer the pangs of hunger. . . . Till when will you go on acquiescing in this utter humiliation, when your honour is made free of, your wives raped, your children orphaned, your money taken to be spent in the palaces of Constantinople, full as they are with intoxicating drink, musical instruments, and all kinds of wealth and luxury, and your young men driven to fight your Arab brethren, sometimes in the Yemen, sometimes in Kerek, sometimes in the Hauran, thus reinforcing the persecutions of the Turks, while you remain silent and accept this monstrous imposition?[7]

The manifesto, conceiving of the Arab nation as founded on community of language, appealed to Jewish and Christian Arabs, whose ancestors studied side by side with Muslims in the mosques of Baghdad and Andalusia, to unite with their Muslim brothers against the foreigner.

For you must know that those who do not speak your tongue are more harmful to you than the ignorant fanatics among the Arabs who are your

---

[7] *Ibid.*, pp. 153–154.

brethren in patriotism and race, while it is difficult for you to reach agreement with these contemptible creatures who are at the same time your enemies and the enemies of the Muslim Arabs.[8]

Common to the various nationalist currents just mentioned is acceptance of the West's judgment that the debility, immobilism, and fatalism of the Islamic world stemmed from Islam itself, and that the remedy was application of the principles believed to be the sources of European power: the development of a sense of nationhood, the vigorous pursuit of the nation's interests, the divorce of religion from politics, representative and responsible civil institutions, civil freedoms, industrialization, and the cultivation of secular, "scientific" modes of thinking. Parallel to this trend of thought was a competing current based on the conviction that the seventh-century revelation was valid for all time; that the integration of faith and state in the early generations of Islam provided the energy and spirit that created the Arab empire, and that the subsequent decline was attributable to distortion, corruption, and abandonment of the pristine ideal of the Islamic community. The remedy for present weakness was therefore to be found in purifying and revitalizing Islam itself.

The pan-Islamic agitator and theoretician Jamāl al-Dīn al-Afghānī (1839–1897) summarily rejected the prevalent Western notion that Islam is inherently inimical to rational, scientific thought. On the contrary, he insisted, it was the religion "demanded by reason," whereas European strides in science and technology had been made only at the price of abandoning Christianity. Islam furthermore demands the mutual solidarity and responsibility from which the strength of nations flows.[9] Restoration of Islamic power is thus to be achieved by a return to the true fundamental principles of the Faith. Not himself an Arab, Afghānī's efforts to revive Islam as a bulwark against the West by working through incumbent rulers extended over a vast territory from India to Egypt, and embroiled him with the Shah of Persia, the Ottoman sultan, the Khedive of Egypt, and the British government. His ideas reached primarily the educated elites and were pan-Islamic

---

[8]Ibid., p. 155.
[9]Albert Hourani, *Arabic Thought in the Liberal Age* (London: Oxford University Press, reprinted with corrections 1967), p. 123.

in character, not specifically Arab. Universal Islamic solidarity, however, presupposes Arab solidarity, and he is rightly acknowledged a precursor of the Islamic strain of Arab nationalism. His pupil, associate, and successor, Shaikh Muhammad 'Abduh (1849–1905), attained to positions in Egypt—as Grand Mufti and as advisor on the administration of al-Azhar University—from which his doctrines could be effectively propagated among substantial numbers of people. Without repudiating change and modernization as such, 'Abduh insisted that a proper and thorough knowledge of the Faith, based on reasoned analysis, was a necessary guide to choice among the aspects of Western civilization of those that could contribute to the integrity, strength, and progress of Muslim society. His influence over an entire generation of Egyptian publicists and politicians was pervasive but dichotomous. On the one hand, the centrality of Islam posited by his doctrine became the major preoccupation of a school of thought, typified by Rashīd Riḍā, that pressed for the repudiation of political institutions and processes copied from, or imposed by, Western secular influence, and a return to the early configuration responsible for the achievements of Islam's first generations. This trend of thought ultimately found practical expression in the militant Muslim Brotherhood, founded in 1929 by Ḥasan al-Banna. Following up the positivist aspect of 'Abduh's thought, other Egyptians became the theoreticians, propagandists, and leaders of a distinct Egyptian nationalism that had begun to assert itself by the 1880s.

Within the permissive limits of Ottoman suzerainty Egypt had its own distinct history during the nineteenth century. Under Muhammad 'Alī and his successors the country pursued age-old imperial objectives in Syria, the Arabian Peninsula, and the Sudan, and developed its own distinct economy and administrative structures inspired from European models. The dynasty never became genuinely naturalized, however, and preferment in high civil and military posts was consistently accorded to Turks, Circassians, and others regarded as aliens by the indigenous people. The notion of an Egyptian nationhood had taken rudimentary form in the press by the 1870s and, toward the end of that decade, a National Party appeared, recruited among native Egyptian army officers as well as civilians. Its leader, Colonel Aḥmad 'Urābī, headed a riot in 1879 against the Turco-Circassian senior officers and, in 1881, forced a nationalist government on Khedive Tawfīq, whose threat to Franco-British control of Egypt's finances led directly to the British occupation the following year. The British regime acted on the principle that Egypt was not a nation capable or deserving of self-rule. Needless to say, this assessment failed to commend itself to the Egyptians themselves. The country's first modern politician, Muṣṭafā Kāmil, preached a nationalism aberrant in that its ideological basis was the typically Western one of patriotism for the territorial fatherland irrespective of language, race, or creed. His successors deflected his ideas toward more indigenous concepts; nevertheless, his Nationalist Party, formally founded in 1907 but already in effective existence for a decade, established enduring patterns of political action: the mobilization of mass sentiment, the organization of student strikes and demonstrations, and the instigation of violence against the foreigners in control of Egypt's affairs. Under successive British mentors as Agents and Consuls General—Sir Evelyn Baring (later Lord Cromer) (1884–1907), Sir Eldon Gorst (1907–1911), and Lord Kitchener (1911–1914)—cautious steps were taken toward the development of democratic, representative institutions. With the general cooperation of the Khedive, jealous of any infringement of his authority, the British repressed overt nationalist action and, with the onset of World War I, forced it underground. After the Armistice it emerged vastly strengthened under the leadership of Saʿd Zaghlūl and the Wafd.

A pupil of Muhammad 'Abduh, Zaghlūl had been more closely associated with the Umma Party of the Shaikh's followers than with Kāmil's Nationalist group. Intermittently at odds with the British and with the Khedive, he nevertheless served as minister of education, where he promoted the expansion of the school system and the replacement of English by Arabic as the language of instruction. Later, as minister of justice, he endeavored to reform the legal system, retaining its Islamic base but making it more responsive to contemporary needs, while placing constitutional curbs on the Khedive's discretionary powers. As postwar nationalist leader, he pressed for absolute Egyptian independence, but also for social reforms, specifically termed "revolutionary," in some respects remarkably anticipatory of those espoused by the military regime thirty years later: Egyptianization of the economy, emancipation of women, the destruction of the aristocratic pasha class, political power to the fellahin, and the removal of the Turkish element from Egyptian politics.[10] While during succeeding decades Wafd leaders succeeded in subordinating their concern for the social element of Zaghlūl's program to their private interests, and even became pashas themselves, their devotion to national independence was unswerving. The goal, however, was independence not of the Arabs, with whom few Egyptians as yet identified themselves, but of Egypt, geographically defined to include the Sudan. Failure to achieve the objective, despite the encouragement of Allied wartime propaganda, intensified the xenophobic element present from the first in Egyptian nationalism and turned it first against Britain, then against the West generally. Identical hopes were frustrated in Syria, Iraq, and the Maghreb. In Arab eyes the West had cynically betrayed its own proclaimed ideals. Thenceforth the various currents of thought might accept or reject Western liberal principles and the social sources of Western material strength and prosperity, or claim that these were borrowings originally indigenous to Arab culture; the West itself was condemned as an adversary. Discussion of Arab national aspirations proceeded against a background litany of execration of Western greed and injustice.

The problem of defining the scope of "Arabism" and formulating a nationalist doctrine with popular appeal arose in Syria, during the interwar years, with a poignancy heightened by the fact that Syrians had led the cultural revival that awakened Arabs to a feeling of common identity. Already fragmented socially among Druze, Alawites, Kurds, Shī'a, and Sunnī Muslims, and a kaleidoscope of Christian sects, the territory was shattered politically and insulated from its Arab neighbors. The process had begun with the institution in 1861, under European pressure, of a separate regime in Mount Lebanon under French influence. The World War I settlement formally detached an expanded Lebanon, Palestine, and Transjordan, and had made a separate entity instead of a sister province of Iraq. In each truncation distinctive legal and administrative forms were being instituted, creating in each a distinctive

---

[10]Ibid., p. 216.

set of circumstances for the independence struggle. In the Syrian heartland a pronounced generation gap emerged within the nationalist movement. The campaign for Syrian independence was waged in the main by well-established local notables, each jealous of his equal status with the others, all agreed in principle on the ideal of Arab unity but preoccupied with the immediate practical Syrian problem, organized in loose and shifting coalitions, such as the National Bloc, with no clear idea of what should be done once independence had been gained.[11] Younger generation nationalists, convinced that the existing parochial loyalties were a source of weakness and that a Syria greatly diminished in area and population could never aspire to power and economic viability, sought some broader concept by which local identifications might be transcended. The problem of defining the Arab nation in such a way as to stimulate a comprehensive solidarity while reconciling sharp differences of religion, sect, and social customs was dealt with in various ways.

In the view of Anṭūn Saʿāda (1904–1949) the descendents of the ancient Canaanites, Arameans, Assyrians, Chaldeans, Hittites, and Akkadians inhabiting Syria, Lebanon, Palestine, Jordan, and Iraq had become a single national entity endowed with genius and mentality superior to those of their neighbors.[12] Its solidarity and strength had been dissipated by its division among many sects, each with its own political aims and its own judicial system. In the interest of national unity, welfare, and power, all religious influence must be rigorously excluded from temporal and political affairs. Judicial and administrative institutions must be unified, feudalism abolished, economic production increased under state auspices, capital nationalized, and a strong army created. To work for the Syrian material power which is "the index and manifestation of an advanced spiritual power," Saʿāda founded in 1932 the Syrian Social Nationalist Party (SSNP), whose disciplined, hierarchical organization recalls the contemporary fascist parties in Europe. The SSNP played an intermittent role in Syro-Lebanese politics. Saʿāda took refuge in Syria in 1949 after an abortive coup

---

[11] Ibid., p. 307.

[12] *The Teaching Book of the Syrian Social Nationalist Party;* text in Kemal H. Karpat, ed., *Political and Social Thought in the Contemporary Middle East* (New York: Praeger, 1968), p. 96.

attempt in Lebanon; the dictator Ḥusnī Zaʻīm turned him over to the Lebanese authorities, who promptly executed him. A Party member retaliated by assassinating Prime Minister Riyāḍ al-Ṣulḥ. The SSNP later figured in the 1958 Lebanese civil war in support of President Chamoun. The Greater Syria notion, however, has generally been superseded by more comprehensive concepts.

Christian Arab theorists, of course, had to come to terms in some fashion with the intimate relationship between Arabism and Islam. Saʻāda found a solution of sorts in a vague, anticlerical, and dubious racism. Others, notably Constantine Zurayq and Edmond Rabbāth, frankly acknowledge Islam as, in the first instance, the national religion of the Arabs. Islamic culture of the golden age is Arab culture, the common heritage of all Arabs regardless of creed. Solidarity in religious faith is one phase through which nations pass toward unity. Islam is the Arabs' past; its political institutions —the *sharīʻa* and the caliphate—have, however, been outgrown, and the modern Arab nation must adopt modern institutions characteristic of the West.[13]

Parallel solutions to the sectarian problem were formulated by Muslim thinkers. Perhaps the purest and most enduring distillation was that of Sati ʻal-Ḥuṣrī (1880–1968). A man marginal to the Arab mainstream in a different way from the Christians of his native Syria, he received a typically Turkish education in Constantinople and loyally served the Ottoman state in responsible civil posts until its collapse after World War I. His choice of "becoming" an Arab instead of "remaining" a Turk was deliberate. He was minister of education in Faisal's ill-fated government in Damascus; he followed him to Iraq, where he continued his service in the field of public education. He ended his career as an official of the Arab League. For many years he was in a position to act on his conviction that national sentiments should be developed through the education of youth. For Ḥuṣrī, political communities are created by the sentiments of nationalism, territorial patriotism, and loyalty to a state. When these all coincide, society is politically stable and loyalties are undivided; otherwise, political beliefs may be dangerously ambiguous and conflicting.[14] The components of

---

[13]Hourani, op. cit., pp. 309–311.
[14]Ibid., pp. 311–316.

nationalism are, first, a common language and, secondarily, a shared history, while religion, material interests and attachment to a fixed territory are at best ancillary.[15] He emphasized the intense Arabization in certain areas during the building of the Islamic empire even when the people did not adopt the new religion, whereas strongly entrenched cultures such as the Persian and Turkish embraced Islam but retained their own languages. The Qur'ān's influence, and that of pre-Islamic and later literature, has kept a pure standard of Arabic in being notwithstanding the proliferation of colloquial dialects. The history that Ḥuṣrī had in mind is not that of scholarly books, but that which lives in the minds of the people, universally known, preserving the national traditions. Ḥuṣrī's theory of Arab nationalism is thus typically secular in character. Arab political unity, he insisted, is both natural and inevitable. Reiterating a common, if debatable, assertion, he considered the present divisions among Arab regions the product of imperialist interests and policies. The resulting regional idologies must be combated and a uniform national sentiment revived, by education, to prepare the way for political unity. Ḥuṣrī's concept of Arab nationalism was widely disseminated, and its continuing appeal is reflected in the frequent reprinting of his writings. It contributed to vindicating the priority of comprehensive Arabism over local patriotisms. Arab nationalism henceforth comprehended without question Egypt, Libya, and the Maghreb.

The contradictions inherent in these various approaches to defining the Arab nation have not been resolved. Several mutually incompatible ideologies have come to assert that specified forms of socio-economic organization, and certain political orientations, are essential elements of Arab nationalism and prerequisite to attainment of its aims. There remains an irreducible core of sentiment that the Arabs are one distinct people confronting together a world environment at least potentially hostile, which seeks to deny to the Arab nation the unity, dignity, and power to which it is entitled by its past and potential contributions to human civilization. While profound differences among the Arab countries in level and quality of education, economic endowment, develop-

---

[15]William L. Cleveland, *The Making of an Arab Nationalist* (Princeton, N.J.: Princeton University Press, 1971), pp. 99 ff.

ment, technology, and administrative and legal structures impede the quest for political unity, actions of their governments must remain within bounds of the popular feeling of Arab solidarity against the outsider. Troubles menacing Arabs in Morocco or Syria touch exposed nerves in Iraq and Yemen. The catastrophe that befell the Arabs of Palestine has lent nationalist feeling a remarkable dimension of emotional intensity from end to end of the Arab world that profoundly conditions relations between the United States and all Arab states.

PALESTINE: THE CATALYST

The land of Palestine belongs of right to a people uniquely favored of God, the vehicle of His revelation respecting the salvation of mankind, charged with a permanent mission for the enlightenment of humanity and the establishment of justice, long the object of repression and injustice, whose enemies are presently sustained by a world superpower for its own imperial interests. The perplexing essence of the Palestine problem is the fact that both Arabs and Jews see themselves exclusively identified by these attributes. "The prospects for settlement would be dim enough were God thought to be a partisan of either protagonist; but alas, he has emerged as the ally of both."[16] The vast literatures defending the justice of one and the other cause argue from *a priori* mystical principles beyond empirical confirmation. Each ideology comprises a hermetic system of which the deductions escape evaluation by external criteria and commands the fanaticism that moves men to disregard selfish material advantage, and life itself, to alter an intolerably unsatisfactory world. The issue transcends the fate of the several million people immediately involved. Seventy years ago an Arab nationalist theoretician wrote,

Two important phenomena, of the same nature but mutually opposed . . . are now emerging in Turkey in Asia: these are the reawakening of the Arab nation and the latent effort of the Jews to reestablish on a very broad scale the ancient monarchy of Israel. These two movements are destined

---

[16]Malcolm H. Kerr, "The Arabs and Israelis: Perceptual Dimensions to their Dilemma," in Willard A. Beling, ed., *The Middle East: Quest for an American Policy* (Albany: State University of New York Press, 1973), p. 31.

to mutual combat until one wins out over the other. Upon the final result of the struggle ... will depend the fate of the entire world.[17]

Insofar as the United Nations mirrors the concern of the world community, Azoury prophesied truly: no other dispute has so absorbed the attention of the Security Council and the General Assembly. Both the Arab and the Israeli conceptual systems have proved impervious to the principles of equity the United Nations has sought to apply. The United Nations pronounced its fateful judgment in the Partition Resolution of November 29, 1947. Neither side has acknowledged the justice of this, or the many succeeding decrees, and both remain in defiance of a long series of United Nations commands. International competence, authority, and wisdom have been repeatedly challenged, conflicting as they do with two national mythologies between which there is no early prospect of reconciliation. No solution yet conceived to the Palestine issue appears just to all those inevitably involved.

The proclamation on May 14, 1948 of Israel's sovereign independence, its recognition by most of the world's governments, and its consolidation by force of arms in the immediately ensuing wars form the watershed of contemporary Arab history. In Arab eyes a wedge, both territorial and psychological, was driven between the Arabs of Asia and Africa with the help of the Western powers, in the face of insistent warnings that vital Arab interests were at stake. It eliminated the possibility that the Arabs might become partners of the Western democracies in the developing cold war and tinged their neutralism with a militancy that some in the West were unable to distinguish from alignment with the East. The Israelis were, as their leaders remain, Western men, in full command of the skills in purposeful social mobilization, technology, and military technique that were the source of Western power. The humiliating defeat sustained by the Arabs led them to an anxious search for the sources of their weakness. Many discovered it in the venality and treachery of their governments, in outmoded forms of social organization, and in their stagnant, unproductive economies controlled from abroad. The Arab world entered an era of revolution that has not yet run its course. Opposition to the

---

[17]Nejib Azoury, *Le Réveil de la nation arabe;* quoted in Hourani, op. cit., p. 279 (translation from French by present writer).

Israeli presence became an attitude on which all Arabs could unite; what to do about it in terms of practical policies, however, raised problems on which Arab leaders differed, and these differences became the subject of passionate contention among them and an obstacle to Arab unity. Within the broad framework of Arabism a new, radical subspecies of nationalism arose among the Palestinian refugees and their descendents.

The significant American role in the creation and survival of Israel should be recalled briefly.

The mass slaughter of Jews in territories under Nazi control before and during World War II and the perils surrounding those remaining alive stimulated the major segment of American Jewry to abandon the concept of Palestinianism and to unite on the policy of the early establishment of a Jewish state. In May 1942 representatives of the major Zionist organizations, meeting at the Biltmore Hotel in New York, resolved that immigration into Palestine should be unlimited, that it should go forward under administration of the Jewish Agency, and that all Palestine should become a Jewish commonwealth integrated in the structure of the new democratic world.[18] The American Jewish Conference, representing 2¼ million Jews, endorsed the Biltmore Program, and sixteen tightly organized Zionist groups with membership totaling over 486,000 began militant activity toward its implementation. This placed the American wing of Zionism in a distinctly more extreme posture than Weizmann and the World Zionist Organization which, despite the 1939 White Paper, still reposed hope in the British government.

At the close of the war President Harry Truman came under intensive pressure from the Zionists, from leaders in both Houses of Congress, and from other leaders of public opinion to throw the full weight of American government influence behind the Zionist program. Having inherited no Palestine policy from his predecessor, he tried to devise an approach to the problem that would take account of the various United States interests affected. Roosevelt, who had given American Zionists vague assurances of sympathy with their aims, had formally pledged to Ibn Saud and other Arab

---

[18]Joseph B. Schechtman, *The United States and the Jewish State Movement* (New York: Herzl Press, 1966), p. 61.

leaders that the United States would take no action affecting Arab interests in Palestine without full consultation with Arabs as well as Jews. During the war years, it became established American policy that the Middle East was primarily a British responsibility. Britain, moreover, was the mandatory power in Palestine; while the 1924 Convention gave the United States a voice in any fundamental change in the terms of the mandate, any American initiative toward change implied some responsibility for its application. Public sentiment was forcing the rapid demobilization of the armed forces, and the President's military advisors warned that few, if any, American troops could be made available to enforce a decision unacceptable to the Arabs. Defense and foreign affairs officials were concerned that alienation of the Arabs might deprive the West of Middle Eastern oil supplies and encourage the Soviet Union to expand southward into the region. Reports of American diplomats, confirmed by urgent representations of Arab legations in Washington, made clear the depth of Arab feeling and the certainty that large-scale Jewish immigration or the establishment of a Jewish state in Palestine would be opposed by armed action. Genuinely concerned with the plight of the displaced Jews in Germany and Austria, numbering about 100,000, Truman adopted and clung tenaciously to the position that their fate should receive first priority, whether by emigration to Palestine or resettlement elsewhere; that this should be accomplished without major military, political or economic commitment by the United States; and that the political future of Palestine was a subject for settlement by the United Nations. As early as the Potsdam Conference, he urged a liberal immigration policy on Prime Minister Attlee. On August 31, 1945 he specifically recommended to Attlee that 100,000 immigration certificates be issued at once. It is doubtful whether Truman saw that such a measure would make the formation of a Zionist state both possible and inevitable.

The Jewish community in Palestine had, under David Ben Gurion and other zealous leaders, "fought the 1939 White Paper as though there was no war and fought the war as if there were no White Paper." The latter's ban on immigration had been regularly circumvented, with emphasis on entry of able-bodied youths. Soon after the war, the Jewish security force Haganah, underground but tolerated by the mandatory, attained an estimated strength of 60,000. Spearheaded by illegal terrorist formations, Irgun and the Stern Gang, the community mounted an intensifying challenge to British authority.

As a preliminary response to Truman's appeal, the British government announced in September 1945 that a maximum of 1500 certificates for immigration to Palestine would be issued monthly. In October Foreign Secretary Ernest Bevin formally proposed that an Anglo-American Committee of Inquiry be formed to examine the entire question of the Jewish refugees, including its Palestine aspects, before any broader action should be settled on. While regretting the attendant delay, President Truman agreed. A twelve-member joint committee was appointed that rendered its report in April 1946. Declaring that Palestine could not absorb all European Jews, the report nevertheless recommended the early admission of 100,000 actual victims of Nazi and Fascist persecution. Palestine should become a United Nations trusteeship, the trustee to prepare the territory for eventual independence as a binational democratic state. Future immigration should be the object of agreement between the two communities. Restrictions on land transfers and the Jewish National Fund's ban on the employment of Arabs on Jewish-owned land should be terminated. Truman publicly endorsed the Committee's recommendation for the 100,000 immigration permits, while reserving judgment on the others.

The Committee's proposals satisfied no one. Senior representatives of Transjordan, Egypt, Yemen, and Saudi Arabia issued a statement from Inchass, Egypt, in May, warning Britain and the United States that, while the Arabs wanted their friendship, such friendship depended on whether the two powers transgressed against the rights of the Palestine Arabs. In June the Arab League Council, meeting at Bludan in Syria, set up a special committee on Palestine. It recommended stiffening the already existing boycott of Zionist goods, measures to prevent the sale of Arab land in Palestine, and improved Arab propaganda efforts in the West. The Council denied any American claim to a voice in Palestine affairs and called on Britain to negotiate with the Arab governments. The Committee's program was equally unsatisfactory to the Zionists, determined on the early foundation of a sovereign Jewish state.

In an effort to break the deadlock Truman, in June 1946, appointed a "Special Cabinet Committee," representing the Departments of State, War, and Treasury, to negotiate with the British on the implementation of the pending proposals. The resulting Morrison-Grady Plan, named for Herbert Morrison, Lord President of the Council, and American Ambassador Henry F. Grady, contemplated a division of Palestine into three areas under British trusteeship: one Jewish, one Arab, and one including Jerusalem under direct administration by the trustee, who would moreover be responsible for defense, finance, and other national functions. The United States would undertake to finance development projects and otherwise assist the Arab sector and to extend substantial loans to the Arab states. Following acceptance of the proposal by the Jews and Arabs, 100,000 Jewish immigrants were to be admitted, with American assistance for the cost of their settlement. The trusteeship might, according to circumstance, evolve toward a binational state, a unitary state, or toward partition.

The new plan was roundly condemned by all articulate segments of American opinion as well as by some senior members of the bureaucracy, and the President was placed in the awkward position of repudiating the work of his own appointees. The British government meanwhile endeavored to reach some solution by direct negotiation with the Arab Higher Committee and the Jewish Agency. The talks, begun in July 1946, were intermittently boycotted by both sides. Their progress was compromised not only by intransigence on either side but also by competitively pro-Zionist expressions in the United States elections of that year. The Twenty-Second Zionist Congress, which met in December, united on the policy of an independent Jewish state. Having failed to achieve Arab-Jewish agreement on any major issue, the British government decided in February 1947 to place the problem before the United Nations.

At a special session in May the United Nations General Assembly appointed an eleven-member Special Committee on Palestine (UNSCOP)[19] to investigate and report on all Palestine-related issues. The UNSCOP report, made public in September, submitted a majority and a minority plan. The former proposed a partition

---

[19]Australia, Canada, Czechoslovakia, Guatemala, India, Iran, the Netherlands, Peru, Sweden, Uruguay, and Yugoslavia.

of Palestine into an Arab and a Jewish state and an independent Jerusalem under United Nations trusteeship, the whole unified economically under UNESCO supervision. The minority (India, Iran, and Yugoslavia), apprehending a permanently unsettling irredentism in case of partition, proposed a federal union of Arab and Jewish states, after a three-year transitional period during which immigration would be allowed within the limits of economic absorptive capacity.

The majority proposal met the Zionists' aim of an independent state, if not their concept of its geographic extent, and they mounted a campaign in the United States in its support that has, for pervasiveness, few parallels in our history. Nevertheless, whereas the General Assembly, convened in regular session September 16, addressed its attention at once to the UNSCOP report, the United States delegation withheld expression of support for partition until October 11. As adopted on November 29, with full support of the Soviet bloc, the Resolution[20] requested the Security Council to ensure its implementation and provided for a five-nation Commission to organize governments in the respective Jewish and Arab states in Palestine, to come into power upon termination of the mandate, not later than August 1, 1948. The Arab states promptly declared they would not be bound by the Resolution and would oppose it by force; they began recruitment of volunteers to serve with Palestine Arab guerrilla formations. The British announced that they would renounce the mandate and evacuate Palestine by May 15; they meanwhile withheld cooperation with the Commission, which was denied access to the territory. Violence and disorder heightened in Palestine, in a triangular struggle among British, Jews, and Arabs.

Although it became more and more apparent that the United Nations plan could be placed in operation only by armed force, the United States opposed proposals in the Security Council for the organization of an international police force, fearing that Soviet participation, which could not be prevented, might give the communists a foothold in the Near East from which they could not be dislodged. One week after the United Nations resolution was

---

[20]Text in Jacob C. Hurewitz, ed., *Diplomacy in the Near and Middle East* (New York: D. van Nostrand Co., 1956), Vol. ii, p. 281 ff.

adopted, Secretary of State Marshall announced an embargo on the shipment of American arms to any Middle East destination; the decision was denounced by the Zionists as discriminating against the ill-equipped Jews, who accepted partition, in favor of the supposedly well-armed Arabs, who rejected it.

Implicit in United States support for partition was the subordination of global strategic considerations, as seen by the Defense and State departments, to those of responsiveness to a vocal, influential, and wealthy sector of the electorate, and to humanitarian concerns. It further assumed that the program could be carried out peacefully. The latter hope was soon eroded. The United Nations Palestine Commission, denied both British and Arab cooperation, reported to the Security Council in February that it would be unable to implement partition unless provided with substantial military forces and predicted an extended period of strife and bloodshed.

Secretary of Defense Forrestal was alarmed by the prospect that access to Arab oil might be shut off from the United States. American petroleum reserves had risen only 6% from 1939–1946, and the country was now importing as much oil as it exported. Middle East oil was essential to the success of the European Recovery Program. In January 1948 Forrestal learned that Aramco had decided to suspend work on Tapline, for which Syria was delaying action on transit rights, and on further development in Saudi Arabia, anticipating protracted disturbances in Palestine with broad repercussions. Air Force planners were at this time projecting an early requirement for American air bases not only in North Africa but in the Middle East itself. Forrestal pressed these preoccupations assiduously before the cabinet and the National Security Council. With the President's acquiescence the Secretary instituted discussions, which led nowhere, with leaders of both major political parties toward agreement to exclude the Palestine issue from domestic politics.

The political atmosphere between the United States and the Soviet Union was moreover rapidly deteriorating. Early in March, one week after the communist coup in Czechoslovakia, the American High Commissioner in Berlin, General Lucius Clay, reported a subtle change in the Soviet attitude that led him to feel that war might erupt with "dramatic suddenness."

These disquieting pressures led President Truman to reexamine the United States position on Palestine. The views of the State Department were placed before the President in a memorandum prepared by Under Secretary Robert Lovett, Dean Rusk, head of the Office of Special Political Affairs, and Loy Henderson, director of the Office of Near Eastern and African Affairs. The partition resolution, it was argued, was simply a recommendation by the General Assembly that had proved unworkable. An effort to impose the plan by force would risk involving the United States in war with the Arab states, with great detriment to American national security. Sacrifice of Arab goodwill would lay the Near East open to penetration by the Soviet Union. The Department therefore recommended that the United States call on the United Nations to set aside the partition plan, to impose a truce among the belligerents in Palestine, and to establish a provisional trusteeship in the territory, to be administered by the Trusteeship Council. By March 8, Secretary of State Marshall informed the American delegate at the United Nations, Warren Austin, that the President had approved these recommendations and instructed him to introduce them at the earliest appropriate opportunity.[21]

The new American proposal, placed before the Security Council on March 19, created consternation and bewilderment. Although mildly encouraging to the Arabs, it was totally unacceptable to the Zionists, who declared that they would oppose it, by force if necessary, and proceed with the establishment of an independent state. It was sharply denounced by Russia and the Ukraine, who insisted on the letter of the partition resolution. While the United States now expressed willingness to provide forces to impose a truce, no positive response was forthcoming even from those United Nations members who remained unconvinced of the feasibility of partition. The State Department's hope that the trusteeship scheme would forestall full-scale war in Palestine appeared more and more unrealistic. The Security Council, unable to take decisive action, voted on April 1 to call the General Assembly into special session, while appealing to both sides in Palestine to agree

---

[21]Recent scholarship has discredited the notion, disingenuously encouraged by Truman in his memoirs, that the State Department acted without the President's authority on this occasion. See John Snetsinger, *Truman, the Jewish Vote, and the Creation of Israel* (Stanford: Hoover Institution Press, 1974), pp. 86–88.

to armistice terms. Time was fast running out as the British mandate drew to its close. As May 15 approached, the United States, like other powers, was obliged to decide what attitude to adopt toward the Jewish state, whose creation was imminent.

Nineteen forty-eight was a presidential election year, and Truman's prospects of reelection were, at best, uncertain. His Republican opponent, Governor Thomas A. Dewey of New York, bid unequivocally for the Zionist vote. A leading Democrat, Henry A. Wallace, had already defected to form the Progressive Party, and his candidacy for the presidency had furthermore been endorsed by the American Labor Party. The rise of the States Rights ("Dixiecrat") Party in July threatened rightist inroads in the South, theretofore solidly Democratic. As early as spring 1948, Democratic Party officials judged that the President might well lose the election if the normally Democratic vote of the Jewish community in several important states, already in doubt because of the administration's reversal on Palestine partition, were alienated. On May 12 the President heard the arguments for and against prompt recognition of the future state of Israel. Secretary of State Marshall and Under Secretary Lovett appealed to Truman not to decide the issue on grounds of domestic politics; they emphasized that recognition, before the new government had proved itself in administrative control of its national territory, would depart from established policy and antagonize the Arabs. Clark Clifford and David Niles, the key White House advisors on campaign strategy, urged the President to redeem his standing with the Jewish voters by immediate recognition, or even by announcing in advance his intention to recognize Israel as soon as it came into being.

Swayed by the latter arguments, Truman arranged the announcement of United States de facto recognition ten minutes after the existence of the State of Israel was proclaimed on May 15. This act was the first in a series of steps during the remaining months of the campaign by which the President demonstrated sympathetic support for Israel and rehabilitated his position among Zionist voters. Before the end of May he received Chaim Weizmann, newly elected President of Israel, on a state visit. He named an enthusiastic supporter of Zionism, James G. McDonald, as American Ambassador to the new state and ordered the arrangement of a substantial loan to Israel. Of more direct concern to the Arabs was his action regarding the Palestine conciliation plan drawn up by United Nations mediator Count Folke Bernadotte shortly before his assassination on September 17. The plan proposed to reduce possible points of Arab-Israeli friction by a readjustment of Israel's borders as defined by the 1947 partition resolution, including the reassignment to the Arabs of the Negev Desert region. The Democratic Party national platform had opposed any change in Israel's boundaries as specified in the Resolution unless fully acceptable to her, which surrender of the Negev most assuredly was not. State Department officials grappling with the Palestine problem persuaded Secretary Marshall to issue a forthright statement of United States support for the Bernadotte program, in the hope that the assassination had created an opportunity to restore peace in the territory. Marshall had moved without consulting the President, who came under immediate pressure to repudiate his act. A week before the election Truman, disregarding the interparty agreement to exclude foreign affairs from the campaign, delivered a strongly pro-Israel address at Madison Square Garden in New York; while avoiding specific mention of the Bernadotte plan or of Marshall, he repudiated his Secretary of State indirectly by declaring his unconditional support for the Democratic party platform. The President was, of course, reelected in one of America's more notable political upsets.

Coming at a time when the United States had been pressing in the United Nations for reappraisal of the concept of partition, and thus of an independent Jewish State, Truman's precipitous recognition of Israel infuriated the Arabs, convinced them that the United States had deliberately deceived them and the world community as to its true intention—supposedly, to make sure that the partition resolution remained in effect at the end of the mandate —and gave rise to the enduring notion that America was chiefly responsible for the creation of Israel at the expense of the Arabs. This was true, in the limited sense that the resources that enabled the Jews in Palestine to build the economic infrastructure and institutions that began to function immediately as an effective government came from private American contributions, and that the American government had, in disregard of Arab concern, forced Britain to relax its policy on Jewish immigration into Palestine, thus promoting the growth of a community large enough to defend itself. Viewed dispassionately, on the other hand, American action during the United Nations handling of the issue exhibited no consistent pro-Zionist policy. Insisting on a decisive role in settling the issue and exercising vigorous pressure on other countries' delegations in the final few days before the partition vote, the United States nevertheless opposed the United Nations measures that might have made it work. Political realities, demonstrated in the history of the British mandate and in the studied assessment of the Palestine Commission, showed clearly enough that a Jewish state could be established only by armed force. An international police force organized to enforce implementation of the partition program on completion of the British evacuation might have induced the formation of the contemplated Arab government that, in contrast with the Jews, the disorganized Palestine Arabs had failed to make ready. Such a force might, furthermore, have deterred the Arab League States from invading Palestine and instituting the first Arab-Israeli war. The abortive trusteeship proposal prevented any realistic international planning for action on termination of the mandate, and the purpose of partition was thus defeated.

The vacillating American position on the issue, resulting from domestic political pressures, may be contrasted with the steadfast Soviet policy during the critical phase. After October 23, 1947, the Soviet Union, subordinating its historical anti-Zionist bias to the objective of reducing imperialist presence in the Near East by procuring the British evacuation of Palestine, and perhaps hoping to achieve influence in the new Jewish state by reason of the East European origin of much of its population, announced and pressed its support of Palestine partition. Without this support, indeed, the partition Resolution would have failed adoption by the General Assembly. With its client states the Soviet Union promptly accorded full recognition to the Jewish state and maintained cordial relations with it for several years. Soviet help was of crucial importance to Israel in its war for survival. Whereas the United States arms embargo remained in effect for both Arabs and Jews (although the latter had considerable success in circumventing it), the Israelis were, through Czechoslovakia, permitted substantial purchases of Soviet arms denied to the Arab states.

THE PALESTINE WAR AND ITS AFTERMATH

Many of the enduring features of the Palestine problem took form as results of the Palestine War of 1948 to 1949. The Arab countries had left no possible doubt of their intention to oppose by force the consolidation of Israel and, on May 15, elements of the Egyptian, Transjordanian, Lebanese, Syrian, and Iraqi armies advanced into areas of Palestine inhabited largely by Arabs. The Israelis were hard pressed for a few weeks, not yet having perfected the organization of their armed forces nor completed the distribution of arms of which delivery had been planned to coincide with the final departure of the British. Israel appealed to the United Nations against the Arab attack, and the United States, the Soviet Union, and Secretary General Trygve Lie took the lead in obtaining the passage on May 29 of a Security Council resolution calling for a four-week cease-fire during which no outside power was to introduce war material or fighting personnel into the area. Although the Arab States were reluctant to lose such momentum as their advance still had, United Nations Mediator Count Bernadotte succeeded in establishing a truce as of June 11. Taking better advantage of the respite than the Arabs were able to do, the Israelis procured quantities of heavy arms, chiefly from Czechoslovakia, and enough aircraft were smuggled from the United States and Britain to form a small but effective air force. Administrative and public services were organized meanwhile, and civilian industries were adapted to the production of military equipment. Consequently, upon expiration of the truce, Israeli forces passed to the attack against Arab troops now largely on the defensive, occupying about 780 square miles of territory before the United Nations Security Council passed a resolution blaming the Arabs for the resumed hostilities and peremptorily ordering a permanent cease-fire, which Israel accepted only under United States pressure. In September the United Nations Mediator proposed the plan already mentioned, incorporating important territorial modifications, favorable to the Arabs, of the original partition plan and recommending the annexation by Transjordan of the Arab portions of Palestine. The cease-fire, at best imperfectly respected by either side, was broken at the end of October by an Israeli offensive to seize western Galilee and parts of the Negev and, in December, Israeli troops took the whole of the Negev. Early in January the parlous situation of Egypt's troops, surrounded and inaccessible for supply or relief, led her to enter armistice negotiations with Israel through the good offices of Dr. Ralph Bunche, the Acting United Nations Mediator. An Israeli-Egyptian Armistice Agreement signed February 24 was followed, after tortuous negotiations, by bilateral arrangements between Israel and Lebanon (March 23), Transjordan (April 3), and finally Syria (July 20).

The central fact emerging from the conflict was the consolidation of Israel, not by international agreement but by force of arms. The new state's territorial configuration embraced all those areas where Jewish settlement was concentrated, as well as extensive desert tracts sparsely inhabited by Arabs. While its area substantially exceeded that allotted by the partition resolution, its boundaries had little strategic logic; they were long and difficult to defend against chronically hostile neighbors. The nation was born, and could survive, only by virtue of a strong military establishment. It became clear during the United Nations debates that the only international intervention considered would have been directed against the Arabs on behalf of Israel. On the other hand, the efforts of the United Nations mediators and truce observers, directed toward a practicable compromise between the belligerents, tended to thwart the Israeli objective of seizing as much land as possible for future colonization. As a result, a deep and lasting suspicion and contempt for the United Nations and its agents arose in Israel, together with the conviction that the nation's interests could be entrusted only to its own armed strength. Israeli leaders made no secret during the war of their dissatisfaction with the extent of the territory reserved to their state; their statements on the subject aroused Arab fears that Israel intended to expand further and further, which subsequent history has done little to dispel.

The struggle for Palestine under the mandate was civil war between two communities within a single political entity. It became international war after May 15, 1948, when the neighboring Arab states moved against Israel. It did not, however, follow the usual pattern of war by culminating in a negotiated treaty of peace in which the vanquished party seeks the best possible terms from the victor. The anomaly stems from the inconclusive outcome of the conflict. In the conventional sense there was no victor. Although the Arab armies briefly occupied portions of the territory reserved for the Jewish state, and Israel made incursions into the Egyptian Sinai, the military engagements took place in large part in Arab sections of Palestine in which there was in effect no government. The Arab states' armies were, indeed, defeated. Their national territory nevertheless remained largely inviolate, and their governments continued to function unimpaired. Israel did not attain a position in which she could impose terms on them. The 1949 Armistice Agreements merely institutionalized the cessation of hostilities, in itself certainly no small achievement for the United Nations mediator. The possible conditions of peace were absent: either the application of overwhelming force by one belligerent against the national territory of its adversary, or vital coincident aims by the warring parties, attainable only through peace, overriding the sources of hostility.

The defeat of the Arab armies in Palestine was nevertheless of momentous consequence for the Arab countries and their political leadership. No government, of course, advertises to its people the weakness and incompetence of its army. The Arab governments erred in the opposite direction by promising, and even claiming, spectacular victories they had reason to know were beyond reach. The Arab countries involved had armies totaling nearly 80,000 at the outbreak of war, of which a significant portion had to be reserved for the maintenance of internal order. Of the forces initially committed in Palestine, the Syrian and Lebanese, numbering no more than 6000, were former territorial troops whose command had been taken over from the French scarcely three years before; they were poorly trained and equipped. The Egyptian and Iraqi forces, no more than 10,000 and 4000, respectively, were badly led and lacked competent technical staffs; they had insufficient weapons and ammunition for sustained combat, since Britain had supplied them sparingly both to preserve a dependent relationship and to prevent their use against her own troops in the area. Only Transjordan's Arab Legion, under British command, was adequately trained; its stocks of arms and ammunition were, on the other hand, insufficient for prolonged operations by the 4000 or 5000 men sent at first into Palestine. Facing inexperienced Arab armies of at most 25,000 at the outbreak of war, Israel's Haganah, which became the Israel Defense Force, had at least 45,000 well-trained men of whom at least half had gained experience in modern warfare with Allied armies during World War II, backed by the terrorist organizations, several thousand strong, which were gradually absorbed into the regular forces. Initially less well armed than the Arab troops, the Jews had the advantages of a compact territory containing the country's best-developed communications facilities, interior lines, unified leadership, high morale, and total dedication to the national cause. When, during the first truce, the Israelis had secured armaments overbalancing those of the Arab states, the latter lost a tactical initiative they were never able to regain. Although the total Arab troops committed in the war, including the few thousand ineffectual Palestinian irregulars, rose to an estimated 45,000, the Israelis could eventually field forces perhaps twice as numerous.

With the possible exception of King Abdullah, the Arab leaders badly miscalculated the quality of their own armies and the capability of the Jews to wage war. They were furthermore divided. Beyond the common sentiment that the Arab character of Palestine should be vindicated, they had no clear joint objective in the war and worked actively to thwart each other's aims. Abdullah sought to increase the territory under his rule as a step toward the creation of a Hashemite Greater Syria, and was prepared to compose to some degree with the Israelis for this purpose. King Farūq, determined to frustrate Abdullah's ambitions, impeded the passage of arms shipped to the Arab Legion; he moreover installed an "All-Palestine" puppet regime in the Egyptian-occupied area that became known as the Gaza Strip, with the cooperation of Ibn Saud, a dynastic rival of the Hashemites. Mutual suspicions and the lack of common purpose contributed as substantially to the failure of the Arab military effort as the absence of tactical coordination in the field.

The Arab peoples had been stirred to an extraordinary degree of emotional involvement in the war. Their leaders had led them to expect early and complete triumph and had carefully concealed from them the successive reverses sustained by their armies. The Arabs were thus unprepared for the defeat implicitly acknowledged by signature of the Armistice Agreements. As the factors that contributed to the disaster gradually became known, popular anger focused on the political leaderships. Civilian and military agitation against the ineffectual Syrian parliamentary regime resulted in the first of a succession of army coups in March 1949. Abdullah's secret, inconclusive negotiations with Israeli officials were seen as betrayal of the national cause; he was assassinated in Jerusalem by a Palestinian refugee on July 20, 1951. Highly placed Egyptians had trafficked in defective weapons supplied to Egyptian troops, and the inefficient government had failed to supply its forces adequately or to rescue surrounded units; the discredited monarchy was overthrown by the military coup of July 1952. It was universally posited that Arab honor and dignity, lost by military defeat, could be recovered only through future military victory. This implied, in the first instance, a new and urgent priority for the development of the Arab military establishments. Many Arabs identified sources of weakness in the existing political, economic, and social institutions and set about working for revolutionary change. The failure of inter-Arab coordination in the war made the necessity for achieving unity of Arab national purpose obvious.

The final major consequence of the war was the intractable problem of the Palestinian refugees. Already, during the communal disturbances of the 1930s, about 30,000 of the more prosperous Palestinians, the natural leadership pool, had moved temporarily to other Arab countries. No paragovernmental agency parallel to that of the Jews developed among the Arabs under the mandate. In the Arab areas the mandatory authorities provided the administrative and public services, and these disappeared as the British departed. After adoption of the United Nations partition resolution, disorder increased rapidly. Terrorized by Jewish attacks, both actual and rumored, an estimated 200,000 Arabs had fled their homes before May 15. After the first truce, when Jewish forces moved into densely populated Arab areas, the exodus increased until a total of more than 750,000 Palestinians had become refugees; the largest concentrations were in the Gaza Strip and the portions of Palestine occupied by the Arab Legion (soon incorporated with Transjordan to compose the Hashemite Kingdom of Jordan), and smaller numbers in Lebanon and Syria. On the mediator's initiative the United Nations acknowledged the international community's responsibility for the plight of the displaced population and its future. Initially the United Nations endeavored to effect the refugees' early return to their homes, now mainly under Israeli control. The Israeli government, however, refused to admit any significant number, fearing that the repatriates would jeopardize the country's security in the absence of a peace settlement and anxious to make available the maximum space feasible for further Jewish immigration and settlement. The enduring attitude of the United Nations on the problem was incorporated in General Assembly 194 (III) of December 11, 1948, providing that those refugees "wishing to return to their homes and live in peace with their neighbours should be permitted to do so at the earliest practicable date, and that compensation should be paid for the property of those choosing not to return and for loss of or damage to property which, under principles of international law or in equity, should be made good by the Governments or authorities responsible."

The same Resolution established the Palestine Conciliation Commission (PCC), composed of the United States, France, and Turkey. The PCC convened Arab representatives in conferences at Beirut, and later at Lausanne with Israeli representation, which made no practical headway toward resolving the problem but produced a clear definition of its essentially insoluble character: Israel insisted that the return of any substantial number of refugees could be considered only after, or in the context of, a final peace with the Arab states, meanwhile taking economic, social, and administrative measures that would reduce the practicability of any repatriation; the Arabs, on the other hand, could not be moved from the position that repatriation, or adequate compensation, was a condition precedent to the discussion of any other peace terms. This impasse remained for a quarter-century the irreducible core of the refugee issue.

Those responsible for United States policy in the Near East considered that the refugees represented a potential threat to the stability of the region and feared that it might, as a result, fall easy prey to communist penetration. In May 1949 President Truman placed exceedingly strong pressure on Prime Minister Ben Gurion for concessions on both refugee and boundary issues; the response was indignantly negative.

The United States cooperated fully in United Nations emergency relief operations for the refugees and made available the services of its ambassador in Cairo, Stanton Griffis, to coordinate an international relief program, beginning in December 1948. The PCC, realistically judging that little progress could be made toward an Arab-Israeli peace without some solution to the refugee problem, itself unresponsive to political action, addressed itself to economic methods, examining the possibility of making the refugees self-sustaining in the countries where they had taken refuge. The Commission's preliminary study resulted in the Economic Survey Mission for the Middle East, known as the Clapp Mission, named for its director, Gordon R. Clapp, Chairman of the Board of the Tennessee Valley Authority. The Mission's thesis, in which a long succession of American policy makers have never finally lost faith, was that the refugee problem could be solved or alleviated by resettlement in the Arab countries adjoining Palestine (except perhaps for already overpopulated Egypt) through large-scale multipurpose development projects undertaken with outside financial assistance and expertise, thus bypassing political issues. The Mission found that this approach, while economically sound, could provide no early solution, in view of the scarce capital, technical, research, and administrative resources in the countries concerned; large-scale programs would have to be preceded by modest pilot projects. It therefore recommended that, while the latter were accomplishing the necessary preparatory work, adequate provision be made for the refugees' maintenance, and that small-scale public works projects be instituted on which some could be gainfully employed. In December 1949 the General Assembly established the Relief and Works Agency for Palestine Refugees (UNRWA) for this dual purpose. The Arab governments concerned, however, withheld cooperation in any programs aimed at "liquidating" the Palestine problem through resettling the refugees (few of whom in any case wished to live permanently elsewhere than in their homeland); their own citizens had prior claims on the available resources and, for differing local reasons, the Palestinians were considered a potentially disruptive political element. The UNRWA's task became limited for the most part to ensuring a minimum of subsistence for the refugees in temporary shelters and the provision of educational facilities that permitted a small number to find work in various Arab states where they became economically, if seldom politically, integrated. From the first the United States has contributed far more than its usual share of United Nations expenses to the Agency's annual budget: never less than half, and often as much as 70%. Few items have been less popular among American legislators responsible for passing judgment on appropriations. Some have proposed a progressive decrease in the UNRWA budget as a device to force the Arab host governments to assume full and permanent responsibility for the refugees. Such suggestions have always given way to the argument that this would do irreparable harm to American interests generally in the Arab world. The case was put, as early as 1950, to the House Foreign Affairs Committee by Assistant Secretary of State George McGhee.

... The political loss of this area to the Soviet Union would be a major disaster comparable to its loss during war. Certainly the political strategic position of the Soviet Union would be immeasurably strengthened by the attainment of its objectives in the Near East, and the cold war materially prolonged. ...

Against this background, our solicitude for the Palestine refugees, partly based on humanitarian considerations, has additional justification. As long as the refugee problem remains unresolved ... attainment of a political settlement in Palestine is delayed ... [and] the refugees ... will continue to serve as a natural focal point for exploitation by Communist and disruptive elements which neither we nor the Near Eastern governments can afford to ignore. ... The presence of three-quarters of a million idle, destitute people—a number greater than the combined strength of all the standing armies of the Near East—whose discontent increases with the passage of time, is the greatest threat to the security of the area which now exists.[22]

From the outset, therefore, the Palestine issue has been seen by American policy makers as one in which major interests of the United States, including its security, were involved. During the concluding years of the Truman administration, reaction to communist probings elsewhere in the world overshadowed problems in the Arab countries: the Berlin airlift, the Kuomintang collapse

---

[22]United States House of Representatives, Committee on Foreign Affairs, *Hearings on Palestine Refugees* (Washington: USGPO, 1950), p. 9.

in China and, finally, the Korean War. The succeeding administration, by contrast, sought as a major objective a form of collaboration from the Arab states for which they were quite unprepared and in which they saw little advantage to themselves. The confrontation of incompatible American and Arab objectives that emerged from the Palestine War inhibited and eventually defeated United States efforts to recruit the Arab states as militants in its crusade against "international communism."

CHAPTER V

The Arabs and Western Defense

A CERTAIN MANICHEISM COLORED THE AMERICAN WORLD VIEW during the 1950s. The dark powers of a monolithic international communism commanded by the Kremlin appeared locked everywhere in struggle with the forces of freedom and democracy led by America. Within the United States demogogic exploitation of the prevailing paranoia enriched the political vocabulary with the term McCarthyism. Abroad, the long series of communist advances and challenges in Eastern Europe, Turkey, Iran, and eastern Asia were conducted by the Red Army or under its shadow. The contest thus presented itself primarily in military and strategic terms, and it seemed imperative to build positions of armed strength that would contain communism within the area it already controlled, block its outward infiltration, and rely on its inherent evil to ensure its eventual internal collapse. No Arab land adjoined the Soviet Union or its satellites. Arab states nevertheless comprised a large proportion of the Middle East, which was thought of as a strategic unit; they moreover contained petroleum necessary for the well-being of Western economies, and flanked the sea-lanes by which it was brought to market over the entire length of the Mediterranean. One major node of international communications, the Suez Canal, lay in an Arab country, protected by a major Western military base whose critical importance had been demonstrated in two world wars. No geopolitical planning could leave the Arab world out of account.

The governments of Western Europe, wartime allies and enemies alike of the United States, generally shared the American apprehension of Soviet expansion and willingly joined in the formation of the North Atlantic Treaty Organization conceived to oppose it. They could not, however, pull their full weight within the alliance in the weakened economic situation in which they emerged from the war, and the European Recovery Program was undertaken to rehabilitate their economic and military strength; economic assistance was thus, in the United States view, intimately associated with factors of security. NATO was designed primarily for the defense of Western Europe. America nevertheless relied in the first instance on its NATO partners to ensure the defense of their dependencies in Africa, the Near East and Asia. Acting on the anticolonialist principles to which it had adhered since the Woodrow Wilson era, the United States at the same time urged these allies to dissolve the formal ties binding these areas to their metropoles, assuming that they would, as free nations, become willing and effective partners in the global defense against communism. The colonial powers, not fully sharing this assumption, endeavored to respond to American sentiment and compose with nationalist movements within their empires while preserving the essential core of political and economic control. These concurrent aims gradually proved irreconcilable, however, and the United States felt compelled to assume a more and more direct and independent role in the effort to organize world defense. In the Middle East, pursuing imperfectly compatible aims, America inadvertently found itself at odds with its European allies; its close association with them, on the other hand, tarred the United States with their "imperialist" brush.

Few Arabs were persuaded by the Western approach to world defense. America and her allies professed to be defending the "free" world. However, the Arabs did not regard themselves as free. Numerous Arab states were linked to Britain or France by agreements, concluded under varying degrees of duress, that denied them full freedom of decision in matters of defense, in external relations, and often in their internal affairs. Americans stressed historic and continuing Russian ambitions to expand southward into the Middle East. The foreign troops in the area, however, were British and French, not Russian, a constant and irritating reminder of the limitations on Arab independence. These same troops helped to keep in power elites now discredited by their failure to eliminate backwardness, disease, and poverty, and by their inability to defend the Arab land of Palestine against Zionism, which itself had flourished under the umbrella of the mandate, a device of Western imperialism. The Soviet Union, which had vigorously supported the partition of Palestine and facilitated the arming of the Jews, had no drawing power for the Arabs. There were, certainly, Arab communist parties, but these had been founded either by Westerners or by Arabs who had become communists while living in Western countries; they had no mass organization or appeal, and represented no discernible domestic threat. While the Arabs thus saw no reason to fear international communism or Russia, they most certainly saw their freedom and independence immediately menaced by the West and by Israel and sought freedom from the influence of any outside power of whatever political orientation.

America's assumption of a firsthand role in Middle East defense coincided with the close of the Stalin era in the Soviet Union. While the Soviet Union's most determined actions were aimed at enhancing its influence in the contiguous, non-Arab countries, it consistently made clear that the Arab East, relatively close to its own borders, was also its legitimate concern. In policy terms this was reflected chiefly in steady effort to reduce the political and military presence of the Western powers in the area. Arab nationalist movements, lacking communist leadership, were doctrinally discounted as bourgeois and inherently ineffectual. Correct, if not particularly close, relations were conducted with the generally conservative Arab governments that chose to maintain them. After Stalin's death in March 1953, a major shift began in the Soviet attitude toward the uncommitted countries of Asia and Africa. In order to contain and reduce Western power and influence it was now perceived to be in the Soviet interest to cultivate close commercial, political, and military ties even with traditional, reactionary governments; movements of national liberation from imperialist control gained a new respectability in communist eyes and even came to be acknowledged as possible avenues toward socialism. In line with the new doctrines, Soviet activities in what was becoming known as the "third" world intensified throughout the 1950s. A corresponding heightening of American apprehension led the United States into a series of actions eminently reasonable on grounds of geopolitics but that, given the conditions of political life in some areas, such as the Arab states, produced results disconcertingly different from those intended.

The point is well illustrated by the Tripartite Declaration on arms shipments to the Near East, issued by the United States, Britain, and France on May 25, 1950, and the consultation procedures established to give it effect. Already in 1949 the three governments had voiced concern before the Security Council at the possible development of an arms race between the Arab states and Israel, leading to a renewed outbreak of war. The incorporation of parts of Palestine in the new Kingdom of Jordan furthermore raised fears of a possible attack on the Kingdom by King Abdullah's Arab enemies. The Declaration expressed the three Powers' recognition of the need of the Near East countries for a certain level of armament to assure internal security and their legitimate self-defense, and to "permit them to play their part in the defense of the area as a whole." Noting that assurances had been elicited that the countries to which arms had already been delivered would not use them for any aggressive purpose, the three governments stated that future shipments would be subject to the same condition. They further declared:

. . . their deep interest in and their desire to promote the establishment and maintenance of peace and stability in the area and their unalterable opposition to the use of force or threat of force between any of the states in that area. The three Governments, should they find that any of these states was preparing to violate frontiers or armistice lines, would, consistently with their obligations as members of the United Nations, immediately take action, both within and outside the United Nations, to prevent such violation.

Both Israel and the Arab states considered the announced policy as discriminatory. The Arabs moreover interpreted it as an effort to infringe their sovereignty and independence, as well as to usurp the function of regional security that, in their view, rested with the Arab League as a regional organization under Article 52 of the

---

[1]Text in J. C. Hurewitz, *Diplomacy in the Near and Middle East. A Documentary Record: 1914–1956* (New York: D. van Nostrand Co., 1956), Vol. ii, p. 308.

United Nations Charter. In a statement dated June 21 the League Council asserted that the Arab need for arms stemmed from

their deep sense of responsibility for safeguarding the internal security of their countries, insuring the legitimate defense of their *neutrality* and fulfilling the obligation of safeguarding international security in this region.[2]

The League Council further contested the three Powers' right to decide the scale of armament appropriate to the Arab states.

It goes without saying that the level of armed forces maintained by every state for defense purposes and for participation in the maintenance of international security is a matter that can only be estimated by the state concerned. It is also subject to various factors, chiefly the size of the population, the area of the country and the length and diversity of its frontiers.

Although, as the Council acknowledged, the three powers had assured the Arab states that they had no intention of dividing the area among them into spheres of influence, it recorded a residue of suspicion.

There is no doubt that action alone will dispel these doubts if it demonstrates that the three powers are in fact concerned with maintaining peace in the Middle East impartially and on the basis of right and justice and respect for the sovereignty of the states and without subjecting them to domination or influence.

The diverging security concerns between the NATO powers and the Arab states emerge clearly from the Declaration and the Arab League's riposte. It is appropriate to emphasize that this contrast was apparent well before the rise of revolutionary regimes in some Arab states and before the Soviet Union had embarked on intensive cultivation of relations with them. The shared conviction of the necessity for joint effort against communist aggression that served as a firm basis for the NATO alliance was lacking in the Arab East. This fact was known and acknowledged by the astute, well-informed men who made policy for the United States during the 1950s. Curiously, they nevertheless pursued the goal of incorporating the Arab states in the Western treaty network with a

---

[2]Text in ibid., pp. 310–311. (Emphasis added.)

single-mindedness that irritated many Arabs, aggravated differences among them, and distorted their comprehension of America's true intentions.

THE MIDDLE EAST COMMAND, THE BAGHDAD PACT, AND THE SUEZ WAR

American strategic planning posited the need to give depth to Western European defenses by the establishment of military installations on the southern shores of the Mediterranean and in the Middle East. By agreement with Britain and France, the respective occupying powers, American air bases were activated in Libya (1948) and later in Morocco (1951). To the east, the United States followed with concern Britain's difficulties in preserving sufficient influence to ensure adequate defense arrangements. In both Iraq and Egypt her position rested formally on locally unpopular treaties by which she had reserved certain privileges, including the use of military bases and airfields; these agreements were coming under increasingly bitter attack from nationalists as derogating from these countries' sovereignty. In 1946 Britain attempted to palliate Iraqi sensitivities by replacing the existing treaty with a new one, the Treaty of Portsmouth, purporting to form an "equal" alliance between the two countries. The agreement, however, failed to provide for the early evacuation of British troops, and violent street demonstrations in Baghdad forced the resignation of the Ṣālih Jabr government that had negotiated it. Order was restored by Iraq's strong man, Nūrī al-Saʿīd, but the British position in the country remained equivocal. In the same year Britain also sought revised treaty arrangements with Egypt. In negotiations with Prime Minister Ismāʿīl Ṣidqī the British made considerable concessions respecting her access to the great Suez base, but declined to give unqualified recognition to Egypt's claim of sole sovereignty over the Sudan. Forced by nationalist pressure to resign, Ṣidqī was replaced by Nuqrāshī Pasha who, in 1947, invited the United Nations Security Council to declare invalid the "unequal" 1936 Treaty, which still had nine years to run. Although supported by the Soviet Union and Poland, the Egyptian case failed to persuade a majority, and the Council was unable to take action beyond recommending further negotiation between the contending parties. British-Egyptian relations remained at stalemate, in a more and more acrimonious atmosphere, until the Wafd Party's victory in the 1950 elections.

Disquieted by the evident decline of British capabilities in the Middle East and by the possibility that the Russians might exploit internal conflicts in the area to press their traditional southward ambitions, Secretary of State Dean Acheson conferred with the Pentagon on means by which the United States might strengthen the British hand and reinforce the Western position in the area. The "northern tier" bordering Soviet territory having been secured by the admission of Greece and Turkey to NATO and by bilateral military arrangements between the United States and Iran, the Arab states and Israel might, American planners thought, be brought into the developing global defense network by a multilateral approach whereby a Middle East Command (MEC), headed by a British officer, would coordinate security arrangements for the countries in the region; the latter would receive training for their armed forces and token quantities of weapons. Innocently,[3] it was assumed that the scheme would remove the stigma of "occupation," repugnant to Arab nationalist sentiment, from the British troops that would remain, since the Arabs would now be participating in their own defense against communist aggression. The Labor Government in Great Britain was meanwhile working on new proposals to Egypt for revised treaty provisions. Details of the MEC idea were perfected by consultation among the United States, Britain, France, and Turkey, and incorporated in British proposals presented to Egypt in October 1951. The NATO powers published a statement in November setting forth the principles underlying the MEC project. The Kremlin responded with a sharp diplomatic protest, also well publicized, portraying the plan as a device to maintain Western forces in the Middle Eastern countries in order to keep them in subjection and to attack the Soviet Union. Soviet propaganda continued to keep these allegations present in the minds of the people of the region throughout the Western endeavor to organize Middle East defense.

---

[3]Dean Acheson, *Present at the Creation* (New York: W. W. Norton & Co., 1969), p. 562.

The moment could hardly have been less propitious for winning Egyptian cooperation. The 1950 elections had returned the Wafd Party to office on a platform including total and unconditional British evacuation and the union of Egypt and the Sudan, both objectives of immense appeal to all shades of Egyptian opinion. No Egyptian perceived a threat to his country's security from the Soviet Union or international communism. Foreign-imposed restrictions on its political freedom and foreign control of its wealth were, on the other hand, constantly and painfully before Egyptian eyes. Poignant above all was the security threat from Israel which, only three years before, had inflicted humiliating defeat on the armies of Egypt and her sister Arab states. The Western powers into whose hands Egypt was now requested to entrust her safety had made clear, in the Tripartite Declaration, that the supply of Western arms would be a function of these powers' own defense interests, not of Egyptian interest in Arab defense against the immediate enemy.

It should have surprised no one, therefore, that Prime Minister Muṣṭafā al-Naḥḥās, although on notice that new British treaty proposals were on the way, recommended on October 7 and 8 to the Egyptian Parliament and King Farūq legislation abrogating the 1936 Treaty as well as the 1899 Condominium Agreement on the Sudan, or that when the MEC project was submitted to him on the October 13 he rejected it without so much as reading it. On October 15 the Parliament denounced the two treaties; Farūq assumed the title King of Egypt and the Sudan. MEC became a casualty of the ensuing impasse that was, moreover, the seedbed of the Naguib-Nasser *coup d'état* of July 23, 1952.

The Free Officers who authored the Egyptian coup had, by their own admission, no comprehensive program for ruling the country. They were fervently agreed on what they were against: the galling outside control of Egyptian affairs; the scandal of a privileged aristocracy, headed by a debauched king; the rapacity of an exploitative high bourgeoisie and landed class; and a political leadership grown opportunist and cynical. The new regime's inner circle, the Revolutionary Command Council revolving around Lt. Col. Gamāl 'Abd al-Nasser, moved deliberately and skillfully to eliminate or neutralize the elements of the *ancien régime* power structure. Farūq was promptly deposed; a regency was installed in the name of his infant son, until Egypt was proclaimed a republic in June 1953. 'Alī Māher, a former Prime Minister, was returned provisionally to that office until September 1952, when he resigned in protest against the agrarian reform introduced to curb the power of the large landowners. The conventional political parties were ordered to purge their membership of corrupt elements; thus enfeebled and disrupted, they were dissolved entirely. The army officer corps was purged of elements identified with the former ruling class or with the political right and far left. The regime's front man, General Muhammad Naguib, a genuinely popular figure with close ties with the old regime, became restive with his figurehead role and sought to escape RCC tutelage by cooperating with the Muslim Brotherhood, the last remaining mass organization beyond RCC control. Following an attempt to assassinate Nasser by a member of the Brotherhood, the organization was outlawed and its leadership executed or imprisoned; Naguib was finally ousted in November 1954. Nasser remained uncontested master of Egypt, with a solid base of popular support in the army, the trade unions, and a highly overstaffed bureaucracy.

The slogans by which Nasser managed to politicize and mobilize the Egyptian urban mass—the end of foreign control, recovery of Egyptian national dignity, the army as embodiment of the people's interests and aspirations—restricted him to certain lines of policy. He could not bind the country to any arrangement by which foreign soldiers would remain on Egyptian soil. National pride, moreover, could not be appropriately symbolized (or public obedience enforced) by a shabby army inadequately equipped with obsolescent weapons; it had to have modern, sophisticated arms. Finally, since Egypt could not achieve the economic expansion necessary even to keep pace with the rapidly expanding population with her own scant resources, substantial aid had to come from abroad. Astutely, Nasser realized that assistance from the great powers would be provided less liberally to a client state, whose policies could be taken for granted, than to an uncommitted country whose friendship had to be courted. To assert herself as a factor to be reckoned with in world affairs, Egypt could draw on her geographic situation including, notably, the Suez Canal; on the genuine, if partial and intermittent, leadership she could exert in the relations between the Arab states and the rest of the world; and on her actual or potential links with the Muslim world and Africa.

Reasonable calculation of United States interests and capabilities in the Middle East had, aside from an aberration on the Palestine issue, tended to be the norm of the Truman administration. The Eisenhower administration, which took office not long after the Egyptian revolution, tended to regard world issues in dichotomous terms of moral right and wrong. Military deterrence of Soviet expansion would not suffice of itself, in the view of the Secretary of State, John Foster Dulles. Believing that the principle source of war was to be found in "a confrontation of universalist faiths: Christianity versus communism, spirituality versus atheism," he felt that the United States must demonstrate itself a "spiritual highland," typifying "the spiritual, intellectual and economic conditions that all men want."[4] The assumption thus expressed—that all men, however morally upright, want the conditions most Americans find desirable for themselves—is rather widespread but demonstrably false. It misled Dulles into a tireless effort to mobilize the noncommunist world against a threat many failed to perceive, encouraged him to regard dissent from his convictions as ignorant, sinful or both, obscured realization that international pacts bind only to the extent that parties to them see their interests served thereby, and inhibited a clear distinction in his mind between nationalism and subservience to communism. As Secretary of State, Dulles combined lofty moral principle with a bewildering virtuosity of tactical maneuver that often left his interlocutors uncertain as to his true intentions and even his sincerity. President Eisenhower's more straightforward and homespun style at times inclined him toward an approach to problems differing from that of his Secretary, despite a general harmony of principle. Dulles tried, loyally if not always successfully, to ascertain and abide by his chief's wishes. It is perhaps unfortunate that the President, suffering from an ileitis attack in the summer of 1956, left his Secretary without specific guidance on the fateful issue of the Aswan High Dam.

---

[4]Townsend Hoopes, *The Devil and John Foster Dulles* (Boston: Little, Brown and Co., 1973), pp. 65–66.

Shortly after taking office Dulles undertook a tour of the Middle East, in a public aura of instituting a new, impartial, American posture between the Arab states and Israel. He returned in May 1953 with the realistic conclusion that there was no present prospect of enlisting the Arabs in the Western alliance system. "Many Arab League countries," he reported to the American public,[5] "are so engrossed with their quarrels with Israel or with Great Britain or France that they pay little heed to the menace of Soviet communism." He noted

. . . a vague desire to have a collective security system. But no such system can be imposed from without. It should be designed and grow from within out of a sense of common destiny and common danger.

While awaiting the formal creation of a security association, the United States can usefully help strengthen the interrelated defense of those countries which want strength, not as against each other or the West, but to resist the common threat to all free peoples.

Dulles did not lose all hope that the British might remain effectively responsible for the defense of the Suez Canal and for the management of the adjacent base. American diplomats discreetly encouraged both British and Egyptians to reach a satisfactory settlement. The negotiations, which took place in an atmosphere of rising Egyptian resentment of the British military presence, culminated in July 1954 in an agreement by which Britain undertook to withdraw all her troops, subject to the right of return only in case of attack on an Arab state or Turkey.

After signature of the Manila Pact of September 1954 establishing the Southeast Asia Treaty Organization, a gap remained in the *cordon sanitaire* around the communist world that the United States and Britain sought to fill with an elaborate series of regional agreements. With American encouragement a mutual defense pact was concluded between Turkey, already a member of NATO, and Pakistan, a signatory of the Manila Pact. Under British guidance, Iraq then entered into a bilateral defense agreement with Turkey. Britain adhered to the Iraq-Turkey agreement in April 1955, thus placing her military facilities in Iraq, of ambiguous status since the failure of the Portsmouth Treaty, on a regular footing. Finally, in

---

[5]Text in *Department of State Bulletin,* June 15, 1953, pp. 831–835.

October 1955 with the recruitment of Iran, now recovered from the Mossadeq convulsion and engaged in military cooperation with the United States, the "northern tier" was organized under the name of the Baghdad Pact. The United States had permitted the signatories to assume that it would join the Pact when it came into being. Coming to a full realization of the Pact's unpopularity elsewhere in the Arab world, however, the United States drew back from entering it as a full member and limited its participation to sharing the work of its military committee. America thus reaped maximum disadvantage from a somewhat ill-conceived structure. Without the American catalyst the heterogeneous organization grew few fangs for free world defense, while incurring the odium both of the Soviet Union and of large sectors of Arab opinion.

The Iraqi alignment exacerbated tensions already rapidly growing among the Arab states. Iraqi Prime Minister Nūrī al-Sa'īd, a close friend of Britain and one of the few Arabs to take the communist threat seriously, had failed in an attempt to persuade Nasser to cooperate in associating the Arab League defense system with NATO. By entering into the Baghdad Pact Iraq did, in fact, depart from the neutralist letter and spirit of the Arab League Pact. This breach of Arab solidarity ran counter to Nasser's ambition to use his leadership of a common Arab front as leverage against the great powers. The Egyptian leader, infuriated, embarked on a bitter and prolonged propaganda assault against Nūrī, the Iraqi government, and the principle of any pacts restricting Arab freedom of maneuver.

The Egyptian settlement with Britain left the United States free to resume discussion, already in an exploratory stage, of economic aid and arms sales to Egypt. The matter of military support became mired in restrictions imposed by American legislation; arms could be supplied on easy terms only in the context of a military advisory mission in the recipient country and under agreed stipulations concerning their use; the Egyptians could reconcile neither condition with their full sovereignty. Powerful American pressure groups moreover found the arming of a hostile neighbor of Israel distinctly distasteful. Although the amounts of arms Nasser sought at this time were modest (in the $20 million range), political reluctance and bureaucratic viscosity so delayed an American decision that Nasser despaired of equipping his army from the West and turned to the Soviet Union.

Soviet policy had now moved away from its exclusive preoccupation with military defense against NATO and related alliances. The "internal contradictions" of capitalism and its imperialist manifestation were henceforth to be encouraged to run their natural course; "improvement" of relations with the Western powers would go forward with efforts to divide them one from another, while countries linked with the West, such as Iran and Japan, were to be courted; states outside the military blocs were to be strengthened, supported, and encouraged to preserve their independence of the "colonial" powers, including the United States. The new Soviet line was proclaimed dogma at the Twentieth Congress of the Soviet Union's Communist Party. The transition was already well along, however, as reflected in the fact that, whereas Soviet propaganda had denounced Nasser as a Fascist lackey of the imperialists during his negotiations with the British, the Soviet Union was prepared two years later to enter into a barter arrangement by which large quantities of Russian arms were provided to Egypt in exchange for cotton.

Announced on September 27, 1955, the deal alarmed Washington officials. An agitated Dulles hastily despatched a special emissary, Assistant Secretary of State George Allen, to remonstrate with Nasser. The mission, which took place at the end of September, was misleadingly portrayed in the news media as the delivery of an ultimatum. Carried out with a farcical want of coordination, it resulted only in the enhancement of Nasser's prestige (for resisting the pressure of a superpower) and in confirming the efficacity of his "positive" neutralism.[6]

Following up its arms agreement, the Soviet Union offered to replace the West in financing the Aswan High Dam. This principal economic project of Nasser's regime was a glamorous conception by which the country's arable land would be substantially increased, more intensive use made of land already under cultivation by a shift from flood to perennial irrigation, and large quantities of hydroelectric power generated. Feasibility studies by the World

---

[6]Miles Copeland, *The Game of Nations* (New York: Simon and Schuster, 1969), pp. 156–159.

Bank begun in 1953 indicated that the project was technically sound and economically justified, given adequate foreign exchange help. In December 1955 a program was worked out in consultation with the Egyptian finance minister whereby the United States and Great Britain would provide respective grants of $56 million and $14 million for the project's first stages; the Bank offered to lend $200 million, while Egypt agreed to pay the local costs of some $900 million over a period of about eighteen years. The terms were formally proposed to Nasser's government which, unused to the procedures of international banking, took exception to some details of the offer as impinging on Egyptian sovereignty. It soon became clear that support of the project entailed domestic political risks for the Eisenhower Administration. Zionist opposition was predictable. Nasser's neutralism, dramatized by his procurement of Russian arms, generated the hostility of hard-core "cold warriors" in Congress and the public. Questions were raised (not, however, by the World Bank experts, who were in the best position to judge) about whether the cost of the arms would make it impossible for Egypt to meet her share of the dam's cost. Finally, a few southern-state legislators deemed it unwise to contribute to Egypt's ability to compete with the United States in the world cotton market. The President and Secretary Dulles endeavored to improve the climate by sending a secret emissary to work out a settlement of Israeli-Egyptian differences. The mission failed to produce results, and the High Dam project rested on dead center for six months.[7]

Close collaboration based on common hostility to Nasser's Egypt meanwhile developed between Israel and France. The former, feeling isolated by the Eisenhower Administration's effort to mend American relations with the Arab states, reacted with a progressively more bellicose posture along the truce lines, climaxed by a massive raid in February 1955 on the Egyptian-held Gaza Strip. She furthermore instituted military planning and collaboration with France. The latter, not yet recovered from her Indochina disaster, faced full-scale rebellion in Algeria from November 1954 onward, as well as turbulent independence movements in Morocco and Tunisia. The Nasser regime's uninhibited

---

[7]Hoopes, op. cit., pp. 331–332.

propaganda support of these movements and its modicum of practical aid to the Algerian insurgency instilled in the mind of Prime Minister Guy Mollet the conviction that the Egyptian President was the sole author of France's North African woes and that his destruction was essential to her position there. France began to ship arms in quantity to Israel, at times in contravention of inter-Allied agreements respecting the shipment of weapons to the Near East, and to explore with Israeli strategists the feasibility of common action against Egypt.

Anthony Eden, who succeeded the octogenarian Winston Churchill as British Prime Minister in April 1955, faced vociferous elements in Parliament and the press who were quick to condemn each new step in dissolving the empire that Britain had become too weak to hold. Her position in the Arab East, attributed by romantics to a mystical understanding of the Arab mind by Englishmen had, in practice, rested on close cooperation with a small traditional elite beholden to Britain in various ways, of a generation now giving way to younger leaders appealing to politicized masses and bitterly resentful both of British influence and of British responsibility for creation of the state of Israel. Successive reverses and merciless criticism dulled the already ailing Eden's judgment until he came to see in the Egyptian President Britain's sole and mortal enemy in the Near East. As Foreign Secretary, Eden had met with Nasser in February 1955 and reached with him a gentlemen's agreement whereby Egyptian propaganda attacks on the Baghdad Pact would cease, while Britain would abandon efforts to recruit other Arab states to its membership.[8] As Prime Minister, Eden, disregarding both this understanding and American misgivings, permitted his Foreign Secretary, Harold Macmillan, to try to bring Jordan into the Pact. When General Sir Gerald Templer, Chief of the Imperial Staff, arrived in Amman in December 1955 to conclude the relevant military agreements, popular demonstrations and divisions within the Jordanian government led King Hussein to abandon the project in order to save his throne. His close association with Great Britain nevertheless remained under violent attack from Egypt and Syria and, on March 1, 1956, he abruptly dismissed his Arab Legion's British commander of long

---

[8]Ibid., p. 322.

standing, Glubb Pasha. The act outraged Eden, who held Nasser responsible and concluded that "the world was not large enough to hold both him and Nasser."[9]

In February 1956 Eden and his new Foreign Secretary, Selwyn Lloyd, conferred in Washington with Eisenhower and Dulles. Differences in approach to Middle East problems were not fully resolved in the discussions. The British remained anxious to preserve the remnants of their imperial position by traditional methods, while the Americans saw more promise in allowing colonial structures to decay and seeking accommodation with the new nationalisms. The British saw in Nasser a danger to Western interests that must be removed at any cost, while the Americans accepted him as a figure of influence who must be kept from going over to the Russian camp. The differences were nevertheless papered over and, on the specific issue of the High Dam, it seems to have been understood that the Anglo-American offer would be allowed to lapse through inaction, but that no public announcement would be made to that effect.[10]

It is not clear exactly when Dulles decided that the United States would abandon the project. His subsequent explanations of his repudiation of the American offer were internally inconsistent and at variance with those of others, including Nasser. Certainly, the already dubious appeal of the undertaking in the United States was further impaired following Egypt's recognition of the Chinese People's Republic in April 1956. The China Lobby was thereupon added to the list of pressure groups opposed to American help for the High Dam. At any rate, Nasser chose to bring the matter to issue and instructed his ambassador in Washington, Ahmad Hussein, to inform the Secretary of State that Egypt accepted without further reservation the conditions of the pending offer. In a July 19 interview Dulles withdrew the offer, perhaps more brusquely than he had intended, after the Ambassador mentioned that the Soviets had offered to finance the Dam. The State Department released an announcement the same day, innocuous except for its

---

[9]Anthony Nutting, *No End of a Lesson: The Inside Story of the Suez Crisis* (New York: C. N. Potter, 1967), p. 18.
[10]Richard Goold-Adams, *John Foster Dulles—A Reappraisal* (New York: Appleton-Century-Crofts Inc., 1962), p. 202.

suggestion that the Egyptian economy had become too weak to support the project's local currency costs. Nasser interpreted the American action, as reported by his Ambassador, as "an attack on the regime and an invitation to the people of Egypt to bring it down."[11] On July 24 he attacked the United States in immoderate terms in a public speech. Two days later, in another intemperate address, he announced the nationalization of the Universal Suez Maritime Canal Company and his government's determination to use the Canal's revenues to construct the High Dam. Simultaneously, Egyptian technicians occupied the Canal's facilities and assumed control of its operations.

Although Egyptian-registered, the Company was a major symbol of both British and French empire; its shareholders included the British government and many French nationals. Nasser's bold move was intolerably provocative to Eden and Mollet, who both called for the prompt use of armed force to restore international control of the Canal and to humiliate, if not to destroy, Egypt's President. President Eisenhower objected strongly to military action and took urgent steps to dissuade his allies from impulsive acts. Dulles, determined from the outset to assert United States control over events, found Nasser's act morally repulsive, if perhaps debatable in law, and shared the Anglo-French attitude that the Canal should not fall under exclusive Egyptian control. Acting within the President's injunction against the use of force, in exchanges with the French and British he nevertheless so hedged the American position that Eden and Mollet realized only too late that the United States would not condone a last-ditch resort to arms.

Urgent consultation between the Secretary of State and the two allied premiers resulted in invitations to the principal maritime nations to a conference in London on August 16. Under Dulles' guidance the meeting formulated a proposal by which the operation of the Canal would become the responsibility of an international board established by treaty and associated with the United Nations. That agreement to such a proposal, which would nullify nationalization of the Company, would be suicidal for Nasser was sensed by Eisenhower, as well as by the Indian representative at the conference, both of whom suggested simply an advisory role

---

[11]Hoopes, op. cit., p. 341.

for the contemplated board. Although strongly pressed by Eden to take the proposal to Nasser in person, Dulles declined. The dubious mission was entrusted to Australian Prime Minister Menzies, whose uncompromising and threatening attitude in his meetings with Nasser merely convinced Nasser that Britain and France were determined to go to war.

This was true. Britain and France were already proceeding with plans whereby European pilots would be ordered off the Canal at a chosen date; the resulting disruption of maritime traffic would provide occasion for recourse to the United Nations to restore international control of the Canal; a Soviet veto, it was assumed, would prevent positive United Nations action; the two allies would then be justified before world opinion in sending troops into Egypt in defense of their vital national interests and the security of international navigation.

Dulles was sufficiently aware of these intentions to realize their final objective, an exceedingly awkward one for the Republican administration. President Eisenhower would shortly embark on his campaign for reelection in November. His foreign policy was under attack from influential quarters as dangerously adventurous, as lacking the flexibility needed to deal effectively with changing world circumstances, or as so badly coordinated as to be disruptive of the Western alliance. The prospect of a United Nations debate of the Suez Canal issue was a forbidding one. No result could conceivably be reached that would be acceptable to Britain and France and also to Egypt. When the inevitable impasse was reached, the United States would be obliged to choose between acquiescence in the use of armed force by its allies or to uphold the principle of peaceful settlement of disputes at the cost of grave strain on the solidarity of NATO. Either position would alienate an important segment of the American electorate. It was desperately urgent for Dulles to find a way of delaying a showdown on Suez until the President was safely reelected. He hastily devised a new proposal, calling for an association among the maritime powers (soon termed the Suez Canal Users Association— SCUA). Members' ships would provide their own pilots for passage of the waterway, and tolls would be deposited in a common fund of which a portion would be paid to Egypt, or withheld if Egypt sought to hinder traffic in any way. Despite the bizarre character of the scheme, Dulles persuaded Eden to sponsor it at a new conference of maritime powers at London that began on September 19. The shaky legal and practical aspects of the SCUA plan were quickly exposed by several delegations (Italy, the Netherlands, Denmark, Norway, and Pakistan), and many participants favored recourse to the United Nations Security Council. Dulles, of course, argued fervently against such action. In a lame compromise the Conference decided to proceed with the organization of SCUA. No sooner, however, had the Secretary left London than Eden and Mollet cut the ground from under his feet by appealing at once to the Security Council.

Franco-Israeli plans for attacking Egypt had meanwhile matured. They included a preliminary Israeli diversion against Jordan, which actually began early in October. King Hussein appealed for help to Britain and Iraq. The latter sent troops into Jordan, and use of the RAF against Israel was imminent. It thus became necessary to bring Britain into the plan; this was accomplished between October 13 and 22, and the British cabinet approved the joint operation on October 25.

In the United Nations discussion, Egypt adopted a posture so reasonable and forthcoming as to jeopardize the tripartite program. Selwyn Lloyd proposed a set of six principles according to which the Canal issue should be settled. Egypt accepted these, in addition to the principle of an international advisory board, such as SCUA. Eden and Mollet, seeing that "the situation had drifted uncomfortably close to a settlement, and one, moreover, that Nasser would survive,"[12] instructed their delegates in New York to introduce further, more onerous conditions, which were promptly vetoed by the Soviet Union. Late in the afternoon of October 29, while United Nations Secretary-General Hammarskjöld was endeavoring to get private negotiations started on the Six Principles, Israel dropped a battalion of paratroops near Mitla Pass, forty miles east of the Suez Canal. Israeli columns advanced along both major roads across the Sinai Peninsula and south toward Sharm al-Shaikh on the Tiran Straits.

The unfolding of the Suez crisis would have to be dismissed as surrealist fantasy were it not fact. Notwithstanding an immediate

---

[12]Ibid., p. 368.

call by the United States for urgent action by the United Nations Security Council, the British and French published a twelve-hour ultimatum to Israel and Egypt demanding that they cease hostilities and withdraw to positions ten miles from the Canal in order to permit Anglo-French occupation of key points along the waterway. Egypt, that is, was required to evacuate about 25,000 square miles of unquestionably Egyptian territory, while her attacker was invited to advance another thirty miles beyond her extreme forward positions. The announced motive of the Anglo-French action being uninterrupted navigation of the Canal, British planes based on Cyprus bombed its terminal at Port Said, its headquarters at Ismailia, and the cities of Cairo and Alexandria on the evening of October 31, depriving Egypt of its air force as well as of its ability to protect the Canal, through which shipping had, in any case, been passing normally. In reaction to the British attack Egypt sank numerous block-ships in the Canal, effectively obstructing navigation. In solidarity with Egypt, Syria thoroughly sabotaged the IPC pipelines on November 3, interrupting the flow of Middle East oil to all of Western Europe and throwing the pound sterling into crisis. Britain and France vetoed a Security Council resolution calling for a ceasefire. The issue consequently went before the General Assembly, which overwhelmingly adopted an American resolution on November 2 calling for an end to hostilities and the despatch of a United Nations force to keep the peace. Britain and France voted against the measure, which both Egypt and Israel accepted the following day. The British invasion force, now logically redundant, was approaching by sea from Malta. The British and French announced that their troops would act in behalf of the United Nations police force until it could arrive. In the face of Soviet saber-rattling and refusal of American support, Eden telephoned Mollet shortly after midnight to say Britain was withdrawing from the operation. He omitted to inform his military commanders, however; British and French forces landed twenty hours later in the Canal zone, made short work of the opposing Egyptian forces, and occupied about twenty miles of the now useless waterway. Israel, meanwhile, having shocked her coconspirators by accepting the United Nations ceasefire, reversed field, resumed operations until Sharm al-Shaikh was captured, then submitted once more to the ceasefire appeal, all within two hours of the landings at Suez. After two weeks of stubborn defiance of the United Nations and the United States, Britain and France announced an unconditional, phased withdrawal from Egyptian territory, which was completed December 22. Israel sought to remain in occupation of the Sinai Peninsula but, under stern American pressure, eventually withdrew in March 1957. Egypt, whose armed forces earned no laurels from the war, gained immeasurably in the esteem of much of the world as the steadfast victim of unprovoked aggression by a powerful coalition; Nasser's prestige and influence with the Arab masses, whatever the unspoken reservations of other Arab leaders, was henceforth unassailable.

Britain and France failed in their objectives, both ostensible and covert, in the Suez affair. They sought to reassert a position of imperial strength; the remnants of their Middle East influence were virtually destroyed. Vital communications and petroleum supplies were cut off, not protected. Nasser, far from being overthrown or humiliated, emerged stronger and more hostile than before. The blunders can be attributed partly to the fact that Eden and Mollet looked at Nasser through distorting lenses and saw Mussolini and Hitler. Theirs were not, however, the only distorting lenses; Dulles, through his own, looked at Nasser and saw Marx and Lenin. He had learned and acknowledged that the defense preoccupations of Egypt and most Arab states were regional, not global. He was genuinely committed to the traditional American support for the freedom and self-determination of peoples and had little sympathy for the pursuit of purely colonialist objectives by America's allies. He did not, however, act forthrightly on these bases, but on abstractions applied, with an able lawyer's virtuosity, to short-term tactical ends. American policy under his guidance left Nasser no choice other than resort to the Soviet Union for both arms and economic aid. The ambiguity of his exchanges with Eden and Mollet, clouded further by his public utterances, permitted them a residue of hope that the United States, through fear of the spread of communism in the Middle East, would not interfere with their Suez adventure. The disaster opened a breach in the Atlantic alliance that required patient effort to rebuild. In the Arab world, any subsequent effort in behalf of Western defense would be strictly up to the United States.

THE EISENHOWER DOCTRINE

As the Suez crisis eased, President Eisenhower set down his thoughts regarding future American action in the Near East in pursuit of the fixed objective of excluding Soviet influence.[13] His understanding of the well-springs of Arab politics does not appear to have been greatly enlightened by the recent events. Every weak country of the region, he posited, must be given clearly to understand the implications of Soviet domination. Egypt might be furnished arms sufficient for its defense and internal security, training missions, and economic aid in return for an agreement that it would never accept any Soviet offer. The Tripartite Declaration might be translated into bilateral treaties with each country in the area. Economic and friendly ties might be cultivated with Iraq, Jordan, Saudi Arabia, and Lebanon (i.e., the Arab states already under conservative, Westward-leaning governments). By implication the United States, acting on its own, would attempt to fill the power "vacuum" left by the eclipse of British and French influence, using some of the methods that had helped to weaken that influence: the creation of formal restrictions on the Arab states' freedom of action. The Eisenhower Administration thus never arrived at a clear distinction in practice between communism and revolutionary Arab nationalism. Its inability to come to terms with the latter quickly erased the momentarily favorable effect of its opposition to the tripartite attack on Egypt. The United States soon permitted itself to be drawn into a series of interventions in largely domestic crises in eastern Arab countries reinforcing its own neocolonialist image and facilitating the infiltration of Soviet influence. The rigid American posture was manifested immediately after the Suez war, when the United States refused either to provide Egypt emergency food and medical supplies or to permit their purchase with Egyptian funds blocked on nationalization of the Canal Company; the Soviet Union furnished the required supplies without hesitation. American policy began to act on the assumption that Nasser's Egypt was "controlled by international

---

[13]Dwight D. Eisenhower, *Waging Peace 1956–1961* (Garden City, N.Y.: Doubleday & Co., 1965), pp. 96–97.

communism," and embarked on a sterile attempt to isolate her from her sister Arab states.

The President and his advisors wove his thoughts into a declaration of policy toward the Middle East and emphasized the significance they attached to it by seeking the concurrence of both houses of Congress. The proposed policy, which as a joint resolution would have the force of law, declared that the independence and integrity of the Middle Eastern countries was vital to the American national interest and world peace. It authorized the President to use United States armed forces, if requested by a state in the region, against armed aggression from any country controlled by international communism. Substantial funds ($200 million in fiscal year 1957) were to be made available to the President to undertake military and economic aid programs in countries that requested such assistance to enhance their self-defense capability.[14]

While no member of Congress questioned the propriety and necessity of American action to resist communist aggression, the proposal appeared to some senators as abdication of the Senate's advisory duties under the Constitution. Senator William Fulbright, already well advanced on his career as gadfly of American foreign policy, questioned the wisdom of giving a "blank check" of such sweeping nature to an executive branch including

a current Secretary of State who greets the dawn with a boast about his triumphs, and meets the dusk with scare words of panic, saying that the Nation will be ruined unless it unites to ratify the mistakes he made during the day.

On more substantive grounds the Senator questioned the resolution's proviso that United States action would depend on a request by the threatened state. "This is a dubious kind of limitation," he suggested,

because our own security may well depend on the use of American Armed Forces against overt armed aggression from international communism—regardless of whether the nation under attack asks for our help or not.

[14]Text in Senate Foreign Relations Committee, *Select Chronology and Background Documents Relating to the Middle East* (Washington: USGPO, 1969), pp. 151–152.

Does it make sense, then, to serve advance notice that America's freedom of action in fighting for its own interest will be at the mercy of how some of the quite unstable Middle Eastern governments react to communist aggression?[15]

It speaks eloquently of Congress' chilly reaction that, while the President set forth his proposal in a special message on January 6, 1957 (giving it precedence over the State of the Union message), the Middle East Resolution was adopted only on March 9 after lively debate and querulous cross-examination of Secretary Dulles.

The Eisenhower Doctrine purported to be a unilateral statement of American policy and intentions in support of Arab independence. To Arab neutralists, it appeared suspiciously like a renewed effort by Western imperialism to restore and maintain its tutelage of the Middle East. Under Nasser's leadership, they attacked it bitterly by publicity, diplomacy, and attempted subversion of Arab regimes closely associated with the United States. Among the Arab states only Lebanon, Iraq, and Libya welcomed it openly. Jordan, Saudi Arabia, and the Sudan, each for its own local reasons, were only cautiously receptive.

The attitude defined by the Doctrine received its first test in Jordan. King Hussein's situation early in 1957 was precarious. Jordan's treaty arrangements with Britain remained in effect, providing for the presence of British troops and a subsidy on which the country's fiscal solvency utterly depended. During 1956 the escalation of incidents on the Jordan-Israel border prompted an offer of Syrian troops, which Hussein accepted on condition that a similar contingent be furnished by Saudi Arabia. In October, under pressure of public opinion, the King embarked on an experiment in representative institutions and permitted parliamentary elections. The resulting assembly had a left-wing majority, mainly from among West Bank Palestinians; a cabinet was installed under the premiership of a fervent Arab nationalist, Suleimān Nābulsī. With the support of the young, Nasserist Chief of Staff, 'Alī Abū

---

[15]Senate speech by J. William Fulbright, January 24, 1957. Text in Robert L. Branyan and Lawrence H. Larsen, eds., *The Eisenhower Administration: A Documentary History* (New York: Random House, 1971), Vol. ii, pp. 713–719.

Nuwār, the new government urged the King to break Jordan's ties with Britain; in the post-Suez state of popular sentiment he was unable to refuse. In mid-January Jordan associated itself with the Arab Solidarity Pact, by which Egypt, Syria, and Saudi Arabia agreed to give Jordan financial support following severance of her links with Britain.[16] The Anglo-Jordanian treaty ceased to exist, and British troops withdrew from the country by mid-March. Meanwhile, the Prime Minister and Chief of Staff purged the government and army of persons loyal to the King, preparatory to deposing him and establishing a republic. In April General Abū Nuwār mounted a revolt, which was opposed by troops, largely East Bank bedouins, who remained loyal to Hussein. Taking note of the deteriorating situation, Eisenhower and Dulles announced that the integrity of Jordan was "vital" to the United States. The Sixth Fleet was ordered to the eastern Mediterranean, and emergency aid of $10 million was extended to Jordan. With this support and his own courage and luck, Hussein managed to weather the crisis. He dissolved parliament and all political parties, dismissed Nābulsī, Abū Nuwār, and other disloyal officers (who took refuge first in Syria, then in Egypt), and reinstated authoritarian rule. The Eisenhower Doctrine thus appeared to be working effectively as a prop for an Arab regime that sought American help for its survival, although involvement of "international communism" in the situation was remote or nonexistent, aside from Hussein's public stand against it.

One result of this outcome of the Jordan crisis was the psychological and political isolation of Syria from her immediate neighbors. Having returned to parliamentary processes in 1954 after a succession of military dictatorships, the country's politics were in remarkable disarray. The old-line Populist and Nationalist parties, although together commanding a parliamentary majority, were paralyzed by mutual hostility and opportunism. The vacuum was filled in part by the left-wing Ba'th Party, whose militantly nationalist, anti-West ideology was abetted by army elements and by an active, ably led, but small communist party. Appealing to the entire Arab nation across state boundaries, the Ba'th made

---

[16]Only Saudi Arabia fulfilled any part of its financial obligation under the Pact.

particular efforts in Lebanon, Iraq, and Jordan to discredit Turkey and her NATO ties and to encourage cooperation with the Soviet Union.

In August 1957 the Syrian government arranged for a sharp increase in the volume of Russian economic and military aid already arriving in substantial amounts; three American diplomats were expelled from Damascus on the charge of conspiring against the regime and General 'Afīf al-Bizrī, widely believed to be a communist, became Chief of Staff of the armed forces. Syria's neighbors suspected, and went far toward convincing the United States, that Syria was on the verge of becoming a Soviet satellite if, indeed, she had not already become one, and that action must be taken to change her government. The United States took some precautionary measures. Arms deliveries to Iraq, Lebanon, and Jordan were accelerated, fighter aircraft were moved to Turkey, and the Sixth Fleet sailed eastward. During consultations in Turkey with a special United States emissary, however, the Arab states mentioned backed off from their charges of communist penetration in Syria, and none had the slightest inclination to institute armed action against her. For several weeks the situation remained tensely static, with Turkish troops massed near the Syrian border. The crisis simmered down by the end of October, when Syria withdrew a complaint lodged at the United Nations against Turkey. Although the United States did not specifically invoke the Eisenhower Doctrine during the incident (there was never a serious possibility of Syrian attack against any of her neighbors), its actions were well within the context of the intent to deny the Middle East to Soviet influence.

The inconclusive crisis served to emphasize Syria's isolation from her Arab neighbors and the fragmented, feeble character of her government. Such effective authority as existed was slipping into the hands of the minority Ba'th, the communists, and competing cliques of army officers. Despairing of gaining effective control of the country and fearing consolidation of communist influence, the Ba'th leaders and their sympathizers in the military turned to Egypt, proposing political unification of the two countries. The move was supported by many leaders of the conventional political parties in the name of Arab unity. President Nasser agreed to the proposal only reluctantly; he had sought a controlling voice in the foreign policy of Syria (and of the other Arab states) but not the burden of responsibility for her internal affairs. He insisted that the union take the form of a centralized, unitary state instead of the looser federation the Syrians had had in mind. He demanded further that the Syrian army renounce its role in politics and that all political parties, including the Ba'th, be dissolved. After plebiscites in the two countries, the United Arab Republic (UAR) was proclaimed on February 22, 1958. The union was to endure less than four years. At the moment of its creation, however, it appeared to the Arab masses a first, momentous step toward realization of the dream of Arab unity. It sparked the formation of a short-lived rival union between the Hashemite regimes in Jordan and Iraq. Even the archaic monarchy in Yemen entered into tenuous association with the UAR: more, however, as insurance against the Cairo propanganda machine than as a step toward genuine union. Creation of the UAR resulted immediately in sharply increased pressure on the frankly pro-West regime in Lebanon, where the Eisenhower Doctrine was to receive its most spectacular test.

The political stability of Lebanon, even its national independence, depends on observance of the National Pact, formulated during World War II by the founders of the Republic, Beshāra al-Khourī and Riyāḍ al-Ṣulḥ. It specifies the broad lines of the country's political orientation and provides a detailed scheme for the allocation of public offices among the various components of this multiconfessional society. Recognizing that the historic outside links of the Maronite Christians with the West, on one hand, and Sunni Muslims with the surrounding Arab world, on the other, constitute an ever-present danger of foreign intervention, the Pact stipulates that Lebanon, while preserving its Arab identity and coordinating its policies with those of other Arab states, should remain independent, neutral, and sovereign. Lebanon's postwar experience indicated that the arrangement was effective in preserving a reasonable balance among the foreign influences seeking to direct the affairs of this extraordinarily heterogeneous polity. Camille Chamoun, who became President in September 1952 for a six-year term and who was ineligible for reelection under Lebanon's constitution, worked constructively to develop the country's economy. He worked imprudently, at the same time, to enhance the powers of the presidency at the expense of the Sunni prime minister and of the recognized leaders of major sectors of the population, including the Druze and his own Maronites. He developed, as dynamic and successful politicians often do, a notion that Lebanon could ill dispense with his leadership, and it seemed plausible that the parliament elected in 1957 under his clever stage management might be persuaded to amend the constitution to allow him to succeed himself. Both Chamoun and his Foreign Minister, Charles Malik, were outspokenly pro-West, and they further upset Lebanon's delicate political balance by enthusiastically endorsing the Eisenhower Doctrine. During the Suez crisis, furthermore, they lost step with the other Arab states by refusing to sever diplomatic relations with Britain and France. The disaffection generated by these policies was encouraged by Syria and Egypt with arms, money, personnel, and propaganda, which increased in scale upon the founding of the UAR. Isolated violence escalated into civil war in May 1958. Chamoun was unable to induce General Fuad Chehab, Commander in Chief of the Lebanese army, small and of questionable cohesiveness, to move vigorously against the rebellion. Entire quarters of Beirut, large Sunni areas in the Biqā^c and the North, as well as the Druze territory of Shouf passed beyond the government's effective control.

On May 13 President Chamoun enquired of President Eisenhower what the United States attitude would be if Lebanon requested aid under the Middle East Declaration. Eisenhower replied that the United States would send troops to assist the legal government of Lebanon and to protect American lives and property, but only if another Arab state concurred, and not for the purpose of achieving an additional term for Chamoun. On May 22 Lebanon complained before the United Nations Security Council that the UAR was arming and instigating the revolt. The United Nations sent military observers to verify the alleged infiltration across Lebanon's borders. Whether the observers had, on arrival, already been prejudiced against the Lebanese case by the United States, the UAR, or by United Nations Secretary-General Hammarskjöld and therefore spent their time on the beaches and at cocktail parties as Chamoun later alleged,[17] or whether because

---

[17] Camille Chamoun, *Crise au Moyen-Orient* (Paris: Gallimard, 1963), pp. 416–417.

they had access to only the border areas that were under government control and limited their observation to daylight hours, their reports were quite inconclusive. The crisis appeared to abate somewhat in June, after Prime Minister Sāmī al-Ṣulḥ stated he would not support a new term of office for the President. On July 14, however, the Iraqi army overthrew the Hashemite monarchy; the royal family, Nūrī al-Saʿīd, and other prominent figures were murdered amid scenes of mob violence. Assuming, as did many observers at the time, that the coup was the work of Nasser's UAR, the alarmed Chamoun requested urgent American assistance. Eisenhower and his advisors, equally disturbed by the destruction of a supposed pillar of American global defense, acted promptly. Marines from the Sixth Fleet landed unopposed the following day at Beirut airport and were reinforced during the next ten days to a total of about 11,000 men—more than the entire Lebanese army. Great Britain, responding to a parallel appeal from King Hussein, airlifted troops to Jordan. American troops remained in Lebanon, without engaging the rebels or, indeed, anyone else, until October 25, by which time the domestic political crisis had been resolved in harmony with the National Pact. The issue before the United Nations was presently resolved by the adoption of a resolution agreed to by all of the Arab states, including the parties to the dispute, and Arab world preoccupation shifted to other concerns.

The form the domestic Lebanese solution took is worth noting. In June President Nasser had expressed to the American Ambassador in Cairo the opinion that a suitable arrangement would be the succession of General Chehab to the Lebanese presidency, with Rashīd Karāmī, Sunni leader of the rebellion in northern Lebanon, as prime minister; he suggested, somewhat outrageously, that the United States and the UAR jointly impose this combination on the Lebanese. Chamoun, rather innocently, assumed that the role of the American forces would be to advance to Lebanon's borders with the Syrian Region of the UAR, evict the foreign "volunteers," force the indigenous rebels into obedience to the government, and perhaps even prolong his tenure as president. This general approach had the support of the large American business community in Beirut, highly influential in Congress and at the top levels of the United States government. On the heels of the marines, however, President Eisenhower had sent a personal envoy, Robert Murphy, with broad authority to "act in the best interest of the United

States." Murphy, with little prior knowledge of the current Lebanese situation, set about conferring with the leaders of major segments of the community including, to Chamoun's disgust, leading figures of the rebellion. He eventually concluded that General Chehab alone was capable of reuniting the country and should become the next president of Lebanon.[18] The rebel leaders, who had insisted that presidential elections could not take place while American troops were in Lebanon, were informed that they would remain *until* a new president was chosen; Chamoun was put on notice that the forces would be withdrawn at once *unless* the election took place on schedule. The parliament convened July 31 and, on the second ballot, elected General Chehab who, upon his inauguration, appointed Rashīd Karāmī prime minister. The suitability of this outcome in the Lebanese situation was vindicated by the progressive return of the country to internal tranquillity, increasing prosperity and the neutrality that is a condition for Lebanese stability. Chamoun and some American businessmen, shocked to see armed insurrection thus triumphant, interpreted the result as a victory for Nasser and an abysmal failure of the Eisenhower Doctrine.[19] Such a simplistic view obscures the fact that the Doctrine was applied flexibly, with concern for political realities, and promoted a workable solution of an essentially local problem. Had the President and his representatives attempted to impose on Lebanon a regime committed to "doctrinaire" principles of anticommunism and Western defense, the problem would undoubtedly have been compounded instead of eased.

The first efforts by the United States to direct single-handedly the course of political events in the Arab world were thus exerted against the background of the Eisenhower Doctrine, if not always specifically in its name, and produced results other than those intended. It was based on rather vulnerable assumptions inherent in the cold war, beginning with the principle that the Soviet Union had no legitimate interest in the Middle East or any right to presence or influence there, and that the United States had both the moral obligation and the capability to exclude it from the region.

---

[18]Robert Murphy, *Diplomat among Warriors* (Garden City, N.Y.: Doubleday & Co., 1964), p. 398.
[19]Chamoun, op. cit., p. 429.

The Administration's world outlook led it to seek military solutions to essentially political problems. Both Eisenhower and Dulles subscribed in principle to the general desirability of social and political change and economic progress in these countries. The changes in train in the Near East, however, were occurring by disorderly means and threatened the position of the Arab leaders who appeared to be the necessary bulwark against communist infiltration. Lacking a sufficient appreciation of the difference (in fact, the incompatibility) of communism with Arab nationalism and neutralism, the United States was led into unilateral actions that, far from shielding the Near East from the cold war, actually tended to draw it into the confrontation and lent substance to communist assertions, eagerly adopted by Arab nationalists, that the United States had become the leader of a Western imperialism opposed to Arab freedom and progress. With the benefit of expanding American experience with emerging peoples, succeeding administrations made somewhat finer distinctions.

SHIFTING COLD WAR PATTERNS

The American and Western European thesis that the Middle East was a preserve of their interests in which the Soviet Union had no rightful concern was, of course, hotly contested from the first by the Soviets, who insisted with some point that, since the region was on their doorstep, they had vital interests in the area. In 1956 and 1958 the Russians had limited means, beyond propaganda and intergovernment transactions, by which to challenge the Western position in the Arab states. The Soviet nuclear arsenal was growing, but the United States still held a clear preponderance. The Lebanese landings gave proof that the United States had a mobile, strategic, conventional military capability of a sort that the Russians could not match. Intervening between Soviet territory and the Arab states, moreover, were Turkey and Iran, both linked with the Western alliance system. Soviet defense doctrine accepted the concept of effort to ensure that the immediate neighbors of the Soviet Union should be satellites if possible, benevolent neutrals at a minimum, and that this protective zone should be progressively deepened. The Arab East thus had a potential defense significance for the Soviet Union, in addition to its economic and political concern. Political changes and the evolution of military technology during the decade of the 1960s rendered the potential an actuality.

Although the Soviet Union made clear its regret at the fall of Mossadeq and the dissolution of the Tudeh Party between 1953 and 1954 and condemned Iran's defense pacts with Turkey and Pakistan, the Soviet effort to establish reliable relations with Iran was not abandoned. An agreement of 1956 intensified commercial exchanges between the two countries. The Soviets proposed a treaty of friendship and nonaggression in 1959 and reacted with violent propaganda attacks when, instead, Iran entered into bilateral defense arrangements with the United States. Within a year, nevertheless, the Shah promised not to permit the installation of nuclear missiles on Iranian soil and, in 1963, the Soviet Union assisted with substantial credits in alleviating the economic crisis accompanying the first phases of Iran's "White Revolution." Irano-Soviet official and state visits multiplied. Iranian dissatisfaction with the Western oil consortium's slow expansion of petroleum exports and the termination of American economic assistance at the end of 1967 were accompanied by further economic links between Iran and the Soviet Union, including a major long-term project for the supply of Iranian natural gas to her northern neighbor.

Following the Cuban missile crisis in the fall of 1962, American missiles were removed from launching sites in Turkey. This raised questions in Turkish minds as to the extent of the American commitment to Turkey's defense and encouraged already existing tendencies to seek independent pursuit of Turkish interests, including the establishment of a *modus vivendi* with the Soviet Union. This became settled policy after 1964, when President Johnson formally notified Prime Minister İnönü that Turkey could not expect the United States to intervene against Soviet retaliation in case of armed action by Turkey in behalf of the Turkish minority on Cyprus. Soviet policy shifted in the following years from unqualified support of the Greek Cypriots to a position palatable to Turkey and, as in the Iranian case, expansion of Turco-Soviet economic exchanges accompanied a decline in American aid.

This easing and strengthening of Soviet relations with the northern tier states went forward with a long series of modifications in the cold war "givens." Fissures in the Atlantic alliance developed and seemed the less worrisome after the Moscow Nuclear Test Ban Treaty of 1963, the prospect of further Soviet-American detente, the relative loosening of Russian discipline over the East European satellites, the Moscow-Peking ideological cleavage, and the resulting confrontation on the border between the Soviet Union and China. Meanwhile, United States reliance on manned bombers as its principal nuclear delivery system gave way to "hardened" missile-launching sites, Polaris submarines, and other devices. The necessity for a worldwide network of American air bases receded. The Nouasseur Base in Morocco, the use of Dhahran Airfield in Saudi Arabia, and Wheelus Field in Libya were successively relinquished with little sentiment that American safety was thereby imperiled. With the appearance of supertankers even the Suez Canal declined in importance as the jugular vein of Western Europe's industry and military capability. In defense terms, the odds changed significantly. The strategic mobility that the Soviet Union lacked in 1958 was by 1967 in being, both in the form of a long-range air transport fleet and of a permanent, sizeable Soviet naval squadron in a Mediterranean Sea where the American Sixth Fleet had formerly had uncontested freedom of action.

CHAPTER VI

America and the Polarized Arab World

T HE UNITED STATES FACED PERPLEXING PROBLEMS in the search for coherent and effective policies toward the Arab states during the years between the Suez War and the renewed conflict of June 1967. The first Palestine war, as war often does, served as a seed-bed for revolution. During the ensuing decade, traditional leaderships in Egypt, Syria, and Iraq gave way to new regimes that, in time, carried out substantial social and economic restructuring. Although the impulse for change pervaded the Arab world, it raised no irresistible challenge in most of the Arabian Peninsula. In Jordan, and to a lesser degree in Morocco and Libya, it was contained by increased authoritarianism. The Arab revolutionary movement was a proselytizing one and rapidly developed an adversary relationship with the traditional regimes; it was not monolithic, however, and competing ideologies disturbed relations even among the revolutionary states themselves.

Arab disunity created pitfalls for United States policy. Close and cooperative relations with one Arab state tended to impair normal intercourse with those of differing orientation, while increasingly intimate American relations with Israel compromised the United States position throughout the Arab world. In 1957 President Eisenhower, in an effort to stem the tide of revolution, briefly tried the tactic of sponsoring King Saud of Saudi Arabia as a sort of American chosen instrument among the Arabs; the King lacked the wisdom and regional stature for such a role, however, and the idea was quickly abandoned. The succeeding administrations made a serious effort to accommodate to the currents of political and social change in the Arab states. It gradually became apparent that Arab progressivism, coincident at some important points with

161

the lines pursued by the Soviet Union, was ultimately incompatible with the objectives the United States set for itself as leader of the "free" world in this era of rapid decolonization in Asia and Africa. By the end of the 1960s, America was maneuvered into a posture of general opposition to the Arab regimes that symbolized progress, and of support for traditional forces apparently seeking to repress mass aspirations toward constructive change.

THE NEW AMERICAN APPROACH

While abandoning the futile objective of forming military alliances among the Arab states, the Kennedy Administration pursued much the same aims in the area as its predecessor. The United States sought to prevent the establishment by a hostile foreign power of a position in the Middle East that would permit it to interfere with the East-West communications of the United States and its allies through the region or with continued Western access to its oil resources, thus seriously upsetting the world balance of power. The United States was considered to be concerned with access to the region's markets, free and safe entry thereto for its citizens, in progress toward a solution of the Palestine problem, in restraining the regional arms race, in the growth of democratic institutions, and in promoting sympathy for America and its way of life.[1]

Although the conception of American interests in the Arab countries remained stable, the mechanism for decision making on major foreign policy issues was significantly altered, in a manner intended to render the bureaucracy more responsive to the President's attitudes. The White House staff concerned with external affairs was greatly increased. Enhanced authority became centered in the post of national security affairs advisor, to which McGeorge Bundy was appointed. The direct role the President intended to play in foreign relations was reflected in his choice of Dean Rusk as Secretary of State: able and experienced, but content with the technician's role of executing instead of initiating policy.

---

[1]John S. Badeau, *The American Approach to the Arab World* (New York: Harper & Row, 1968), pp. 15–33; William R. Polk, *The United States and the Arab World* (Cambridge: Harvard University Press, rev. ed., 1969), pp. 315–316.

Agencies, both civil and military, for the gathering of intelligence and for the conduct of unorthodox political action, were substantially expanded. The humanitarian, idealistic image projected by the young President has somewhat obscured the preoccupation of his tragically curtailed administration with American armed might, both conventional and unconventional; whereas the previous administration's brinkmanship fell short of the commitment of American forces in hostilities abroad, the use of military power under Kennedy and his successor in the pursuit of American cold war objectives became an alternative to be deliberately weighed on grounds less of scruple than of estimated effectiveness. The institutional changes had definite impact on United States relations with the Arab states. The use of coercion by a great power in Africa and Asia was resented by broad sectors of Arab opinion. The middle levels of the State Department's bureaus of Near Eastern and South Asian Affairs, and of Intelligence and Research, the locus of the government's expertise on Arab affairs, were little consulted in the formulation of policy. Decisions tended to be swayed by the advice of those—the White House staff and the Congress—most sensitive to the pressure of the efficient Zionist lobby, and thus to minimize factors affecting American relations with the individual Arab countries.

With its generally liberal outlook the new administration had some sympathy for the social and political changes in train in some Arab states and adopted the principle that the provision of American economic assistance should not be governed by the recipient's form of government or political orientation, nor simply for the purpose of inducing a pro-West attitude. Aid, it was assumed, would promote stability, even in revolutionary countries, by alleviating the economic distress that breeds popular dissatisfaction and violence, by focusing government attention on development and away from disruptive external action, and by bringing people into the political process in sufficient numbers to inhibit irresponsible government policies. Conversely, American influence would be exerted toward persuading the Arab states and Israel to reduce to a minimum their military expenditures so that the greatest possible proportion of their assets might be devoted to constructive purposes. The United States would, as a matter of principle, avoid taking sides in local disputes where its vital interests were not at stake in view of the possibility that its involvement would encourage others to intervene, at the risk of grave international escalation of conflict. Realistically assessing as quite limited its means of influencing Arab policies, the United States would intervene by force only to protect its few vital interests and, to avoid miscalculation, these would be made unmistakably clear.[2]

The assumptions underlying American aid programs in the Arab countries and elsewhere in the third world were drawn from the successes of the Marshall Plan of economic rehabilitation in postwar Europe, where the restoration of prosperity appeared to have stopped the spread of communism, promoted stability, and strengthened democratic institutions. It was therefore deeply disappointing to learn by experience that assistance as applied to countries already industrialized, with strong traditions of representative government, did not produce the same results in economically backward societies with different political experiences. The hypothesis that since people are the same all over the world they seek above all a fuller life, and that increasing satisfaction of material wants is the best antidote to unrest and disruptive policies, failed to hold universally. Development itself set in motion social dislocations that were reflected in political instability and dissatisfactions. Whole peoples, not merely a few "irresponsible" leaders, gave precedence to goals of status and prestige over the enhancement of material welfare. The expectation that aid wisely apportioned and administered was an avenue to the friendship and cooperation of the beneficiaries often proved illusory. These unpalatable lessons, which reduced the readiness of the American people and Congress to donate wealth and talent to the underdeveloped countries, were learned gradually, during a period when American resources were coming under pressures from our own urban poor, a deteriorating balance of trade and payments, and the increasing involvement in Indochina, and when our substantial annual agricultural surplus—a key aid tool—was disappearing.

The attitude assumed by the Kennedy Administration toward the Arab world was no doubt the best possible adaptation to a difficult set of circumstances. The hard fact was that in several Arab states governments were pursuing revolutionary, socialist,

---

[2]Badeau, op. cit., p. 221.

and neutralist aims sufficiently responsive to their peoples' aspirations to maintain themselves in power, and that some of these aims ran directly counter to important American interests in the Arab world and elsewhere. Much of the American public and some of its elected representatives came to view these states as satellites or allies of the Soviet Union. In point of fact, the Arab countries arrived at radicalism by their own independent and several routes.

ARAB RADICALISM

Since the words referring to the content of radicalism—"revolution," "socialism," and "neutralism"—tend to be laden with as much emotion as information in causal American parlance, their connotations in the Arab context must be made clear.

The Arabic term commonly translated as "revolution"—*Thawra*—generally refers to revolt against existing authority. Thus the Arab Revolt against Ottoman rule in 1917, in the name of an Arab monarch, was "revolution," as were the various movements toward liberation from colonial rule during the ensuing decades. The term applies also to insurrection against indigenous authority, whether to shift the locus of power or to achieve some change in the allocation of resources among the classes of society. By any usual standards of equity, it can scarcely be questioned that countries such as Egypt, Iraq, and Syria needed sweeping change. Political independence left broad economic sectors (utilities, banking insurance, etc.) in foreign hands; such local industrial enterprise as had developed was of such a nature as to perpetuate dependence on outside capital; a disproportionate share of agricultural land was held by large proprietors whose overwhelming economic power over the masses of peasants gave them control over their political expression as well. Democratic forms were, indeed, inherited from the colonial regimes. While personalities alternated in high office, however, effective control remained in the hands of small elites whose interests would be jeopardized by any structural change of consequence. Gradual, orderly reform was not a feasible proposition within the existing political framework. Inevitably, the intrusive political processes became discredited among Arab intellectuals and the masses as true democracy; their repudiation was one effective way of rejecting the imperialist West. Furthermore, the weakness of these regimes was cruelly exposed during the Palestine war of 1948, when they proved incapable of coordinated effort in a cause publicly proclaimed as vital, of fielding trained, efficient military forces, or of providing them logistic support. It is not surprising that impetus for basic change came from the humiliated armies that were, furthermore, the sole source of the necessary physical force to effect change.

The usual Arabic word for socialism—*ishtirākiya*—does not come from the same linguistic root as *mujtama'*—"society." Sa'ada's para-Fascist SSNP—*al-hizb al-qawmī al-ijtimā'i*—which identified itself by the latter term, preached a Syrian nationalist ideology in which individual interest and welfare were expressly subordinated to the power of the state. *Ishtirākiya,* on the other hand, carries connotations of participation and sharing, with overtones relating to early Islamic principles, including the apportionment of war booty and the sharing of private wealth through *zakāt,* the charity tax. As a term of modern theory, it became current only at the beginning of the present century. It was employed by Shiblī Shumayyil, a controversial proponent of "science as religion," to refer to positive intervention of the state in social affairs for the general welfare by such means as providing employment, fair wages, and public health services. The word came to embrace a wide spectrum of attitudes and ideologies ranging from systematic Marxism to a generalized liberalism. Some apologists for Islam, arguing from the Koranic prohibition of interest, the cornerstone of capitalism, and from *sharī'a* principles of wealth sharing, asserted that socialism is, in fact, synonomous with Islamic concepts of social justice.

In the sense relevant here, neutralism, with its nonalignment and anticolonialist aspects, is a phenomenon of the cold war. Its essence is rejection of the notion that the cold war is a basic concern of all states and that all must participate in it. It arose during the 1950s and early 1960s primarily among the nations of Africa and Asia, which had in common the economic and social experiences of colonialism, a sentiment of racial separateness from European whites, and the determination to assert their sovereign status. The neutralist attitude may be reflected simply in passivity and aloofness toward the great-power rivalries, in a more "positive" exploitation of the cold war situation for national advantage, or in a "messianic" agitation for an end of cold war problems and the emergence of a pluralistic international order free of competing blocs. The Afro-Asian states, with a few exceptions, were until recently dependencies of Western powers and thus "aligned" with them. It is observable that both major cold war rivals are more zealous in obstructing movement away from alignment toward neutralism than movement in the other direction. The neutralist states are consequently particularly sensitive to Western "imperialist" or "neo-imperialist" efforts to preserve or reestablish positions of political, military, or economic influence. Conversely, the Soviet Union, not having commanded such positions in the past, has been able to exploit Afro-Asian neutralist sentiment for its own ends without incurring much odium for its own repression in Eastern Europe.[3]

The neutralist movement took form at the Bandung Conference of April 1955, held largely to protest the formation of SEATO and the Baghdad Pact. The Colombo powers and the Arab states expressed exceedingly diverse views at the meeting, and its concluding declaration was left sufficiently vague to allow a variety of interpretations. The "spirit" of Bandung, however, had strong appeal to the new nations and those soon to attain independence. The Afro-Asian context of Bandung had the effect of excluding the Soviet Union, with its vested interest in antiimperialism, and Yugoslavia, a leading exponent of nonalignment. Both were concerned to place these movements on an ideological instead of a geographical basis and succeeded in winning the cooperation of Egypt's President Nasser for this purpose. The Belgrade Conference of chiefs of state and government of nonaligned countries in September 1961, sponsored by Tito and Nasser, took place in a year of cold war crisis: the break in United States-Cuban relations followed by the Bay of Pigs fiasco, tension in Laos, the beginning of the American buildup in Vietnam, the assassination of Congo Premier Patrice Lumumba, the failure of the Kennedy-Khrushchev meeting at Vienna, renewed disputes over Germany, and the building of the Berlin Wall. In this atmosphere the preoccupation

---

[3]Fayez A. Sayegh, *The Dynamics of Neutralism in the Arab World* (San Francisco: Chandler Publishing Co., 1964), pp. 1–104.

of Tito and Nehru with general international questions—peaceful coexistence, disarmament, and the prevention of war—prevailed over the militant antiimperialism of Sukarno and Nkrumah. The second nonaligned conference, at Cairo in October 1964, was held in a markedly relaxed general international climate, following the Moscow Test-Ban Treaty, but at the peak of the Congo crisis. Instead of the cold war, as at Belgrade, imperialism now received blame for all international tensions, and the United States, to the exclusion of other great powers, was repeatedly condemned in the final communique.

Reacting to its exclusion from the Bandung Conference, the Soviet Union inspired the formation by the Stockholm World Peace Organization of a series of "Asian Solidarity Committees." These were extended to Africa in 1956. At the end of 1957, the committees, under Egyptian, Soviet, and Chinese sponsorship, held a motley get-together of "delegates" from forty-four countries. While invoking Bandung, the meeting was something totally different; the participants were not designated by their governments, against which many were in active revolt, but representatives of "progressive" groupings, including many communist-front organizations. The conference passed numerous anti-Western and antiimperialist resolutions and decided to promote these causes through a permanent secretariat. Staffed and financed jointly by Egypt, the Soviet Union, and China, the headquarters sponsored the formation of "solidarity" committees and the holding of an eventual total of forty-two conferences of writers, women, lawyers, economists, and the like, principally devoted to the dissemination of ideas common to neutralism and communism. An effort was even made to extend the movement to Latin America; a conference was held in Havana for this purpose in 1966. The "solidarity" movement declined before the end of the 1960s, both because it became a major forum for the Russian-Chinese ideological dispute and because the newer nations gradually realized that poverty, ignorance, and disease were problems that survived imperialism.[4] The prominent role played by Nasser

---

[4]David Kimche, *The Afro-Asian Movement: Ideology and Foreign Policy of the Third World* (Jerusalem: Israel Universities Press, 1973), passim.

and Algeria's Ben Bella, however, did much to cloud United States relations with the radical Arab states.

The United States had an interest tinged with romanticism in the emerging African countries heightened by the growing self-consciousness of its own Black community, and hoped that they would evolve as moderate states firmly associated with the West. Nasser, on the other hand, regarded the African continent as a sort of Egyptian eminent domain and sought to ensure that as the African territories achieved independence, they would look to Cairo for political leadership and exert their influence to further Arab causes. At the end of the 1950s, at least thirteen headquarters of liberation and dissident movements, mostly African, were installed in Cairo, financed by the Egyptian government and provided with generous facilities for propaganda and subversion.

Egypt's international outlook thus conflicted at a number of points with American aims and objectives. President Nasser's efforts to assert leadership within the Arab world provided further points of friction. By the early 1960s, having failed to impose his policy discipline on moderate Arab regimes with close and friendly ties with the United States, he concluded that Arab unity and coordinated action could be achieved only when the entire region possessed revolutionary, socialist institutions like Egypt's own, and he embarked on an intensive campaign to overturn the more conservative governments by propaganda and subversion. Since these activities seriously damaged Nasser's image before the American public and compromised his relations with the United States government, it is relevent to describe briefly the nature of the socialism he sought to extend throughout the Arab world.

Nasser and his junta brought to the 1952 coup no well-defined program of action beyond faith in economic planning and in the justice of some restriction on the size of agricultural estates. The junta did declare that a social revolution was equally necessary with the political revolution, and proclaimed that its criteria should be the eradication of imperialism in all its forms, an end to feudalism and to control of government by capitalists, the destruction of monopolies, the creation of a strong army, the establishment of social justice, and a sound democratic society. These rather unexceptionable principles did not constitute a doctrine or a guide to action, although they served, in Nasser's words, as "signposts along a difficult road." The regime's social and economic actions were for nine years a process of experimentation and improvisation. Its first significant responsibility in state economic control was assumed upon nationalization of the Suez Canal, followed several months later by sequestration of French and British financial, commercial, and industrial enterprises after the Suez war. It is pertinent to emphasize that expansion of the public economic sector thus began fortuitously, not for doctrinal reasons; also, it stemmed from a move against foreign capital, which in Egypt had been exploitative by any objective criterion, instead of against domestic enterprise. The practical experience gained, the continuing interest in consolidating the regime's power base and, gradually, the genuine appeal of socialist ideas, culminated in 1971 in a reasonably distinct pattern of economic and political organization and social interrelationships that Nasser named Arab Socialism. Action and experience preceded theory, in line with Nasser's essentially pragmatic bent.

As set forth in the Charter of National Action, Nasser's 1962 socialist "manifesto," Arab Socialism is distinctly oriented toward the individual instead of toward an abstract state, although the freedom and well-being of both are interdependent. The objectives of socialism are the pursuit of "sufficiency," justice, and freedom. Sufficiency, in the context of an underdeveloped country, implies the increase of production, including the provision of education, medical, employment, and social security services. Such an increase alone renders meaningful the equal opportunity for a share in the nation's wealth that constitutes social justice: without the enlargement of wealth, redistribution would merely mean the spreading of poverty. Nationalization of means of production must lead to increased production: otherwise, state exploitation would simply replace class exploitation. In planning, the interests of the present generation are not to be unduly sacrificed for those of future generations; social values take precedence over economic. The notion of class warfare is rejected. Class stratification and distinctions are to be dissolved; interclass misunderstanding and conflict must be resolved within the framework of national unity. Socialism contemplates the alliance, not the fusion, of popular forces. The exploitative alliance of feudalists and capitalists is not simply to be replaced by an equally dictatorial alliance of, for example, farmers and laborers. Nationalization of property must be in the interest of equity and must be compensated; it must be neither vengeful nor confiscatory. Socialism is not incompatible with private ownership, provided it is not exploitative.[5]

Arab Socialism thus emerges as a pragmatic ideology rooted in Egypt's own distinctive and monumental problems, however much its language owes to foreign socialist theorizing. It is, in fact, so specifically tailored to Egyptian circumstances that it is not readily exportable; the effort to extend its application to the entirely different Syrian environment was a major factor in Syria's secession from the United Arab Republic in 1961.

The general configuration of Egyptian society was not at issue between Nasser's regime and the United States and would not of itself have precluded cordial relations and substantial continuing American assistance. At issue, on the other hand, were the enormous Egyptian bureaucracy and military establishment. American aid officials felt that these absorbed a highly disproportionate share of Egyptian resources and were used in adventurous activities abroad, which diverted energies and talent from the country's orderly economic development. From Nasser's point of view, however, these establishments were the base of his domestic power, as well as the instruments by which Egypt asserted itself as a force to be reckoned with in world affairs and thus to be wooed with substantial aid by the great powers.

Shortly after assuming office, President Kennedy instituted with Nasser, as with other Arab leaders, a personal correspondence in which views were frankly exchanged. At Nasser's invitation, Kennedy sent a trusted personal representative to study at first hand Egypt's economy, administration, and domestic and foreign policies. The conclusion reached was that while Egypt's nationalization policies, industrialization programs, restriction of civil freedoms and dissent, large military and civil establishment, vigorous assertion of leadership among the Arab states, and quest for influence in the Afro-Asian world were all logical and inevitable

---

[5]Fayez A. Sayegh, "The Theoretical Structure of Nasser's Socialism," in Sami A. Hanna and George H. Gardner, eds., *Arab Socialism—A Documentary Survey* (Leiden: E. J. Brill, 1969), p. 104.

in the Nasser regime's circumstances, the policies were generally hostile to United States interests and did not offer a reasonable basis for substantial assistance to Egypt.

By far the largest American assistance program in the Arab world was already under way in Egypt. During the ensuing years, Egyptian adventurism in the Arab states, notably in Yemen, and in Africa, culminating in 1965 in a sharp public confrontation over the Congo civil war, and Nasser's provocative anti-American, anti-Israel, and pro-Soviet posturing, progressively increased the domestic political liabilities of the Democratic administrations in continuing aid to Egypt. In 1963 there was strong Congressional support for outright termination of assistance, which Kennedy succeeded in overriding. In 1965 an amendment to Public Law 480 explicitly excluded the United Arab Republic from the category of "friendly" countries eligible for local-currency purchases of American agricultural commodities and restricted the President's discretion in continuing the PL 480 program in that country; in fact, after some vacillation, it was terminated the following year.[6]

Beginning in October 1965, Nasser briefly tried the experiment of an "Egypt first" policy under a new prime minister, Zakariya Muḥyī al-Dīn, widely assumed to be pro-American. Prestige expenditures in Egypt and abroad were curtailed, a broader role was assigned to the private economic sector, and a serious effort was made to retrieve a rapidly deteriorating economic and financial situation. One last PL 480 agreement was signed in January 1966. However, the expected influx of aid from official and private American sources and the international financial institutions in which the United States had a decisive voice failed to materialize and, by spring, Nasser was again concentrating his energies on the Arab and Afro-Asian revolutionary struggle. Nasser's extravagant denunciations of the United States, amply publicized by the press, turned the American public, the business community, and the Congress against Egypt. Administration spokesmen, on the other hand, reacted in low key or not at all; the implication that the United States government now regarded him as at most a minor nuisance wounded Nasser's pride.

---

[6] *Legislation on Foreign Relations* (Washington: USGPO, 1969), pp. 224–226.

Whereas theory grew from practical experience in Egypt, social-ist practice in Syria lagged far behind theory. The ideology that eventually became dominant is that of the Arab Socialist Renais-sance (Ba'th) Party, synthesizing Arab nationalism and principles of radical social transformation. The nucleus of the Ba'th was formed about 1943 by Michel Aflaq, a Syrian Christian, who had joined the communist party as a student in France. He later shared the movement's leadership with Ṣalāḥ Bitār. Unable to reconcile communist doctrines with his fervent Arab nationalist beliefs and his veneration for Arab-Islamic culture, Aflaq fused the latter with a somewhat ethereal socialism, the spirituality of which he de-fended by asserting that whereas socialism in the West was mate-rialistic by reaction to the perversion of spiritualism by capitalism into exploitation, enduring Arab national values can revivify the Arab world, unify it, and establish social justice and freedom. In 1953 the Ba'th merged with the Arab Socialist Party of Akram Haurānī. Of a formerly wealthy but recently impoverished land-owning family, Haurānī early distinguished himself as a leader of rebellion among the advanced but severely exploited peasants of the Hama area and of a group of young malcontents, some of whom opted for an army career. The merger gave Ba'thist social-ism a somewhat more earthbound flavor. The Ba'th's Constitution asserts that the Arab homeland is an indivisible politico-economic unit whose special merit is reflected in its periodic resurgences based on individual freedom and the national interest. The Arab nation's mission is "the reform of human existence" and, to this end, it will combat colonialism and all its works by all possible means. Socialism, which is "necessarily derived" from Arab na-tionalism, will guarantee Arab spiritual and material development; it can be achieved only by revolution and class struggle. Private property and inheritance, however, are admissible if not used for exploitation. Wealth and natural resources are the property of the nation. Public utilities and large industrial enterprises are to be administered by the state. Ownership of agricultural land is to be limited to what the owner can himself till, while ownership of small industries is to be regulated according to the economic level of the citizens generally. Lending at interest is to be abolished. The state will supervise foreign and domestic commerce in the interest of consumers and of the national economy.

Such a program, naturally, represented a threat to deeply entrenched Syrian interests both large and small. The Ba'th made slow headway in creating a mass base, but recruited sympathizers in the Syrian armed forces who were later to become decisive for the Party's fortunes. A pan-Arab party, it established branches of some influence in Iraq and Jordan and gained a scattering of adherents as far afield as Yemen. As Arab organizations are prone to do, it developed schisms that compromised its effectiveness. Within Syria, after secession from the UAR, the Ba'th participated in successive governing coalitions, all ultimately backed by unstable army cliques, and achieved a position in which it could institute its economic and social reform programs only toward the end of the 1960s; by then a neo-Marxist faction had displaced the founders in control of the Party.

Syria's fiercely anti-Western neutralism is firmly rooted in her preindependence history. The original Ottoman vilayets in Syria were progressively fragmented by Western pressure or action: the formation of the special nineteenth-century regime in Mount Lebanon, the detachment of Palestine after World War I, the cession of the Sanjak of Alexandretta, and the regional administrations set up by the French mandatory regime. The surviving feeling that Palestine is Janūb Sūriya—Southern Syria—is a major factor in Syria's hostility to the state of Israel and to the latter's Western friends.

In Iraq a socialist movement—the Ahālī—arose in the mid-1930s, led by young Iraqis, some of them educated in England and America. It collaborated in the Bakr Sidqī military coup of 1936. The alliance was a highly artificial one, the dominant sentiment in the army being authoritarian as well as fervently nationalist. Party activity was soon proscribed, but a fragment of the Ahālī that had become organized as a true communist party survived and formed an underground mass base during World War II. Overt, meaningful political debate and organization continued to be repressed, with particular vigor after Iraq's entry into the Baghdad Pact, which was bitterly opposed by large segments of civilian and army opinion. After the July 1958 revolution successive military regimes relied for mobilization of popular support on the communists, on Nasserist Arab Socialists, and ultimately on Ba'thist factions, of which the common denominator has been a strident anti-Western neutralism.

The historical origins of neutralism and socialism emerge with special clarity in the case of Algeria, which was long claimed by France as an integral part of her national territory. Its involvement in the cold war was formally asserted in the North Atlantic Treaty, which specifically named the "Algerian Departments of France" in the area to be defended. In the earlier years of the Algerian war of independence, the United States gave general political support to the French contention that the territory was hers and assisted the French repressive effort both by economic aid and by countenancing the diversion to Algeria of arms and troops earmarked for use in Western Europe. Following the Sino-Soviet schism, the Soviet Union lent political support to de Gaulle's program of settlement with the Algerians by negotiation, whereas the Chinese, hewing to the hard line that colonial control can be terminated only by armed struggle, emerged as the principal non-Arab allies of the Algerian National Liberation Front. Ahmad Ben Bella's regime, which became independent in 1962, was thus predisposed toward a hard, militant neutralism. During a colonial regime lasting well over a century, the traditional Algerian indigenous leadership had been systematically destroyed. The country's bourgeoisie, numbering nearly a million, composed mainly of Frenchmen and other Europeans, withdrew on the heels of the French armies, leaving a fairly complete vacuum at the center and right of the political and economic spectrum. The new Algerian elite formed during the bitter eight-year war for independence was composite, incorporating liberals, radicals, and revolutionaries of several shades of opinion. With its heterogeneous composition, the NLF had no common social ideology beyond nationalism, a populist inclination, and acceptance of a strong state role in planning and development. Ben Bella professed socialism and employed Marxist advisors; the society and economy have been run, however, along rather pragmatic, statist lines, with collegial procedures among the governing elite for the making of important decisions.[7]

The principal members of the Arab radical camp thus arrived at neutralism and socialism by various routes, by their own choice in

---

[7]For a perceptive analysis of the Algerian leadership see William B. Quandt, *Revolution and Political Leadership: Algeria 1954–1968* (Cambridge: M.I.T. Press, 1969), passim.

the light of their respective national circumstances. Under colonial rule their economies were oriented toward a foreign state and closely related to the interests of foreign capitalists and entrepreneurs; this impeded the rise of a dynamic local entrepreneurial class as well as the formation of indigenous private capital devoted to productive investment. After gaining political independence, Arab leaders regarded the colonial powers as responsible for the economic backwardness of their countries; preservation of the existing economic links entailed the perpetuation of under-development; the rejection of economic dependence thus implied rejecting the traditional capitalist pattern of growth and development. Once these principles were accepted, it was natural both to take inspiration from the Soviet example as a model of the rapid development to which the Arab states aspired and to move toward cooperation with the Eastern states in terms of trade, technical assistance, and cultural exchange.[8] In no case have socialist principles or measures been imposed by Soviet force or pressure on an Arab state. Socialism has taken several distinct forms, some of which are ideologically integrated with versions of Arab national-ism that assert opposition to the West as a matter of doctrine. The problems such ideologies raise for United States policy are com-pounded by the fact that they are not shared by all Arab states but, on the contrary, are a source of deep division and acrimonious strife among the Arabs themselves.

THE MODERATE ARAB STATES

Except for Iraq's brief membership in the Baghdad Pact, no Arab country has, of its free will, formally aligned itself with a great-power bloc, whether East or West. The "progressive" states' con-viction, rooted in their colonial and postindependence experience, that the West seeks to deny them freedom of action and thwart vital Arab aspirations, has tended to inhibit cooperative or even cordial relations with the United States. Encounter with the West

[8]Tareq Y. Ismael, *The Middle East in World Politics* (Syracuse: Syracuse University Press, 1974), pp. 216–219.

has, however, not been uniform throughout the Arab world. A number of Arab states have entered the contemporary era with self-confidence, a firm sentiment of identity, and reasonably stable institutions; these have been able to base their policies on rational calculation and to maintain neutral postures in the ordinary sense, as distinct from the "neutralist" biases we have discussed.

The contrast is striking among the three Maghreb countries. Tunisia and Morocco had been protectorates, not colonies or otherwise constitutionally integrated with the metropole and, while French control was firm, this status preserved symbols of an independence that was eventually vindicated by political agitation and negotiation instead of by protracted violence, as in Algeria's case. The independence movement raised delicate questions for American policy; no completely unequivocal compromise was possible between general American sympathy with the aspirations of dependent peoples and the solidarity of the Atlantic Alliance. Thus, while grudgingly assisting France in obstructing United Nations debate of the Tunisian and Moroccan issues, the United States defended with determination against French encroachment its treaty position in Morocco, thus easing the loosening of the French ties. Since their independence in 1956, both states have followed a neutral line, "positive" in the sense that cooperative dealings with the Soviet Union and Eastern Europe are welcomed, while close and cordial relations are maintained with the West. American air bases, for which agreements had been negotiated with the French, did not long survive Moroccan independence; the Moroccan government, on the other hand, has accorded the United States facilities for military communications on its territory. These two Maghreb countries followed different paths in their internal sociopolitical organization. In Morocco the traditional indigenous elites remained substantially intact, and the monarchy itself was a prime mover in the struggle for independence, which was attained without prolonged strife. The king's legitimacy, based on historical and religious factors, has thus far proved sufficient bulwark against revolutionary agitation, and the regime has succeeded in resisting pressures for socialization. Tunisia is a somewhat unusual case of thorough acculturation to European ways of thought. In one sense the Tunisian revolution preceded independence. The latter was won under leadership of a modernized elite already in possession of a cogent program for administering the country along étatist lines under direction of a single, disciplined political party, the Neo-Destour. French withdrawal left no political vacuum and no identity crisis necessitating emotional rejection of the West.

Of the major Arab states, only Saudi Arabia has had no direct encounter with the European colonialism that elsewhere provided the catalyst for rapid social and political change. The Saudi dynasty's rule is based on religious revivalism, and it feels definite responsibility toward the world's Muslims to maintain in the holy land a regime guided by the Qur'ān and the Sunna. Saudi monarchs have sought and obtained general assurances of American protection against unprovoked attack by their neighbors. This cannot properly be construed as alignment with the United States, although it has been so portrayed by the Saudis' radical Arab rivals. Saudi representatives in the United Nations, who have usually been Palestinians recruited specially for the job, have been among the most vociferous in pressing Arab causes and, on cold war issues, have maintained a common, often anti-Western, front with other Arab League states. Saudi Arabia has, on the other hand, normally eschewed direct political relations with the (atheist) communist states. The Islamic solidarity program that King Faisal has pressed since 1965 aims essentially at forming a common Muslim front against communism and against both the Christian West and the irreligious East. It is the pure expression of the negative neutrality to which Saudi Arabia has consistently adhered.

Of particular concern to the United States was the Hashemite regime in Jordan. As a result of the first Palestine war, West Bank Palestinians became a majority of the population in the expanded Kingdom. They were generally less attached to the dynasty than the East Bankers, more sophisticated, and far more receptive to the revolutionary and socialistic currents that were gaining the upper hand in neighboring Syria, Iraq, and Egypt. Above all they sought active policies toward Israel that King Hussein feared would provoke retaliation, result in disastrous military defeat, and cost him his throne. The King learned, by his 1957 experiment in parliamentary democracy, that disaffection could be kept within manageable bounds only by authoritarian methods of rule, which he applied energetically, at great cost to Jordan's relations with the progressive Arab governments. American officials had good reason to believe that a revolution in Jordan by which the King were overthrown would be followed at once by Israeli invasion and occupation of the West Bank. As this would likely touch off a full-scale regional war, the United States considered it in its interest to provide Hussein with the resources he required to maintain his regime. From 1961 to 1971 Jordan received budget support, military assistance totaling over $220 million, and economic development aid sufficient to enable the King to stave off rebellion and to persevere in realistically moderate policies.

The division of the Arab world into mutually hostile radical and conservative camps posed delicate problems for American policy. Action to protect American military, economic, and political interests by strengthening the moderate governments was denounced by the progressive Arabs and at times appeared to constitute American opposition to progress and reform. Efforts to cultivate and improve United States relations with the radical regimes were perceived by the conservative leaders as weakening their own position. Furthermore, since both Arab camps were united in hostility toward the state of Israel, some influential segments of American public opinion did not welcome the fostering of ties between the United States and any Arab country. Most Arab issues of concern to the United States involved not one single American interest, but a complex set of considerations and attitudes in which the most advantageous course of action was seldom self-evident, even among all elements of the American bureaucracy. Decisions consequently tended to be the resultant of various conflicting principles and aims and to give a superficial appearance of incoherence. To illustrate the ramified dynamics of inter-Arab relations and their implications for American policy, it is interesting to recall United States actions with respect to the civil war in Yemen during the 1960s.

INTERVENTION IN YEMEN

The last imams of Yemen endeavored to insulate their country from disruptive outside influences, maintaining their rule by firm repression in the Sunni regions of the south and the coastal plain and by astute manipulation of the complex relations among the more restive, warlike Zaidi tribes in the northern highlands. The aged Imam Yahya was murdered in 1948 in the course of an attempted coup in which a rival aristocratic clan, a revolutionary movement operating chiefly abroad, and army officers who had been cadets in Iraq at the time of the Bakr Sidqī coup all figured prominently. The Crown Prince, Ahmad, was obliged to seek Saudi Arabian financial aid, raise a tribal force, and fight to consolidate his succession. He resumed his father's isolationist and immobilist style of rule. Pressures for political, social, and economic modernization were increasing, however, and Imam Ahmad was the object of repeated assassination attempts. His son, Muhammad al-Badr, was won over to progressive ideas and to Nasser's nationalist ideology and, in the 1950s, he persuaded Ahmad to enter into agreements for economic development programs with China and with the Soviet Union, which had already sold Yemen arms with which to press its irredentist claims against British-held Aden and the Protectorates. In 1958 Badr furthermore induced Nasser to establish a loose federation between Yemen and the newly formed United Arab Republic; the Imam acquiesced in this ill-assorted alliance largely as insurance against Cairo propaganda against his reactionary regime and to enlist Nasser's aid in obliging the British to abandon plans to federate the South Arabian sultanates, under their traditional rulers, with Aden Colony. The Imam made sure that nothing substantially affecting his domestic affairs came of the union and, when Syria seceded from the UAR, took occasion to denounce Nasser's socialism as atheistic. Thenceforth the Egyptian President was an implacable foe of the Yemeni monarchy and lent generous support to the Yemeni movement seeking its overthrow.

The United States had no direct stake in this impoverished, resourceless country nor in its eccentric, archaic regime. The country was, however, on the doorstep of Saudi Arabia, where the United States had vital petroleum interests; Yemen was moreover creating difficulties for our British ally in Aden, the site of the most important Western military installation east of Suez, supporting the Anglo-American naval presence in the Persian Gulf. According to the analysis of "working-level" American diplomats the Yemeni imamate could not, and probably should not, survive much longer in its existing form in a twentieth-century world. The general Western presence in the country was slight, providing no effective balance to that of the major communist powers, which might thus be in on the ground floor of any successor regime, whether headed by Badr, one or other of his rivals within the royal family, or some civilian or military revolutionary figure. The United States decided that in the general Western interest, it should demonstrate to the Yemeni public that there was an alternative to exclusive reliance on the communist world for assistance in their economic development, and thereby to build a store of goodwill against the day when Imam Ahmad passed from the scene. A resident American diplomatic mission was opened in Yemen in 1959, and a program of famine relief, road construction, and water resources development was instituted.

The disparate revolutionary groups in Yemen coordinated plans for a revolt against Imam Ahmad's regime toward the end of September 1962. The aging monarch succumbed to emphysema, rather than to an assassin's bullet, on September 19, however, and the conspirators were divided on whether to allow Prince Badr, who succeeded to the imamate, an opportunity to carry out his proposed reform program, or to proceed with the overthrow of the monarchy. The more extreme element seized the initiative and, on September 26, bombarded Badr's palace in Sanaa, seized the national radio station, and proclaimed Yemen a republic with Brigadier Abdullah al-Sallal as President. Badr, at first presumed dead, escaped north toward the Saudi border, called on Saudi material aid and began rallying the Zaidi tribesmen in a counterrevolutionary movement. The outcome of the ensuing civil war became a hotly contested international issue.

At this particular time Egypt, smarting from the late Imam's provocative denunciation and having openly supported revolution in Yemen (and in the other Arab kingdoms), could ill afford to permit the collapse of the new Yemen republic. Nasser's fortunes as aspiring leader of a unified Arab world were at low ebb. Syria had repudiated union; Iraq's "sole leader," 'Abd al-Karīm Qāsim, was as outspokenly his enemy as the late Nūrī al-Sa'īd had been; in all the Arab world Nasser was on friendly terms only with the newly independent government in Algeria. His own entourage was, furthermore, disunited; an army faction, led by 'Abd al-Hakīm 'Amir, had advocated preservation by force of the union with

Syria and favored vigorous pursuit of Egyptian ambitions abroad; an "Egypt first" faction, identified with Zakariya Muḥyi al-Dīn, opposed squandering the country's resources in foreign adventures and pressed for their concentration on its own development and strength. The Yemeni conspirators had kept Egypt aware of their intentions and had received assurance of Egyptian support in case of interference either by Saudi Arabia or by the British in Aden. Egyptian military advisors and aircraft proceeded to Yemen within a few days of the coup. Evidence of Saudi aid to the royalists as well as less conclusive indications of assistance by certain South Arabian sultans was shortly apparent. Sallal called for the promised Egyptian reinforcements, which Nasser could not withhold without unacceptable loss of prestige and risking the loyalty of his own army, which anticipated no trouble in the role of protecting the new Yemeni regime. At the same time, Nasser reassured the United States and Britain that the sole object of his intervention was to preserve the Yemeni republic and that it was directed neither against the Saudi regime nor against the British position in Aden.

Initial British views on the situation diverged. The Yemeni imamate's claim to South Arabia had given them serious problems, and it had no particular stake in the monarchical regime. The Foreign Office, acknowledging the popular base of the Yemeni revolution and its relatively substantial control of the national territory following the coup, favored recognition of the new regime. The Commonwealth Relations and Colonial Office, on the other hand, and senior British officials in Aden, were preoccupied with plans to effect a federation between the Western Protectorate states and Aden Colony which, after independence, would become a member of the Commonwealth and ensure the future of the Aden military base; for this they needed the cooperation of the Protectorate rulers, who felt their position threatened by the Yemeni revolution. The latter view prevailed. Britain refused to countenance Nasser's intervention by recognizing the Yemeni republic, accelerated organization of the South Arabian Federation, which he had stridently attacked, and turned a blind eye to such assistance as the rulers saw fit to extend to the Yemeni royalists.

Middle-level American officials recognized the Yemen revolution as an expression of indigenous dissatisfaction, and diplomats on the spot recommended the prompt establishment of normal relations with the new regime. Much of the press, the oil industry, and the Congress had become accustomed to attribute any disorder in the Arab world to Nasser's influence; the immediate manifestation of Egyptian sympathy and support for Sallal's government appeared to confirm the assumption that he had instigated the coup, and the Kennedy Administration felt obliged to adopt a cautious approach. The locus of decision on Yemeni matters was moved from the State Department to the White House, where the civil war became informally known as "Komer's War" in honor of the responsible staff functionary. Of overriding concern were the possible repercussions in Saudi Arabia, where a similar revolution might jeopardize American oil interests, and where King Saud's extravagance and ineptitude appeared to offer ample motive for revolt according to the Yemeni example. The King's initial impulse was to keep hands off the Yemen situation. Some royal princes and other notables, however, took the initiative in supplying funds and arms to the royalist side. Badr's uncle, Prince Hasan, who had been Yemen's United Nations delegate, flew to Riyad after receiving news of the coup in his country and succeeded in persuading Saud to give full backing to the counterrevolutionary movement. The rise of an effective royalist opposition compromised the issue of United States recognition of the Yemen republic, under the traditional criterion of substantial control of the national territory. Saudi intervention was soon reflected in the capture of American-made weapons by Yemeni republican troops, and observation of Saudi liaison officers with royalist partisan formations. This provoked forays into Saudi territory by Egyptian aircraft based in Yemen, embarrassing as well as alarming to Saud. King Hussein of Jordan had also impetuously intervened by sending aircraft to Saudi Arabia in support of the Yemeni royalists and instructors to train them in the use of modern arms. The unpopularity of the two monarchs' apparent stand against modernization and progress in Yemen was shortly reflected in the defection to Egypt of the commander of the Jordanian air force, and of seven Saudi pilots with their planes, and in a public break with Saud by several of his younger half-brothers, who took asylum in Cairo with considerable fanfare.

At the time of the Yemen coup Faisal, Crown Prince and titular Prime Minister of Saudi Arabia, was in the United States to attend the annual United Nations General Assembly session. Anticipating that Egypt, a declared enemy of the Saudi dynasty, might use Yemen as a base for attack on his country, he sought assurances that the United States would defend Saudi Arabia; these were given him in a letter of October 25 from President Kennedy that was soon made public. As the Egyptian buildup in Yemen continued, with the attendant threat to Saudi Arabia and to Aden, the President wrote in November to Prince Faisal, King Hussein, and President Nasser, proposing that the issue be settled by the simultaneous evacuation of Egyptian forces from Yemen and cessation of Saudi-Jordanian assistance to the royalists, it being understood that the United States would then recognize the Yemen republic. Faisal and Hussein, however, were not inclined to assist the consolidation of an antimonarchical regime closely allied with Nasser, while the latter, aware that the future of Sallal's government in the face of mounting tribal opposition was problematical, felt unable to risk his prestige by withdrawing the military support on which its survival might depend. The United States then concentrated its diplomatic effort on Cairo and Sanaa. Its recognition of the Sallal regime on December 19 was coordinated with a public statement by the Yemen republican government that it intended to honor Yemen's existing international obligations (including, by implication, an Anglo-Yemeni treaty of 1934 acknowledging British rights in South Arabia) and live in peace with its neighbors, and would, as soon as outside intervention on behalf of the opposition was terminated, request the withdrawal of foreign troops; a concurrent declaration from Cairo undertook to repatriate Egyptian forces on the request of the Sanaa government.

The broad pattern of the Yemeni civil war quickly emerged. Although some elements among the northern tribes were staunch partisans of the republic from the first,[9] others were attached to

---

[9]In 1959 Imam Ahmad summoned the paramount shaikh of the Ḥāshid confederation for discussion of the unrest then current among the tribes, under a safe-conduct carried by Crown Prince al-Badr. During a heated argument, the Imam rashly ordered the shaikh and his son decapitated. Some key Ḥāshid tribes were thereafter irreconcilable enemies of the royal family.

the imamate by religious conviction, while many switched sides according to competing offers of money and weapons. As the indigenous republican army proved unreliable, the military effort against the tribesmen mobilized by Imam al-Badr fell chiefly to the Egyptians, whose modern, mechanized forces were at a disadvantage in Yemen's roadless mountains. Although the Egyptian strength was built up to a total fluctuating between 40,000 and 70,000, increasing reliance was placed on punitive air strikes, including the use of poison gas bombs. The Shāfi'ī areas and principal urban centers were strongly held, but no all-out effort was made to occupy the entire country.

As the civil war dragged on, at great cost to the Egyptians in lives and money, Nasser and Sallal made more and more explicit threats to invade Saudi Arabia and destroy the monarchy there. The Saudi army, which had by policy been kept weak and poorly organized, was incapable of providing any effective border defense against determined attack. The royalist position in northern Yemen became a buffer zone of critical importance to Saudi Arabia's security. Thus Faisal, who in 1963 replaced Saud as effective head of the Saudi government, considered his brother's commitment to the Yemeni ruling family not only a matter of honor and a defense of the institution of monarchy, but also a necessary measure to protect the realm.

As Saudi, Jordanian, and soon Iranian aid continued to the royalists and the Egyptians showed no signs of withdrawing, plans were carefully worked out in the National Security Council for a renewed American effort to dislodge Nasser's forces from Yemen. Ambassador Ellsworth Bunker, an able diplomatic troubleshooter, was assigned the task of negotiating an agreement for simultaneous disengagement between Nasser and Prince Faisal. Renewed promises were given the latter that the United States would defend Saudi Arabia against unprovoked aggression, and American fighter aircraft would be stationed in the country as an earnest of this intention. A program of administrative liberalization and reform was, at the same time, recommended to Faisal, in harmony with the then current conventional wisdom that this would tend to forestall popular rebellion in the Kingdom. The United Nations had meanwhile been brought into the mediation effort and undertook to furnish military observers to enforce termination of outside aid to the royalists and to supervise a phased Egyptian evacuation. Although neither Nasser nor Faisal had the slightest confidence in the other's good faith, their agreement to this program was, in principle, obtained in April 1963. The United Nations force was ridiculously small for its purpose, ill-composed in that its Yugoslav component predictably worked as partisans of the Egyptian interest, and inadequately supported by the United Nations Secretariat. Its command was entrusted to an officer whose political sensitivity bore principally on matters relating to his own ego.[10] Its presence served to reduce somewhat the intensity of the fighting; it failed in its mission, however, and was withdrawn in the fall of 1964.

The Arab summit era, of which more will be said in the next chapter, forced on Faisal and Nasser a symbolic resolution of their differences over Yemen, embodied in the Jidda Agreement of August 1965, by which the Yemenis were to be left to resolve their own internal dispute at a conference at Harad in November. The composition between the two leaders was, however, mere ritual. During the fruitless Harad meeting, Faisal (now King in his own right) concluded a deal with Britain and the United States for an elaborate air defense establishment, an act that Nasser saw as directed against his presence in Yemen. At the same time, Faisal inaugurated, during a state visit to Iran (a country bitterly hostile to Nasser), a vigorous and sustained campaign for a common front among Muslim nations against the spread of communism and, by implication, Nasserism. Any possibility that Nasser might willingly abandon Yemen evaporated in February 1966, when the British made public their intention of evacuating the Aden base and withdrawing from South Arabia by 1968. Thenceforth Yemen was indispensable to him, to ensure that the successor regime should be responsive to his leadership. Unluckily for him, Nasser backed the wrong horse in the three-cornered South Arabian civil war. The relatively moderate nationalists of the Front for the Liberation of Occupied South Yemen, whom he at first supported, proved no match for the flaming radicals of the National Liberation Front, who were in substantial control when the British de-

---

[10]See his memoirs: Carl von Horn, *Soldiering for Peace* (New York: David McKay, 1967), pp. 310–393.

parted in November 1967. His eleventh-hour switch to support of the NLF came too late. Nasser's position in Yemen became untenable after the June 1967 war. The Yemen adventure had helped to render the Egyptian economy nearly bankrupt. Saudi Arabia emerged a stronger, more self-confident adversary. South Arabia shifted leftward beyond Egyptian reach. Sallal fell with the departure of the unpopular Egyptian forces. And, when the Yemenis themselves, who had been pawns in the Nasser-Faisal rivalry, worked out their own national reconciliation in 1971, they did so through the Saudi government's good offices alone.

United States policy toward the Yemen war was little admired by those journalists, oilmen, and Congressmen who, unaware of or ignoring the history of the Yemeni ruling house and its past relations with the United States, convinced themselves that since the Yemeni royalists were fighting Nasser, they were defending American interests. For them, the failure to dislodge the Egyptian army from Yemen seemed a signal defeat of American policy, and entering into official relations with the Yemeni republic seemed to be a serious error. Such a view mistakes a tactical aim for a policy objective. The United States was concerned primarily with the stability of the Saudi regime as it affected our oil interests, which appeared threatened by an inter-Arab quarrel in which King Saud had rashly involved his kingdom, and secondarily with the British position in Aden. Our persuasive leverage was insufficient to induce either Faisal or Nasser to retreat from his intransigent position; while Faisal was convinced that a simple United States threat to withhold the American surplus wheat on which the Egyptian urban population depended would suffice to force Nasser out of Yemen, Nasser was equally certain that a firm word from the United States would oblige its Saudi Arabian "client" to cease aid to the Yemeni royalists. On the heels of the Cuban missile crisis, no responsible Washington official thought of attempting to evict Nasser from Yemen by force, and there was at no time real danger that the Yemen dispute might escalate into a great-power confrontation. A patient and consistent show of American concern, coupled with carefully measured practical indications of support for Saudi security, eventually secured the realistically limited objective the United States was pursuing from the first.

The Yemen incident has been discussed in illustration of the intractable character of the issues arising from the polarization among the Arab states during the 1960s, and the limited means available to the United States in protecting its own basic interests where these were affected by inter-Arab disputes. If the Yemenis had been left to determine their own future, the outcome would have been of only marginal concern to America. Egypt and Saudi Arabia intervened, however, for opposing ideological reasons that, in both cases, developed into interests perceived as vital. As long as both remained firmly committed to the respective Yemeni factions, neither a military nor a political solution was possible. The royalists were never able to mobilize sufficient strength to force the Egyptians out of Yemen; on the other hand, they did maintain a position in northern Yemen strong enough to place a serious Egyptian invasion of Saudi Arabia out of the question. If the safety of American oil interests depended on the survival of the Saudi dynasty, as both the industry and American government officials certainly assumed they did, this was accomplished primarily through the dynasty's own self-preserving action, although its hand was considerably strengthened by a carefully qualified demonstration of American support. The internal threat to the Saudi regime receded as the royal family, in November 1964, deposed King Saud and entrusted rule to Faisal, whose wise and orderly administration corrected many abuses and gradually disarmed effective dissidence. The Egyptian presence in Yemen served to aggravate the situation in South Arabia, where the United States had an important, if indirect, interest in continued British tenure of the Aden base. The failure of the South Arabian Federation—a mismatched union of the politically advanced Aden Colony and the traditional Protectorate regimes—was due mainly to its innate inconsistency. America acknowledged the problem as strictly a British one, recognized that the base had little value in a militantly hostile local environment, and had no leverage on either of the rival movements for control of the successor regime.

The unfolding of the Yemen drama took place according to the dynamics of inter-Arab politics, with only incidental reference to the question of Arab-Israeli relations. The impulse toward a solid Arab front against the common enemy did produce pro-forma and short-lived reconciliations between Nasser and Faisal, resulting in temporary abatement of hostilities in Yemen and efforts toward a negotiated solution. The problem remained insoluble in its own terms, however, and only the *deus ex machina* of the June War altered the terms in such a way as to reduce outside intervention to a point where the Yemenis could decide for themselves how they were to be governed.

CHAPTER VII

The June War and the Failure
of American Policy

THE BACKGROUND OF THE WAR

T HE PROXIMATE ORIGINS OF THE THIRD ARAB-ISRAEL WAR were essentially fortuitous. The conflict was not premeditated or purposefully planned by any of the major participants. By chance or fate, several sets of contentious relationships reached a critical phase simultaneously, each of which in isolation might have been contained without catastrophe. Of these, the problems of utilization of the Jordan River and the Israel-Syria Demilitarized Zone were directly related to the chronic hostility between Israel and her neighbors. The ideological cleavages between the Arab conservative and progressive blocs, and among the more radical states themselves, had reached a peak of intensity. Evolution in the status and aspirations of the Palestine Arabs had begun to create new and destabilizing situations. Finally, reverses sustained by the Soviets in their quest for influence in the "third world" enticed them into ill-calculated moves in the Arab world that helped to produce an explosive atmosphere. Preoccupied by Vietnam and domestic troubles, the United States lacked the moral authority to forestall acts that made collision inevitable.

Well before Israel became a state, the Zionists, anticipating the needs of future immigrants, had studied Palestine's water resources and proposed a comprehensive regional program for the use of the Jordan River system* and, somewhat gratuitously, the Litani, which is wholly within Lebanon. By 1950 Israel had prepared a plan to make maximum use of the water to which she had practical access, involving diversion from the Jordan north of Lake Tiberias, within the Demilitarized Zone, southward toward the

---
*See map p. 200.

191

Negev. The diversion point was on Arab-owned land, and armed clashes occurred in 1953 when work began; under strong United Nations and American pressure, Israel revised her project so as to draw slightly more saline water from Lake Tiberias, whose shore was fully under her control. In 1952 UNRWA had commissioned a study of the Jordan system that resulted in a coordinated plan for its development providing for sharing the available water between Israel and the riparian Arab states. In October 1953 President Eisenhower recruited Eric Johnston, then head of the Motion Picture Association, as a special envoy to seek cooperation of the governments concerned in carrying out a modified version of the UNRWA plan under some form of neutral, international management. In two years of negotiations Johnston managed to narrow the Arab and Israeli differences concerning the technical aspects of the program. The Arab governments ultimately rejected the proposal, however, since in their view it implied a de facto recognition of Israel, while the latter refused any United Nations supervision of the plan and was dissatisfied with her alloted share—40%—of the available water. In the absence of agreement on coordinated use, Israel proceeded with her diversion works. In 1958 Jordan, with American assistance, instituted the East Ghor project, by which water was taken from the Yarmuk, a Jordan tributary rising in Syria, to irrigate land east of the lower Jordan. Both undertakings were generally compatible with the allocation of water envisaged by the Johnston plan.

The Arabs were nevertheless more and more disturbed as the Israeli project neared completion. In their view there was no effective restraint on the amount of water Israel could draw from the total flow, and Jordan might therefore be deprived of vital supplies. More particularly, they feared that the Israeli irrigation operations would enable Israel to absorb large numbers of new immigrants, develop an enhanced military capability, and settle the land so closely as to make impractical the repatriation of any significant number of Palestine Arab refugees. They regarded the Jordan waters as an asset to be held in trust for the Palestinians and therefore to be denied to the Israelis. In late 1963, as the 1964 date approached when the Israeli project would begin operation, Arab public sentiment became more and more aroused, and the

Syrian government began agitating for military action to prevent the diversion.

The first Arab-Israel war left the border area between Syria and Palestine, including the eastern shore of Lake Tiberias, in an ambiguous status. The 1949 Israel-Syria Armistice Agreement, according to the interpretation of Ralph Bunche, the United Nations mediator who negotiated it, left the question of sovereignty over the zone to be settled by an ultimate peace treaty. Meanwhile, its civil administration was to be organized locally by the Chairman of the Israel-Syria Mixed Armistice Commission (MAC) without intervention by outside police or military personnel; neither Syria nor Israel was to seek strategic advantage or undertake any significant activity in the Zone. Israel nevertheless asserted full sovereignty over the Zone, pressed Jewish settlement eastward, evicting Arab farmers and appropriating their land, erected fortifications, embarked on drainage and other development works, denied use of Lake Tiberias to Arab fishermen, impeded the movement of United Nations observers, and generally refrained from cooperation or communication with the MAC. The encroachment produced a long succession of armed clashes of escalating magnitude and frequent condemnation of Israeli actions in the United Nations Security Council which, leading to no practical alleviation of the situation, tended to promote contempt for the United Nations among both Arabs and Israelis and disregard for its dictates. By March 1962 Israel had begun to retaliate against shooting incidents by mounting raids into Syrian territory proper. The United States followed a general policy of judging each incident according to its own circumstances, while vainly exhorting Israel to cooperate with the MAC. Following the killing by Arab gunfire of two Israeli farmers who had entered the Zone to cultivate disputed land in August 1963, Israel, with United States and British encouragement, refrained from armed reprisals and complained to the Security Council instead. An Anglo-American resolution condemning those responsible and laying the responsibility on Syria received nearly unanimous support but was thwarted by a Soviet veto.

The years preceding the June War saw the rise of a new generation of leadership among the dispersed Palestinians. After the first Palestine war, those refugees who were politically aware and active, lacking their own political institutions, gravitated toward membership in the existing regional parties covering a broad spectrum from the Muslim Brotherhood, the ANM,[1] the SSNP, Nasser's National (later Arab Socialist) Union, to the Ba'th. All these espoused Arab unity in some form[2] as a prerequisite to achievement of Arab goals, including the recovery of Palestine. They were at the same time competing, mutually hostile ideologies, and each worked to recruit a maximum of allegiance among the Palestinians as well as to pose as their most effective champion. Nowhere was there an organized, independent Palestinian political voice. In 1959 Iraq's "sole leader," 'Abd al-Karīm Qāsim, then odd-man-out in inter-Arab politics, put forward the notion of a Palestine "entity" whereby the refugees would form their own government-in-exile and a military force that would serve as an army of liberation. Qāsim's move was a challenge to King Hussein and President Nasser, who controlled those parts of Palestine not occupied by Israel and stimulated the multilateral competition for control of the Palestinians. In 1960 Hussein summoned a conference, carefully orchestrated, at which the Palestinian participants affirmed their acceptance of his rule. Cairo retorted with the establishment of the "voice of Palestine" broadcasting service, under Egyptian guidance. Finally, in 1963, an older-generation Palestinian, Ahmad Shukayri, was admitted as Palestinian member of the Arab League Political Committee, which Qāsim was then boycotting.

As early as the 1956 Sinai defeat, some younger Palestinians had begun to lose faith both in the Arab governments and in their traditional leaders as instruments for liberating the homeland and started forming secret political cells and paramilitary formations to pursue their aims by direct terrorist and guerrilla action. Fatah—the Palestine Liberation Movement—which achieved considerable success in these organizing efforts, insisted that the Palestinians themselves must take the lead in armed action against Israel, while counting on the Arab states for aid and protection and, if need be, for the support of their armies. During its first decade, Fatah

---

[1]The Arab Nationalist Movement began as a right-wing Nasserist party before shifting to the extreme left, where it became associated with such radical movements as the South Arabian NLF.

[2]The SSNP, of course, sought primarily the unity of the Fertile Crescent.

avoided embracing one or other of the current Arab ideologies in order to avoid alienating other sources of possible support. Its tactical aim of instituting and escalating armed action against Israel, however, coincided more and more exactly with that of successive postsecession Syrian governments. By the end of 1964, Fataḥ commando squads and other *fadayeen* groups based on Syria had begun incursions into Israel for purposes of sabotage and terrorism. Such incidents, together with Israeli retaliatory action, proliferated during the ensuing years and contributed substantially to the rising tension. A new dimension was thus added to the Arab-Israel dispute. The Arab governments were no longer sole and undisputed custodians of the Palestinian cause. The Palestinians themselves had begun to formulate their own aims and policies and to take actions independent of the will of their hosts but nonetheless engaging their responsibility.

Global politics, furthermore, played a definite role in the shaping of the 1967 crisis. A revised Soviet strategy, originated in the Khrushchev era and formalized by his successors, abandoned the concept of a monolithic movement toward world revolution under the leadership of the CPSU in favor of a coalition among the existing socialist camp in the Soviet Union and Eastern Europe, the communist parties in the West, and "revolutionary democratic" regimes in the third world, which might be expected to evolve toward socialism. The Soviet role was envisaged as to support such regimes and to protect them from successful attack or overthrow by pro-West or neutral forces. Effective performance of this role became essential to the preservation of discipline among the East European satellites, whose peoples had to be convinced of the Soviet Union's determination and ability to enforce this doctrine of "irreversability." The credibility of the Soviet deterrent was seriously eroded in the years preceeding the June War. In 1965 Ben Bella was overthrown in Algeria; the Congo's Patrice Lumumba was assassinated and his regime supplanted by an outspokenly pro-Western one. Early the following year Nkrumah was deposed in Ghana and the student revolts leading to the fall of Sukarno began in Indonesia. These leaders and their parties were all publicly identified as Soviet clients in some significant degree. The conjunction of setbacks led the Soviets to suspect that the CIA was leading a worldwide plot against "progressive" forces and to assume that the United States and its allies were reverting to a policy of "rolling back" the borders of the Soviet sphere of influence. In the Middle East this assumption appeared to be confirmed by the Islamic solidarity movement launched by King Faisal, supposedly as an American "agent," during his visit to Iran at the end of 1965, and soon after by his contract with Britain and the United States for a large-scale air defense system. It became a matter of importance to the Soviet Union to bolster Nasser's regime and its Yemeni puppet as well as other revolutionary democratic Arab states; Moscow sought to enhance their strength by encouraging them to join formally as a politico-military bloc, presenting a common front vis-à-vis the supposed hostile alliance among the Unites States, Israel, Iran, Turkey, and the "reactionary" Arab countries.

President Nasser, who never quite transcended the "politics as conspiracy" outlook that assisted him to power, shared this interpretation of American intentions. A series of events convinced him that the United States was bent on his destruction: American efforts to dislodge him from Yemen, support for Hussein, Faisal, Bourguiba, and other Arab rivals, the sharp 1965 confrontation over the Congo, the ensuing suspension, and eventual termination, of American aid to Egypt. Above all, it seemed that the United States had been secretly supplying Israel with arms. At the beginning of 1965, it became public knowledge that the Federal Republic of Germany had included weapons of United States manufacture under its program of reparations to Israel and was about to deliver 200 Patton tanks. Nasser and other Arabs assumed that Germany was acting merely as agent for the United States in these transactions, which was true at least to the extent that American approval was required for the arms transfers. The news leak precipitated a crisis between West Germany and the "liberated" Arab states in which the tank deal was canceled, but Egypt and others nevertheless severed diplomatic relations. The United States, while seeking to maintain a balance of military capability between Israel and her possible Arab adversaries, had theretofore tried to avoid offending the Arabs by making direct arms shipments to Israel. Fearing, furthermore, that Israel might devote her nuclear reactor at Dimona, constructed with French help, to the production of atomic weapons, the United States sought, unsuccessfully, the right to inspect the installation. In the face of growing Israeli and domestic pressure to arm Israel, the Administration endeavored to elicit assurances and inspection privileges from Egypt respecting her own nuclear activities, arms procurement, and rocket production. President Johnson sent Nasser a letter in these premises in the spring of 1965 with Assistant Secretary of State Phillips Talbot, implying that in the absence of cooperation, the United States would feel obliged to supply Israel with weapons. Nasser interpreted the demarche as an attempt to restore the pre-1955 Western arms "monopoly" in the Middle East and refused to agree. In February 1966 the State Department confirmed that the United States had sold tanks to Israel and Jordan and Hawk missiles to Israel and Saudi Arabia. America thus appeared to Nasser to be working in close collaboration with his chief regional enemies.

The Arab states of both conservative and radical wings had meanwhile tried and failed to address effectively the problem of the Jordan waters and the broader question of Israel by firsthand consultation among their chiefs of state. Toward the end of 1963, as the Jordan waters issue became a pressing one, Syria began agitating for immediate war, of which, in practice, the brunt would fall on Jordan and Egypt. King Hussein had no appetite for such a war, which would most likely cost him his territory west of the Jordan and perhaps his throne. Nasser was content with his border with Israel, quiet since 1956 behind its shield of United Nations blue berets; his standing as the first champion of the Palestine Arabs was preserved by effective jawboning; the flower, finally, of his army was mired in the interminable war with the Yemeni royalists. His current estrangement from most other Arab leaders and his intention of appealing directly to their peoples had been clearly reflected in the 1962 UAR National Charter, which declared that "The concept of Arab unity no longer requires meetings of the rulers of the Arab Nation to portray solidarity among governments."[3] Under the circumstances it was necessary for Nasser both to find an alternative to going to war with Israel and to ensure that the responsibility for not doing so was comfortably

---

[3]Malcolm Kerr, *The Arab Cold War 1958–1967* (New York: Oxford University Press, 1967), p. 127.

diffused. On December 23 he publicly stated his conviction that Arab unity must precede military action against Israel and invited the Arab chiefs of state to meet together to determine how the threat could be met by means short of war. They responded with remarkable unanimity, considering that only Kuwait, the Sudan, and Libya were on polite terms with all other Arab League members, that Saudi Arabia and Egypt were opponents in the Yemen War, that Egypt and Syria were at ideological odds, and that Algeria was then engaged in border disputes with both Morocco and Tunisia. At the first Arab summit, held at Cairo in mid-January 1964, the chiefs of state agreed to submerge their differences and cease propaganda warfare; to undertake engineering works to divert the Jordan River's tributary streams rising in the Arab countries so as to diminish the supply within Israel's reach; that all Arab states would contribute to financing this project as well as to strengthening the armed forces of Jordan, Syria, and Lebanon; and that the Arab League's moribund unified military command would be revived to coordinate defense against possible Israeli retaliation. Finally, the conference encouraged the Palestinian diplomat Ahmad Shukayri to organize a Palestine Liberation Organization through which his countrymen might participate effectively in the confrontation with Israel.

The last-mentioned decision developed into a serious problem for King Hussein. Shukayri's efforts were concentrated on the Palestinians in Jordan, and his attempt to organize them, impose taxes, and recruit and train personnel for a Palestine Liberation Army were a clear challenge to the sovereignty of the King's regime. He soon found it prudent to terminate these operations and expel Shukayri, with great detriment to his standing among the Palestinians and among other Arab leaders.

The Cairo conference was followed by a second summit at Alexandria in September 1964 and a third at Casablanca the next year at which an Arab Solidarity Pact was signed by the kings and presidents forswearing mutual propaganda and interference in one another's domestic affairs. Reality, however, could not be made to approach the ideal. The sources of disharmony were intensifying. The conservative-revolutionary cleavage remained a barrier to loyal cooperation between the leaders of Egypt, Syria, Iraq, and Algeria on the one hand and those of Jordan, Saudi Arabia, Tunisia, and Morocco on the other. The Arab left was itself divided. The Ba'th Party and Arab Socialism were competing pan-Arab movements, in total disagreement on the approach to the Israel problem. Between March 1963 and February 1966 the neo-Marxist wing of the Ba'th consolidated its position in the Syrian army, eliminated Nasser's sympathizers as an effective political force, ousted the founders Aflaq and Bitār from power, and increasingly contested Egyptian leadership among the Arabs. In Iraq a coup in February 1963 destroyed Qāsim's isolated regime and brought to power a Ba'thist-sympathizing regime headed by 'Abd al-Salām 'Arif; the latter shortly moved to reduce Ba'th influence and, while his relations became cordial with Nasser, those with Syria rapidly deteriorated. Peaceful coexistence and cooperation thus proved an elusive aim. They acted as a protective shield for the traditional regimes and emboldened them to actions and policies highly provocative of the leftist states. At length, Nasser publicly renounced summitry, refusing to attend a fourth conference that was to have been held in Algiers in September 1966.

At the Alexandria summit the Arab states adopted a plan for diversion of the Jordan's headwaters whereby dams on the Hasbani and Banyas rivers would shift water into an eighty mile canal terminating above the proposed Makheiba dam on the Yarmuk in Jordan, permitting the expansion of irrigation in Jordan and the generating of hydroelectric power for both Jordan and Syria, as well as providing a potential means of reducing the flow of water to Israel. As Israel began drawing water from Lake Tiberias in 1964 and as desultory work began on the Arab scheme the following year, attempts on both sides were made to interfere with their progress by sabotage and terrorism across the borders. After the 1966 Syrian coup, incidents proliferated as a result of the enthusiastic support of the new government for Fataḥ and its commando arm, *'Aṣifa* ("storm").

THE SIX-DAY WAR

The Syrian regime that assumed office in March 1966 was headed by President Nūr al-dīn al-'Atāsī and Premier Yūsif Zu'ayyin, backed by the army leaders Ṣalāḥ Jadīd and Ḥāfiẓ al-Asad. Its fiery radicalism scarcely concealed the lack of a responsi-

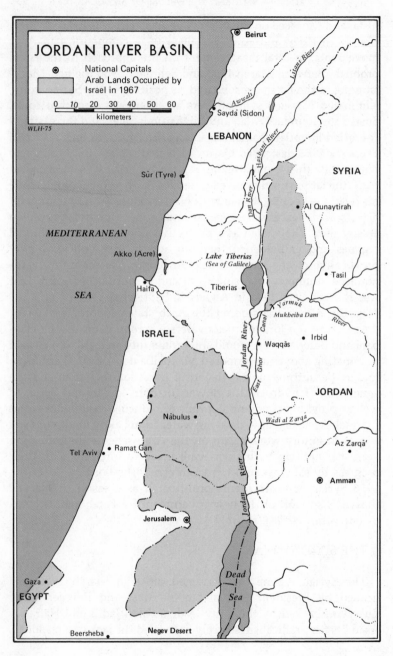

JORDAN RIVER BASIN

◉ National Capitals

Arab Lands Occupied by
Israel in 1967

0 10 20 30 40 50 60
kilometers

WLH-75

◉ Beirut

Litani River

Awwali

Saydá (Sidon)

LEBANON

Súr (Tyre) •

Hasbani River

SYRIA

Dan River

• Al Qunaytirah

MEDITERRANEAN

Akko (Acre) •

Lake Tiberias
(Sea of Galilee)

• Tasil

SEA

Haifa •

• Tiberias

Yarmuk

Mukheiba Dam

River

Jordan River

ISRAEL

East Ghor Canal

Waqqás •

• Irbid

JORDAN

Nábulus •

Wádi al Zarqá

• Az Zarqá'

Tel Aviv • • Ramat Gan

Jordan River

◉ Amman

Jerusalem ◉

Dead

Gaza •

Sea

EGYPT

Beersheba •

Negev Desert

200

ble, coherent policy, and it sought remedy for its weak popular situation by espousing the Fataḥ program of military action against Israel and by proclaiming its desire for close relations with the Soviet Union.[4] The Soviet Union responded with alacrity and promptly stepped up both economic and arms aid. At the same time, the Russians feared that Syrian impetuousness respecting Israel might touch off a major armed class leading to an undesired Soviet confrontation with the United States. As early as May 1966, Premier Kosygin, while visiting Cairo, urged Nasser to join Syria in a mutual defense agreement, by which he calculated that Syrian actions would be placed under some restraint and the Soviet Union relieved of sole responsibility for its client's defense. Despite Syria's disposition to follow a line independent of Cairo, the suggested pact was signed in November 4, 1966, Nasser having concluded that this would deter a large-scale Israeli attack and thus stave off a war for which the Arabs were as yet unprepared. However, instead of producing a moderating influence, the pact encouraged the Syrian regime to a still more active commitment to Fataḥ's militancy.

Beginning in February 1965, Fataḥ had undertaken raids into Israel from its Syrian bases, primarily directed against water diversion works and other irrigation facilities. Since the Syria-Israel truce line was relatively short and closely defended on both sides, the commandos found it tactically expedient to enter Israel by way of southern Lebanon or northwestern Jordan. Neither of these countries wished to exacerbate tension with Israel, and both restrained guerrilla activities to the extent permitted by their coercive ability and by the risk of alienating public opinion. King Hussein's situation in this regard was precarious; the Palestinians, a majority of his subjects, were wooed both by PLO, which sought to usurp essential functions of his government, and by Fataḥ, whose avowed aim was to subvert and overthrow it. He endeavored to minimize the danger of border incidents by keeping guerrilla formations well removed from the truce line, which was left lightly defended.

Western opinion was therefore astonished and shocked when,

---

[4]Itamar Rabinovich, *Syria under the Ba'th 1963–66—The Army-Party Symbiosis* (Jerusalem, Israel Universities Press, 1972), passim.

shortly after signature of the UAR-Syria mutual defense pact, Israel executed a raid of unprecedented scope and violence not against Syria, the principal instigator of commando operations, but against Jordan. The attack of November 13 on the town of Sammū' and neighboring Jordanian villages was severely censured by an overwhelming majority of the United Nations Security Council. Hussein, whose policy had left his West Bank territory poorly defended and denied its Palestinian residents the privilege of defending themselves, was widely discredited and came under pressure from Syria and Egypt to permit the stationing of their troops in Jordan, a move that his regime might well not have survived. The United States, hoping to forestall the regional crisis that could be expected to ensue from the King's downfall, strengthened its naval forces in the eastern Mediterranean and airlifted arms to Amman in order to fortify his position as a caution to his Arab adversaries and as a rebuke to Israel.

Tension relaxed somewhat along the armistice lines for a few months after the Security Council action, although the clashes that had become an annual occurrence in the Syro-Israeli Demilitarized Zone during the winter planting season took place as usual. The Sammū' raid, at the same time, further envenomed relations between Hussein and Faisal, on the one hand, and Egypt and Syria on the other. The two monarchs' propaganda services reproached the "progressive" alliance for its failure to react while Jordan was under attack. Cairo and Damascus broadcasts, and eventually Nasser in person, scathingly denounced the two kings for their alleged collaboration with imperialism and Zionism. Amman and Riyad responded by jeering at Nasser's pusillanimity in permitting the UNEF shield to relieve him of the duty of confronting Israel and to excuse the unmolested passage of Israeli shipping through the Strait of Tiran. Even the Syrians joined in these taunts. These rash affronts to Nasser's honor and courage, and his own bellicose posturing, contributed greatly to the atmosphere that produced the war. They enhanced Israel's sense of insecurity and vastly strengthened the case of Israeli proponents of preventive war. The often reiterated prediction that "Arabism" would presently attack and annihilate its enemies became, in the eyes of the Arab peoples, a promise that finally had to be acted on by the leaders who uttered it. The rhetoric ended by distorting Nasser's normally cunning and sober judgment; the Syrians and Palestinian activists lacked that faculty to begin with.

On April 7, 1967 an attack by Syrian MIGs on Israeli tractors in the demilitarized zone escalated into an engagement involving artillery, tanks, and aircraft; the Israelis shot down six Syrian planes and then conducted a triumphant demonstration over the outskirts of Damascus. Both parties submitted complaints to the United Nations; although the Security Council did not discuss the problem, Secretary General U Thant issued a quiet appeal to all parties to the dispute to refrain from provocative action.

Syria's internal politics became relevant to the regional situation with the publication on April 25 in the army newspaper *Jaysh al-Sha'b* of an atheist article ridiculing Islam and other religions. Indignant reaction by the ulama and mosque orators touched off popular demonstrations, clashes between civilians and security forces in the major cities, and strikes and seizures of business establishments, all aggravated by a current shortage of foodstuffs. (With a very Syrian consistency and plausibility the government attributed the article to a plot among the CIA, Zionists, and two Syrian officers who had fled to Jordan after an abortive coup seven months before.) Anxious to assist the Syrians in their difficulties, Nasser sent his chief of staff, General Muhammad Fawzi, to Damascus to discuss how the UAR might help. It seems likely that the Damascus talks established a scenario whereby Egyptian troops would move into Sinai ostensibly to deter a supposed Israeli attack impending against Syria. This demonstration of Arab solidarity would unite the Syrian people behind their government. For the UAR move to be credible, Nasser would have to demand the removal of the UNEF screen. This would, however, be rejected by the United Nation General Assembly, under whose authority the Force was constituted, and by bowing magnanimously to world opinion in the cause of peace Nasser could portray the operation as a political victory without undue risk of war.

However this may be, the Israelis furnished ample pretext for Egyptian action. Following two Fataḥ incursions in the first week of May, Prime Minister Levi Eshkol and Chief of Staff Itzhak Rabin on May 12 and 13 uttered public threats of action against Syria, widely interpreted as intent to overthrow her government. The Russians, apparently in an effort to create artificially a situation in which they could pose as effective champions of Syria, meanwhile fed to the Egyptians and Syrians reports (discredited by United Nations observers on the spot) of massive Israeli troop concentrations on the Syrian border in preparation for an attack to be launched on May 17. Egyptian troops began moving across the Suez Canal on May 14. Two days later the UAR requested the UNEF commander to withdraw his personnel from certain border posts and, on May 18, demanded the evacuation of the entire force. United Nations Secretary General U Thant consulted with the UNEF Advisory Committee (composed of representatives of Brazil, Canada, Ceylon, India, Norway, and Pakistan), which was divided on the propriety and legality of the UAR demand but united on the impracticability of keeping the force in place over the objection of the host government. U Thant accordingly ordered it promptly withdrawn. Whether Nasser genuinely expected such easy acquiescence is questionable.[5] In any event, once his own forces were at Sharm al-Shaikh, overlooking the Strait of Tiran, he had no choice but to deny its passage to Israel. In a speech at the UAR advanced air force headquarters in Sinai on May 22, he declared the Strait closed to vessels flying Israel's flag or carrying strategic materials to its port of Elath. He furthermore asserted the existence of a "political alliance" against the progressive Arab states by which the United States and Britain were furnishing military equipment to Israel.[6] (Israel, it should be recalled, had stated repeatedly since 1957 that it would consider interference with shipping through the Strait an act of war.)

Nasser's proclamation instantly revived the Arabs' shattered solidarity and restored him to their unquestioned leadership. Cairo was flooded with special emissaries and messages of congratulation and support from all the Arab countries, including even Tunisia, which for the past two years had not been on speaking terms with Egypt. In further speeches during the following week Nasser insisted that the Arabs did not intend to attack Israel, but that if the latter opened hostilities, there would be full-scale war in

---

[5]Robert Stephens, *Nasser: A Political Biography* (London: Allen Lane, The Penguin Press, 1971), p. 471 ff.

[6]*American Foreign Policy: Current Documents 1967* (Washington, D. C.: USGPO, 1967), p. 492.

which the Arab objective would be re-creation of the situation as of 1956, or even 1948.[7] He appears then to have been counting on the United States and the United Nations to deter Israel from going to war simply to reopen the Gulf of Aqaba.

Closure of the Strait and Israel's vigorous reaction thereto alerted the world community to the explosive nature of the situation. On May 23 President Johnson addressed the American public, expressing his concern that the General Armistice Agreements had failed to prevent warlike acts across borders in the Middle East, his dismay at the hurried withdrawal of UNEF without action by either the Security Council or the General Assembly, and his apprehension at the current concentrations of troops. He reiterated the United States position that the Gulf of Aqaba was an international waterway of which the blockade to Israeli shipping was illegal and potentially disastrous to peace and asserted, as his predecessors had done, that the United States was committed to support the political independence and territorial integrity of all nations of the Middle East.[8] On the same day the Soviet government issued a statement condemning "imperialist circles" for Israeli actions calculated to bring back colonial oppression to Arab lands and pledging strong opposition to aggression from the Soviet Union and all peace-loving states.[9] President de Gaulle asserted that all Middle Eastern states had the right to live, and that the country that first resorted to armed force would not have the approval, much less the support, of France.[10] The United Nations Security Council held its first meeting on the dispute on May 24 in the absence of U Thant, who had belatedly realized the gravity of the crisis and gone to Cairo, and over the Soviet delegate's protest that the situation was being overdramatized. The Council's deliberations were, in fact, surprisingly dilatory during the ensuing weeks. Much of its time was given over to hearing charges and countercharges by Israel and the Arab states, in which none demanded urgent action. "The emphasis of each side was on the

---

[7]Stephens, op. cit., p. 479 ff.
[8]Ibid., pp. 494–496.
[9]Ibid., p. 494.
[10]Arthur Lall, *The UN and the Middle East Crisis, 1967* (New York: Columbia University Press, 1968), pp. 42–44.

threats of the other side, and on its own determination to fight and destroy." In the absence of will among the parties to seek a peaceful solution, the Council simply failed to take consequential action.[11]

Both the United States and the Soviet Union, when the latter realized that events were getting out of hand, worked anxiously to avert an explosion by trying to ensure that neither Israel nor the Arabs would launch an attack. Washington and Moscow exchanged assurances that the situation would not be permitted to involve the great powers in a major clash. President Johnson sought, and obtained on May 28, Prime Minister Eshkol's undertaking to abstain from military action for two weeks to give diplomacy a chance to ease the crisis. He sent an experienced diplomat, Charles W. Yost, to Cairo for a similar purpose, back-stopping a new American noncareer ambassador who had not yet presented his credentials, and also a special envoy, Robert Anderson, former Secretary of the Treasury. Finally, he attempted to mobilize the maritime powers in support of the United States position on the status of the Gulf of Aqaba and Strait of Tiran; the notion of an international naval force to convoy ships through these waters was floated, of which the realism was reflected in the faintly derisive title—the "Red Sea Regatta"—by which it became known. The Russians faced a dilemma that precluded any very coherent policy: how to give Syria and the UAR full support without a confrontation with the United States; and how to withhold full support without playing into China's hand. Misjudging both their Arab clients and Israel, they had contributed to a crisis they could no longer control, even with American help, and that threatened the outbreak of a war they did not want. Under the circumstances, they began urging Nasser not to strike the first blow.[12]

On May 31 the American-Egyptian discussions in Cairo resulted in an understanding whereby UAR Vice President Zakariya Muhyī al-Dīn would visit Washington and Vice-President Humphrey would visit Cairo in an effort to find a solution short of war

---

[11]Ibid., p. 45.
[12]Walter Laqueur, *The Road to Jerusalem* (New York: The Macmillan Company, 1968), p. 167.

while preserving Nasser's face. The previous day, however, an alarmed King Hussein had flown to Cairo, agreed with his recent mortal enemy that Jordan would join the UAR-Syria mutual defense pact, place her armed forces under UAR command, and accept the stationing of UAR troops on her territory. He returned to Amman in the company of Ahmad Shukayri, with whom he had been hastily reconciled. Iraq announced its adherence to the pact a few days later. It would, in the most favorable circumstances, have taken months for this consolidation of Arab ranks to be reflected in appreciable enhancement of Arab military capabilities; it was thus largely symbolic as an emergency measure. It nevertheless had decisive results in Israel, where Eshkol and his moderate colleagues could no longer withstand the clamor of a broad segment of opinion, articulated by powerful opposition leaders, for immediate military action. When Eshkol reorganized his government, naming Moshe Dayan defense minister and Menahim Begin minister without portfolio, the die was cast. On June 3 the new cabinet voted overwhelmingly for initiating war. Thus "two great peoples, who were both trying to escape from the humiliations inflicted by European society, were unable to help each other but instead were thrown by historical fate at each other's throats."[13]

On the morning of June 5 the Israeli air force, taking the UAR by complete tactical surprise, demolished most of its planes and rendered its airfields inoperative, then turned to repeat the operation against the Jordanian, Syrian, and Iraqi air arms. Under unchallenged air cover, Israeli ground forces advanced into the Sinai Peninsula, completing its seizure to the eastern bank of the Suez Canal within three days. Other Israeli forces defeated Jordanian troops, now commanded ineptly by an Egyptian general, and occupied all the territory west of the Jordan, including the Old City of Jerusalem. Regrouping its forces, Israel stormed the Golan Heights and, having advanced to Quneitra on the Syrian plateau, accepted the next day the insistent United Nations appeal for a ceasefire.

The remarkable skill of the Israeli air force in the first hours of battle, notably the rapid turnaround achieved between sorties,

---

[13]Stephens, op. cit., p. 492.

made possible an attack greatly exceeding in intensity what Hussein and Nasser believed possible with the number of aircraft known to be in Israel's inventory. They leaped to the conclusion that American planes from Sixth Fleet carriers and British aircraft from Cyprus were participating in the onslaught. Without regard for the publicly known disposition of the Sixth Fleet, whose fighting units the United States had carefully kept well west of the troubled area, and without consulting the Russians, who as usual were keeping the American fleet under tight surveillance, Nasser declared to the world on June 5 that the United States and Britain were assisting in the Israeli operations. Within forty-eight hours the entire "progressive" wing of the Arab world severed relations with America and Britain: the UAR, Algeria, Iraq, Sudan, Syria, and Yemen, plus Mauritania, which had long but vainly petitioned for membership in the Arab League. United States diplomatic relations with the moderate states—Jordan, Libya, Morocco, Kuwait, Saudi Arabia, and Tunisia—were preserved over the opposition of some segments of opinion in these countries. At the outbreak of war, the Arab petroleum ministers were meeting in Baghdad; after the broadcast of Nasser's canard, they proclaimed an embargo of Arab oil shipments to Israel's backers, including specifically Britain and the United States.

The melancholy balance sheet of the state of American interests in the wake of the war may be briefly summarized.

1. The United States had sought, in the interest of its own security, the maintenance of stability in the Middle East and the settlement of disputes by peaceful means. Instead, the region was rocked by a war from which America's moral authority, compromised by its own warlike actions in southeast Asia, was helpless to deter even Israel.
2. Whereas free communications across the area were acknowledged to be a major American interest, the principal surface artery, the Suez Canal, was closed at the onset of war by the sinking of block-ships held in readiness for the purpose; thenceforth shipping between Atlantic and Mediterranean waters to the Indian Ocean and adjacent seas was forced to circumnavigate the African continent.
3. Access to Middle Eastern oil, recognized as a vital interest, was denied entirely by the Arabs for a time to the United States and its major ally. Added impetus was given to the movement to alter, to Western disadvantage, the terms of its availability.

4. The territorial integrity of all countries in the area, for which the United States had consistently proclaimed support, was sharply impaired by Israeli occupation of significant portions of Syria, Jordan, and Egypt.

5. Whereas the United States had sought to contain the expansion of Soviet influence in the Middle East, the Arab defeat forced Syria, Egypt, and Iraq into sole and urgent reliance on the Soviet Union for their national security and the rehabilitation of their armed forces; in exchange, the Russians acquired the use of important naval and aviation facilities as well as an enhancement of their political position. In countries such as Yemen and the Sudan, American aid was no longer an alternative to dependence on Soviet, Chinese, and East European assistance for purposes of economic development.

6. The United States had failed to win practical support from either its allies or the communist countries for its long-standing policy of limiting the Middle East arms race, unsettling both to inter-Arab and Arab-Israel relations, or even to abide by it itself.

7. The United States had sought friendly relations with all Arab states regardless of ideological orientation; it now had no official contact with half the Arab countries, representing a substantial majority of the Arab peoples.

The war's outcome was not seen in these bleak terms by much of the American public, whose empathy with the Israeli cause eclipsed concern for American strategic, commercial, and cultural interests in the Arab countries. The Israeli victory and the Arabs' humiliation were greeted with popular jubilation and with scarcely concealed satisfaction at the highest official levels. The Administration, leaving out of account both some familiar truths of Arab psychology and the firm commitment of Soviet prestige to its Arab clients, assumed that the postwar situation presented an opportunity for a definitive settlement of the entire Arab-Israel issue according to conventional concepts of equity and that Israel's enhanced position would oblige her defeated adversaries to negotiate with her face to face. Addressing a conference of educators on June 19, President Johnson set forth five principles defining American attitudes toward the problem: the right of all peoples of the area to their own national life; a just settlement for the Palestine refugees problem; freedom of innocent passage by all nations through international waterways; limitation of the wasteful and destructive arms race; and political independence and territorial integrity for all. A year later the President supplemented these morally unexceptionable theorems, which nevertheless impinged on aspirations the Arabs regarded as vital to them, with more specific comment on the territorial aspect of the problem.

... the political independence and territorial integrity of all the states in the area must be assured.

We are not the ones to say where other nations should draw lines between them that will assure each the greatest security. It is clear, however, that a return to the situation of June 4, 1967, will not bring peace. There must be secure and there must be recognized borders.

Some such lines must be agreed to by the neighbors involved as part of the transition from armistice to peace.

At the same time, it should be equally clear that boundaries cannot and should not reflect the weight of conquest. Each change must have a reason which each side, in honest negotiation, can accept as a part of a just compromise.

... it is more certain than ever that Jerusalem is a critical issue of any peace settlement. No one wishes to see the Holy City again divided by barbed wire and by machineguns. I therefore tonight urge and appeal to the parties to stretch their imaginations so that their interests, and all the world's interest in Jerusalem, can be taken fully into account in any final settlement.[14]

While the United States thus avoided formulating a detailed peace program, it rejected as unsatisfactory the borders existing as of June 4, 1967. These were lines resulting from the 1948–1949 war, which had been defined as truce lines under the General Armistice Agreements. Israel now denounced these Agreements and furthermore instituted administrative and economic arrangements in the newly occupied territories, including the establishment of agricultural settlements and expropriation of Arab urban property, which confirmed the Arabs' belief that she intended not only to retain them but to encroach still further on their territory. In the United Nations debates following the war the United States consequently appeared to the Arabs to support Israel's gains by conquest, while the Soviet Union was able to assume the role of their champion.

---

[14]Speech on September 10, 1968 before the B'nai B'rith, Washington, D. C. Text in *Department of State Bulletin,* October 7, 1968, p. 347 ff.

THE WAR'S AFTERMATH

Once the Soviet Union realized the magnitude of its Arab clients' defeat and of its own miscalculations, the United Nations Security Council was able to exercise its influence in effecting a ceasefire. The irreconcilable positions of the great powers and their proteges prevented its acting toward a more durable and stable situation between Israel and the Arab states. On June 13 Soviet delegate Federenko introduced a resolution vigorously condemning the Israeli aggression and demanding the immediate and unconditional withdrawal of its forces behind the 1949 armistice lines, and insisted on pressing it to an unsuccessful vote. United States representative Arthur Goldberg had on June 9 proposed a more comprehensive resolution, along the lines set forth by President Johnson, calling for discussions among the parties directly involved looking toward disengagement of all forces, withdrawal, renunciation of force, the maintenance of vital international rights, and the establishment of a stable and durable peace. The Soviet Union expressed its intention of vetoing the United States draft or any revision thereof, thus blocking further action by the Council and, by a somewhat unusual procedure, requested U Thant to call an emergency special session of the General Assembly, which convened on June 19 over American and Israeli objection.

The Soviet Union sought to retrieve its failure in the Security Council by placing before the Assembly a stringently worded proposal condemning Israel's aggression, demanding her withdrawal to the June 4 lines, and calling on her to pay compensation for Arab material destroyed during the hostilities. This draft, which went far toward satisfying Arab demands for United Nations action, gained little support. A United States proposal, which made no clear-cut demand for withdrawal of forces, was not pressed to a vote. Alternative drafts were introduced by a group of nonaligned nations headed by Yugoslavia and by the Latin American powers. The former called for immediate withdrawal of Israeli forces to positions held prior to June 5, requested the Secretary General to ensure compliance of all parties with the General Armistice Agreements (which Israel had declared void as a result of the war) and the appointment of a special representative of the

Secretary General to assist in implementing the resolution. The Latin American draft went beyond a call for full Israeli withdrawal to seek an end to belligerency and the threat of force, utilization of United Nations procedures for peaceful settlement and coexistence in the Middle East, guaranteed freedom of maritime transit, a full solution of the refugee problem, and the independence and territorial inviolability of all states in the region. Both of these resolutions received a clear majority of votes short, however, of the two thirds necessary for adoption. The Assembly unanimously passed a resolution (the United States abstaining) demanding that Israel rescind the measures it had taken to annex the Old City of Jerusalem but, like the Security Council, was unable to come to effective grips with the central issues.

Following the meeting between Alexei Kosygin, Chairman of the Soviet Council of Ministers, and President Johnson at Glassboro, New Jersey from June 23 to 25, their respective United Nations delegations sought some basis for a viable peace. Ambassadors Goldberg and Dobrynin agreed on a draft resolution by which the Assembly would reaffirm the United Nations Charter declaration against the conquest of territory by war, call for withdrawal from all territories occupied after June 4, and urge all parties to acknowledge the right of each to maintain, in peace and security, an independent national state.[15] The text had been deliberately worded to avoid reference to the rights of belligerents, to which the Arabs clung despite their implied renunciation in adhering to the United Nations Charter. The Arab delegations nevertheless rejected the draft, since it clearly recognized Israel's status as a national state. The proposal, furthermore, did not and could not break the deadlock between Israeli insistence on direct negotiations with the Arabs and the latter's refusal to deal with her at first hand. The draft was not laid before the General Assembly, which terminated its special session September 18 without affirmative action.

The fundamental change resulting from the war was the Israeli occupation of the Sinai Peninsula and the Golan heights, unquestionably Egyptian and Syrian territory, respectively, and of the West Bank, which had been administered as Jordanian territory

---

[15]Lall, op. cit., Appendix 25 (p. 312).

for nearly two decades without challenge by the international community. Israel found that the ceasefire lines along the Suez Canal and the Jordan River and on the Syrian plateau simplified the strictly military problems of her defense and amply justified those of controlling the Arab population of the areas seized. The reverse of this coin was that the enhancement of Israel's security deprived the Arab states of theirs. Egypt, moreover, lost the production of her Sinai oilfields and revenue from the Canal, which had reached an annual rate of $230 million. Defense of their remaining territory and recovery of the lost areas became vital Egyptian, Syrian, and Jordanian national objectives, taking precedence over, but not extinguishing, the general aim of restoring Palestine to its native Arabs. The Arab governments directly involved drew quite different lessons from their defeat, however, and proved unable to arrive at a common policy to deal with the situation. King Hussein, whose position was most seriously damaged, endeavored unsuccessfully to have an Arab summit conference convened to concert plans, and also failed, during a tour of Western capitals, to obtain either military equipment or political support to recover his lost territories. 'Atāsī of Syria, Boumedienne of Algeria, and Shukayri of PLO rejected the notion of compromise with Israel or of abandoning armed action against her. On the other hand, Hussein was at length able to persuade Nasser to seek a political solution.

Practical effect was given to this moderating trend at the Khartoum summit conference held at the end of August 1967, in the absence of the Syrian and Algerian chiefs of state. The conferees felt obliged to placate Arab public opinion by rejecting recognition of, or peace with, Israel, and by insisting on the rights of the Palestinians. Tacitly abandoning the call for extinction of the Zionist state, however, they committed themselves to diplomatic efforts to eliminate the "consequences of the aggression" and to procure the withdrawal of Israeli forces. Kuwait, Saudi Arabia, and Libya agreed to subsidize the victims of the war at an annual rate of $266 million to Egypt and $100 million to Jordan until the effects of the war had been removed. The embargo on shipment of Arab oil to America and Britain was lifted.

Numerous violations of the ceasefire meanwhile occurred and reached grave proportions when, on October 21, Egyptian missile boats sank the Israeli destroyer *Elath* and, three days later, Israeli artillery fire destroyed Egypt's two principal oil refineries, in the city of Suez. Both sides, for the first time, requested action by the Security Council, which again addressed the dispute on October 25 with a general sense, previously absent, of the urgency of a long-term settlement. The Council's Resolution 242, adopted on November 22, was skilfully drafted by Lord Caradon, its British member, who endeavored to reconcile the vital interests of the opposing sides: evacuation of the invaded Arab territories and satisfaction of the Palestinians' rights on one hand and, on the other, Israel's need for peace with her neighbors, secure and recognized boundaries, and free navigation of regional waterways. The resolution incorporated the idea of the nonaligned states for a personal representative of the Secretary General to promote a peaceful, enduring settlement. U Thant selected for this mission an experienced Swedish diplomat, Gunnar Jarring. The task, unfortunately, proved to be an impossible one. The resolution was undoubtedly the best formula of which diplomacy was capable. The same broad wording that commended it as reasonable and equitable to the world at large, however, made it susceptible to sharply varying interpretations by the parties directly involved. The fundamental question whether Israel was required to relinquish all territory seized in the war was obfuscated. For reasons of sentiment Israel clearly intended to retain the Old City of Jerusalem and to achieve more readily defensible borders by annexing parts of Syria and Jordan. In the Arab view, by contrast, the resolution clearly demanded a return to the General Armistice lines existing on June 4. The Council specified no sequence in which its specified aims were to be accomplished. Israel adhered rigidly to the attitude that firm, guaranteed peace agreements must be negotiated before any withdrawal. The Arabs, with the support of the communist and nonaligned states, were equally adamant in maintaining that, since acquisition of territory by war was acknowledged as inadmissible, full Israeli withdrawal must precede any negotiation toward the resolution's other objectives. Ambassador Jarring's persistent if intermittent efforts over a period of several years regrettably failed to find a way out of the impasse.

A NEW POLARIZATION

Before the outbreak of the June War the Johnson Administration recalled a distinguished diplomat, Ambassador Julius Holmes, from retirement to conduct a searching inventory and appraisal of American and other Western interests throughout the Middle East as a basis for a review of United States policy in the region. American interests were concluded to be vital and moreover to be dangerously jeopardized by the Soviet Union's penetration into the area and its collaboration with the "progressive" regimes in Iraq, Syria, Yemen, Egypt, the Sudan, and Algeria. NATO military positions had already been outflanked to the east and south by the Soviet Union, which now had a naval squadron regularly stationed in the Mediterranean with access to Arab ports. Western Europe's communications with Asia and Africa appeared threatened. It seemed likely that the rising tide might soon overwhelm the moderate Arab governments in Tunisia, Jordan, Lebanon, and eventually Saudi Arabia and Kuwait. Arab oil in radical hands would then be used as an instrument of political pressure on Europe and Japan as well as the United States. The President and the White House staff concluded from the study that without Soviet aid and support the Arab states would long since have been forced to make peace with Israel. The Egyptian President was assumed to have unlimited expansionist ambitions in the Arab world as well as against Israel, and it seemed probable that when Nasserist regimes were in power in all the countries adjoining Israel, a full-scale Arab attack would occur. The Soviet Union and the "progressive" Arab states were perceived as pursuing a common policy of weakening the Zionist state, in contemplation of its eventual extinction. Since the United States could not permit the destruction of Israel, it would be obliged to intervene, at the risk of precipitating a confrontation between the superpowers that might develop into general war.

Viewed in this manner, the Arab-Israel dispute became a global military-strategic problem, not a regional, political one. Any increment of Arab strength constituted a weakening of Western democratic forces and an advantage for the Soviet Union and communism. Conversely, a strong Israel served as a barrier to Soviet expansion, effective protection for Western interests, and a powerful encouragement to steadfastness among the moderate, pro-West regimes, both Arab and non-Arab, in the Middle East, which desired to block the flow of radical influence. American interests would consequently not be promoted by pressing Israel into concessions without which a peaceful settlement was unattainable, since these would simply stimulate further Soviet and Arab demands ultimately disastrous to Israel's survival, to Western interests in the Middle East, and to world peace.[16]

Although the fact that the United States and the Soviet Union reached, and respected, an understanding to abstain from direct intervention in the Six-Day War might have raised some questions concerning this rationale, it continued to inform American policy during the remaining year and a half of the Johnson Administration. The War had amply demonstrated that the Israelis, given access to modern arms, were more than a match for any Arab coalition that might be brought against them, without necessity for direct American military intervention. The President's determination to ensure that this "balance" should be preserved had the full support of Congress; the Foreign Assistance Act of 1968 stated that

It is the sense of the Congress that the President should take such steps as may be necessary, as soon as practicable after the date of enactment of this section, to negotiate an agreement with the Government of Israel providing for the sale by the United States of such number of supersonic planes as may be necessary to provide Israel with an adequate deterrent force capable of preventing future Arab aggression by offsetting sophisticated weapons received by the Arab States and to replace losses suffered by Israel in the 1967 conflict.[17]

The sale of fifty F-4 Phantom jets was promptly negotiated and announced by the State Department in December. Since France, which had warned Israel against initiating hostilities, was no longer an available source, the United States became the principal

---

[16]Eugene V. Rostow, "American Foreign Policy and the Middle East", in Louis Henken, ed., *World Politics and the Jewish Condition* (New York: Quadrangle Books, 1972), pp. 63–101.
[17]*Legislation on Foreign Relations* (Washington; USGPO, 1969), p. 84.

purveyor of weapons to Israel. The United States furthermore abstained from the effective pressures on Israel for which the Arabs had, perhaps unrealistically, hoped, toward full cooperation with the United Nations Mediator and against actions provocative to Arab sentiment such as the annexation of Jerusalem, the extension of Jewish settlement in the occupied areas, and obstacles to the repatriation of June War Palestinian refugees. In Arab eyes America became more closely allied with Israel in opposition to vital Arab interests.

The flaws in the new American approach gradually became apparent. America's assumptions concerning the nature of the Arab-Israel problem were not fully shared by her West European partners, who considered that the battle to keep the Middle East a Western strategic preserve from which Russia was to be excluded had been lost, largely through American actions, in the Suez War of 1956. They considered their interests in the area, including access to its oil, were thenceforth to be pursued primarily by political and diplomatic means, while NATO's role was to be strictly limited to West European, not global, defense. It was expedient, in terms of their Arab relations, for the European countries to leave to the United States the problem of Israel's survival, while encouraging a political settlement in diplomatic forums. The European drift away from close identification with Israel after the June War coincided with a progressive deterioration, fostered by vigorous Arab diplomacy, of Israeli relations with third-world countries, notably the African states, where Israel had striven to cultivate cordial relations through trade and technical assistance. The American posture thus promoted a new polarization in the Middle East whereby the United States and Israel, on one hand, were ranged against the Arab states and the communist world on the other. The wartime demonstration of Israeli strength failed to weaken radicalism within the Arab world. The defeated states included countries of both conservative and "progressive" orientation. A major result of the war was the relative subordination of inter-Arab differences to rebuilding shattered economies and military forces; the wealthy, conservative regimes—Saudi Arabia, Kuwait, and Libya—contributed even more generously to Egypt than to Jordan. Little more than two years later, military coups brought flaming radicals to power in Libya and the Sudan, which promptly entered upon a program (that proved abortive after much negotiation) of union with Egypt and Syria.

Egypt and Jordan earnestly sought a bearable political composition during the United Nations debates after the June War, and through less conspicuous diplomatic channels. For the restoration of a substantial part (not necessarily all) of their territory and some just provision for the Palestinians, they were prepared to renounce belligerent rights as well as to accept Israel's presence and right to live in security. In this spirit they accepted Security Council Resolution 242 and Ambassador Jarring's mediation effort. Inflamed domestic and general Arab opinion placed further concessions out of the question, particularly the face-to-face negotiation and formal treaties on which Israel insisted. The change of attitude was not merely tactical. During the year and a half following the war, Egypt's captured or destroyed military equipment was replaced by the Soviet Union, which undertook an intensive program to retrain the Egyptian forces. Early in 1968, the United States, in order to enable King Hussein to resist Egyptian, Syrian, and Iraqi pressures to procure arms from the Soviet Union and thus to standardize the equipment of the Arab armies, agreed to provide weapons for the Jordanian army. Although Nasser and Hussein were thus in a markedly improved defense posture by the spring of 1969, they persevered in their cautiously conciliatory policy. Speaking for Nasser as well as himself before the National Press Club in Washington on April 10, the King reiterated the offer of a just and lasting peace on the basis of the integral program of the Resolution. Israel, he emphasized, could have either peace or territory, but could never have both. The government of Israel, however, was determined to have some territory, although it refrained from stating publicly the minimum extent of its demands; it was moreover confident that, victorious in war and assured by American backing of a lasting military superiority over any feasible combination of Arab forces, it could have peace also, negotiated substantially on its own terms directly with the Arabs. Mediation and diplomacy found no way to construct a bridge between the Arab and Israeli positions, and further recourse to war became virtually inevitable.

The American representative in the United Nations Security Council spoke forcefully on June 13, 1967 against a Soviet-proposed resolution demanding total Israeli withdrawal from the territory seized in the Six-Day War, terming it a "prescription for renewed hostilities." The altered situation proved to be fully as explosive as the previous one, and it had two exceedingly short fuses. Previously, Israel had been in occupation only of land within mandated Palestine. She now held portions of Syrian and Egyptian national territory, whose recovery was a vital national aim entirely apart from the Palestine issue that had theretofore been the core of the Arab-Israel problem. The Arabs saw clearly that if the new ceasefire lines were, for lack of political or military challenge, allowed to endure, the world community would soon come to regard them as normal and even legitimate. Having failed to achieve results by diplomatic action, President Nasser proceeded to an escalating armed confrontation with Israel that culminated in the commitment, for the first time, of Russian combat troops in significant numbers in the Arab world. The Palestinians, among whom a fully differentiated nationalism was now maturing, mounted a determined campaign to supplant the existing regime in Jordan. The United States saw its vital interests engaged in both situations; its response is the subject of the following chapter.

CHAPTER VIII

Dress Rehearsal for Confrontation

THE FRAGILE TRUCE

F ROM THE OUTSET THE SUCCEEDING RICHARD NIXON ADMINIS-
TRATION emphasized its deep apprehension at the danger to world
peace represented by the uneasy truce in the Middle East, and its
conviction that the United States must act to forestall the major
clash among the nuclear powers that it might precipitate. Before
his inauguration President Nixon sent a personal emissary, former
Governor of Pennsylvania William Scranton, to the area to make
known his intention of adopting an objective, "even-handed"
attitude among the parties to the dispute: an initiative that aroused
hopes in Arab capitals and nervous misgivings in Israel. Speaking
to the press on January 27, 1969, the President described the situation as very explosive, a "powder keg" that, unless defused, might
lead to a great-power confrontation, which he wished to avoid.[1]
The President decided to entrust primary responsibility for the
handling of Middle East issues to the Secretary of State, William
Rogers, and Joseph Sisco, Assistant Secretary for Middle Eastern
and South Asian Affairs, and to keep his Advisor on National
Security, Dr. Henry Kissinger, a Jew, in the background. An intensive review of United States policies and possible lines of action
established the general objective of containing the rise of Soviet
influence in the Middle East. The Soviet Union was nevertheless
acknowledged to have important interests in the region, and must
consequently be brought into the process of search for a solution
to its problems. United Nations Resolution 242 appeared to remain

---

[1]Senate Foreign Relations Committee, *A Select Chronology and Background Documents Relating to the Middle East* (Washington USGPO, 1st revised ed., 1969), pp.
274–276.

the soundest possible basis for a settlement, and revitalization of United Nations mediator Gunnar Jarring's mission seemed the most promising procedural line of approach. The Arabs would have to be convinced that the new Administration would act impartially toward the issue, and Israel had to be persuaded to withdraw from Arab territories, with only minor border rectifications, under assurance that her security would be internationally guaranteed.

Acting on a pending French proposal for discussions among the permanent members of the United Nations Security Council (minus China) on Middle East peace, the United States instituted negotiations in New York with Britain, France, and the Soviet Union, and bilaterally with the latter, on the basis of an American working paper. In order to enhance the possibility of a favorable outcome the President deferred action on an Israeli request for fifty additional Phantom aircraft and proposed (without favorable result) to the Soviet Union a mutual reduction in the level of arms shipments to the Middle East. During the ensuing months, some progress was achieved in narrowing the wide gap between the American and Soviet views of an appropriate solution. The Soviets tended to favor the concept of a program agreed between the great powers and imposed on the parties concerned, while the United States preferred the establishment of a general framework of which the details would be negotiated among the states directly concerned. The United States agreed that Israel must evacuate the whole Sinai Peninsula, while Russia accepted the principle of demilitarized zones in the border regions. However, the two sides could reach no meeting of minds on the timing of the Israeli withdrawal, on the nature of a security guarantee to Israel, on the disposition of Jerusalem, or on the status of the Arab Palestinians, and the talks eventually broke down. On the President's instructions Secretary Rogers made public the American position, which became known as the Rogers Plan. Four principles underlay the approach: nations not directly involved could not make a durable peace for the nations and governments directly concerned, but could be of help to them in doing so; a durable peace must meet the legitimate concerns of both sides; the entire text of United Nations Resolution 242 would constitute the only feasible framework for a negotiated peace; a protracted period of no war, no peace, recurring violence, and spreading chaos would serve the interest of no one.[2] American policy was "to encourage the Arabs to accept a permanent peace based on a binding agreement and to urge the Israelis to withdraw from occupied territory when their territorial integrity was assured as envisaged by the Security Council Resolution." The intention was to assist the stalled United Nations peace-making effort and to provide Ambassador Jarring with fresh ideas for a renewed attempt.

While well received in Western Europe, the Rogers Plan was roundly condemned by the Soviet Union and rejected by both parties to the dispute. Israel accused the United States of "moralizing," and her Ambassador in Washington, General Itzhak Rabin, led an extraordinarily undiplomatic campaign to mobilize American public opinion against Secretary Rogers and his views. The President nevertheless reiterated the American position in his Report to Congress in February 1970. Like the Israelis, President Nasser feared that the four-power consultations represented an effort to impose a solution in the Middle East from the outside. As early as March 1969, he warned that the attitudes of the participating states in the discussions would determine for each "the extent of their relations with our Arab nation for years to come"; he asserted

that the destiny of the Middle East will be determined in the Middle East itself and that nobody can dictate to the Arab nation what this nation regards as against justice or its lawful, historical rights. Peace cannot be imposed, but peace can come by itself if justice forms the basis. We should always remember that the balance of power may change but the foundations of justice are always firmly rooted and perpetual.[3]

Events on the ground in the Middle East were already outpacing the course of great-power diplomacy. Nasser had emerged from the 1967 disaster with a regional prestige impaired but, in default of another leader with popular appeal throughout the Arab world, not destroyed. His domestic position was similarly weakened. On

---

[2]Text in *United States Foreign Policy 1969–1970* (Washington: Department of State Publication 8575, 1971), pp. 409–412.

[3]Speech before Arab Socialist Union National Congress, March 27, 1969. Text in Walter Laqueur, ed., *The Arab-Israel Reader* (New York: Bantam Books, revised ed., 1970), p. 408.

the eve of the Khartoum conference he was obliged to crush a conspiracy within his immediate entourage. Riots and demonstrations, notably among students, occurred for the first time since the consolidation of his rule in 1955, reflecting frustration at the nation's demonstrated weaknesses and the loss of Egyptian territory. The prompt rebuilding of his armed forces was essential to the reassertion of his leadership: for this he was utterly dependent on the Soviet Union. The latter had no politically feasible alternative to cooperation. Its outspoken support for the Arab cause had raised expectations, not fulfilled, of direct Soviet help in the War. The defeat by a small power, identified with the United States, of two larger states closely associated with the Soviet Union, equipped with Soviet arms and trained by Soviet advisors, was acutely embarrassing. The conclusion that the third world at large was free to draw—that the Soviet Union was neither a useful nor a reliable friend—was potentially damaging not only to Soviet policy among the nonaligned nations but also among its satellites in eastern Europe; it may, indeed, be recalled that a massive Soviet repression in Czechoslovakia followed closely after the June War. The Russians resigned themselves to the costly task of rehabilitating and endeavoring to improve the defense establishments of Egypt and Syria. They moreover adopted a much more forward global naval doctrine; the Soviet fleet's mission would no longer be confined primarily to their own coastal defense; it would thenceforth challenge American mastery of the seas throughout the world. Soviet warships began to appear with greater frequency in the Indian Ocean, the Persian Gulf, and the Red Sea. The Soviet Mediterranean squadron, which until 1967 had consisted of units temporarily detached from the Black Sea, became a permanent fleet, with docking and repair facilities under its own management in Egyptian and Syrian ports. Soon it was in a position not only to afford a credible measure of protection for Soviet client states on the shores of the Mediterranean, but also to neutralize the United States Sixth Fleet, which could thenceforth intervene in area conflicts only at the risk of a superpower confrontation of proportions difficult to predict.

The Egyptian leadership saw clearly that indefinite prolongation of the ceasefire along the Suez Canal in the absence of any progress toward a political settlement with Israel would encourage world indifference to the situation, permit the ceasefire lines to become tacitly accepted as permanent boundaries, and dim the prospect of recovering the occupied Egyptian territory. In the early spring of 1969 Nasser instituted a campaign of frequent small-scale encounters with the Israeli forces east of the Canal, artillery exchanges, and occasional commando probings into the Sinai Peninsula. In June he declared the 1967 ceasefire no longer valid. His press, with characteristic hyperbole, explained the new policy as a "war of attrition" calculated to sap Israel's military, economic, and demographic strength, to restore the June 4, 1967 situation, and eventually to force Israel back within the borders contemplated by the United Nations Palestine Partition resolution. Israel reacted with more and more intensive air strikes, extending deep into the Nile valley and delta, against both military and civilian targets, in the hope of breaking the will of the Egyptian people and forcing their government to plead for peace. The Egyptian economy was further strained by the necessity to provide for a half-million refugees evacuated from the urban centers along the Suez Canal. Alarmed by the incursions, against which Egypt could oppose no adequate defense, Nasser paid a hasty visit to Moscow in January 1970 to appeal for Soviet help.

The Soviet Union responded promptly and vigorously. Large quantities of sophisticated surface-to-air missiles, tanks, and late-model supersonic MIGs were shipped to Egypt. Russian personnel arrived in thousands to man antiaircraft defenses, fly tactical air missions, administer airfields, and occupy operational posts in Egyptian army units, at least down to the battalion level. Soviet and Israeli personnel frequently came face to face in armed engagements.

The unprecedented commitment of Soviet operational troops to action in the Middle East raised in Washington the alarming prospect of a decisive shift in the balance of forces in the region. The State Department determined to undertake unilaterally an American peace-making initiative. A proposal, which became known as the Second Rogers Plan, was formulated whereby Israel, Egypt, and Jordan would be persuaded to "stop shooting and start talking." All parties would renew their acceptance of United Nations Resolution 242 in its entirety and agree to engage in discussions under Ambassador Jarring's auspices, looking toward a just and lasting peace based on mutual acknowledgment of each other's sovereignty, territorial integrity, and political independence. A ninety-day ceasefire and military standstill between Israel and Egypt, within an agreed zone extending to a depth of fifty kilometers on both sides of the Suez Canal, was to be instituted. In carefully calculated public statements the President and other high Administration officials warned the Soviet Union against disturbing the existing balance of military forces in the Middle East, or any effort to establish a preponderant position there. By the end of July, after persistent diplomatic effort, including talks with Soviet representatives, Assistant Secretary Sisco succeeded in obtaining the three governments' agreement to the proposal, and the truce took effect on August 7. Whether or not the Egyptians and Soviets understood the full implications of the standstill agreement, which the United States and Israel took to preclude any military move or buildup within the specified zone,[4] the installation of surface-to-air missiles went forward on the west bank of the Canal. Israel, accusing Egypt of bad faith, suspended discussions with Jarring after a single meeting confined to procedural matters. The ceasefire nevertheless held and was extended by a United Nations General Assembly resolution in November 1970, on Egyptian initiative. Reacting to the UAR violation of the standstill, the United States extended a $500 million military procurement credit to Israel and expedited the shipment of additional Phantom aircraft.

King Hussein's acceptance of the American peace proposal at once exacerbated his already parlous relations with Syria, and particularly with the Palestinian activist movement operating in Jordan. During the ensuing crisis, into which the United States was drawn, the White House assumed direct responsibility for American actions. These were predicated on the sort of cold-war assumptions that had guided policy at the end of the Johnson Administration instead of persisting in the regional-political approach that the State Department had been following. A superpower confrontation was narrowly averted. The long-term result, however, removed any remaining chance that the Arab-Israel problem might eventually be solved by agreement among the

---

[4]Marvin Kalb and Bernard Kalb, *Kissinger* (Boston: Little, Brown, 1974), p. 195.

existing sovereign governments in the area; the Palestinians were henceforth an indispensable party to any lasting settlement.

PALESTINIAN NATIONALISM COMES OF AGE

At the time of the June War the Palestine Arab people were estimated at 2.35 million persons, of whom 57% were refugees. Of the total population 52% lived in Jordan, 13% in Syria and Lebanon, 17% in the Gaza Strip, and 12% in Israel. Since the War, 1.4 million, or nearly two thirds, of all Palestinians have lived under Israeli rule. In the now-truncated Kingdom of Jordan Palestinians outnumber the native East Bank population two to one. Palestinians of military age—fifteen to forty-five—are believed to number between 200,000 and a quarter million.[5]

The 1967 debacle greatly stimulated the determination of the Palestinians to combine among themselves in pursuit of their national aspirations. Given the large fraction of their community under enemy occupation, the dispersion of the rest in many Arab countries with differing ideological orientations, and the large number of candidates for leadership, obstacles to common effort were many. Of immediate urgency was a decision whether organization for armed struggle should take first priority, or whether unity and national mobilization would naturally ensue from militant resistance undertaken immediately. The question was decided in the latter sense, as a by-product of rivalry between PLO and Fatah, in which the latter gained the upper hand.

As a creature of the Arab League, PLO was, in practical terms, under preponderant Egyptian influence, and Nasser had made sure that the Palestine Liberation Army (PLA) refrained from action from its Gaza base that might provoke Israeli retaliation against Egypt. Shukayri's talents ran less to effective administration than to hollow bombast; the PLO executive committee was paralyzed by dissension and rivalry, while the PLA was in a state of near insubordination. Neither the civil nor the military wing made any noticeable contribution to the Arab effort in the War, and both emerged widely discredited.

---

[5]Hisham Sharabi, *Palestine Guerrillas: Their Credibility and Effectiveness* (Washington, D.C.: Georgetown University Press, 1970), p. 21 (fn.).

Fataḥ, by contrast, appeared to the demoralized Arab world, particularly the Palestinians, to be the only dynamic force active against the enemy. Already in existence for a decade, its cohesive, anonymous leadership had foresworn any narrow ideology or involvement in inter-Arab disputes that might damage its broad appeal to Palestinians and the Arabs generally, or divert its energies from the purpose of armed action against Israel. Its sporadic prewar incursions had contributed to the tensions that precipitated the conflict; these were now intensified from a Fataḥ base at Karameh, on the Jordan side of the ceasefire lines. In March 1968 Israel mobilized a large task force to destroy the base. The Fataḥ commandos mounted a stiff resistance and were shortly reinforced by units of the Jordan army. The Israelis leveled Karameh and neighboring villages before retiring; they sustained sufficient casualties, however, that Fataḥ could plausibly represent the engagement to Arab opinion as a military success. Palestinian volunteers appeared in larger numbers than Fataḥ could equip and train. Contributions flowed from well-to-do Palestinians throughout their diaspora, and both arms and funds came from Arab governments of all political persuasions. Although lacking as yet a solid organizational base, Fataḥ attained a position of leadership among Palestinians that could be maintained only by persevering in the armed struggle, or appearing to do so. Militancy, moreover, was the best insurance against sacrifice of Palestinian interests through peace agreements between Israel and the Arab governments.

After the spring of 1968, when Yāsir 'Arafāt appeared publicly as the Fataḥ spokesman, the organization developed from a simple guerrilla formation into a political movement that gradually asserted its ascendency over PLO. The latter had instituted the Palestine National Congress, a sort of broadly representative constituent assembly composed of organized social groups such as labor unions, student and women's societies, and ascriptive notables. In preparation for a Congress meeting held in February 1969, a large bloc of seats was allocated to Fataḥ. 'Arafāt was elected chairman of PLO (Shukayrī having been eased out of the organization some months before), and four Fataḥ representatives were elected to the eleven-man executive committee.

The resistance movement had meanwhile ramified into a bewildering complex of commando organizations parallel, or in opposition, to Fatah. Whether organized on Palestinian initiative or at Syrian or Iraqi inspiration, the larger groupings were dependent for material support on the competing branches of the Ba'th Party ruling those two countries, and, therefore, generally followed their ideologies. The latter varied somewhat in doctrine, but their broad tendency was to assert that only revolution throughout the Arab world could produce the unity required for effective struggle against the Zionist state; the "liberation" of Amman, Beirut, Riyad, and so on was prerequisite to the liberation of Palestine. In 1970 the larger organizations included the Liberation War Vanguard, with its commando arm Sā'iqa ("thunderbolt"), and the Popular Democratic Front for the Liberation of Palestine (PDFLP), both supported by Syria, and the Popular Front for the Liberation of Palestine (PFLP), backed by Iraq, the remnant of the organization of that name founded in late 1967 by Dr. George Habash, which had now split into several factions.[6] These various militant groupings grew to be a more serious menace to the internal security of Jordan and Lebanon than that of Israel. They were moreover essentially beyond the discipline of Yāsir 'Arafāt who, as chairman of PLO, was in theory responsible for their acts.

The Karameh incident was by no means an isolated one but, instead, one event in a continuing alternation of commando incursions into Israel and retaliatory raids into Jordan by the Israeli Defense Force. Apprehending a further all-out Israeli invasion, King Hussein ordered the removal of the commando headquarters from the border area to Amman, to the general indignation of the Palestinians. In the Jordanian interior, however, the guerrillas gradually came to constitute a state within a state, exercising powers of police, taxation, and vehicle registration and eventually controlling large sectors of the capital. Hussein's conciliatory attitude toward Israel, expressed in Washington and elsewhere in the spring of 1969, exacerbated Palestinian animosity against him, and the country was in virtual anarchy by the following summer. The King, who hesitated to move decisively against the Palestinians for fear of alienating general Arab opinion, had difficulty in restrain-

---

[6]William B. Quandt, Fuad Jabber and Ann Losely Lesch, *The Politics of Palestinian Nationalism* (Berkeley and Los Angeles: University of California Press, 1973), pp. 55–77.

ing the Jordan army, fiercely loyal to him personally and bitterly resentful of the Palestinians' provocations. Armed clashes between commandos and regular troops intensified until the summer of 1970. An Arab League-sponsored delegation composed of high-level representatives of Algeria, Tunisia, the Sudan, Libya, and Egypt spent a fortnight in Amman in June and July, succeeding in patching up a tenuous truce. When, in early August, Jordan and Egypt accepted United States proposals for an Arab-Israeli cease-fire, however, no common ground remained between Hussein and the commandos, whose activity against his regime promptly redoubled. On September 13 the King appointed a military government and moved the full strength of his army against the guerrillas, who then occupied a major portion of the capital.

On September 17 the Syrian regime formally declared itself on the side of the Palestinians. The next day President 'Atāsī publicly proposed to Iraq (15,000 of whose troops, stationed in Jordan during the June War, were still in the country) a joint intervention on their behalf. Syrian tanks, with Palestinian markings, had already begun moving toward Jordan and crossed the border on September 18. Hussein's plight appeared desperate; he appealed for immediate help to the United States and other Western countries.

President Nixon had discussed the ominous situation with his senior advisors on September 17. Secretary Rogers favored dealing with the problem by diplomatic procedures, if possible in cooperation with the Soviet Union. The President was, however, won to Kissinger's contrasting view that the crisis represented a Soviet challenge to vital American interests that had to be met by the show or, if need be, the use of military force. The assumption prevailed that Syria was acting in harmony with Soviet desires, even at Soviet instigation; this judgment was fortified by intelligence reports indicating that Russian advisors had accompanied the Syrian armor up to (but not beyond) the frontier and had thus presumably participated in planning the attack. Hussein's firmly pro-West regime was in itself considered to be a valuable American asset; its survival furthermore was deemed vital in order to prevent the outbreak of a new regional war on Israeli initiative. At the same time, direct American intervention on his behalf, it was acknowledged, would probably discredit him so irretrievably within the Arab world at large that his future would be highly problematical. Secretary of Defense Melvin Laird was moreover disturbed at the prospect of a new military venture abroad only four months after the commitment of American forces in Cambodia, public outcry over which had barely subsided. The President decided to persuade Israel to undertake the intervention in Hussein's behalf, in the meantime mounting a show of American force of sufficient dimensions to make clear to the Soviet Union and its presumed Syrian and Palestinian agents the United States determination to protect its own interests.

Nixon approved immediately a long-deferred Israeli request for Phantom aircraft and $500 million in aid, announcing his decision in person to Prime Minister Golda Meir, who was then in the United States. Within the next few days Kissinger and the Israeli Ambassador worked out a plan whereby Israeli troops, after preparatory air action against the Syrian forces that had now occupied the Jordanian town of Irbid, would make a two-pronged attack on Irbid, through both Jordanian and Syrian territory; the United States would stand ready to defend Israel against any retaliatory moves by Soviet or Egyptian forces, or both. Israeli preparations were quickly observable on the ground. The Sixth Fleet was substantially reinforced and ordered to the eastern Mediterranean (inducing a similar beefing-up of the Soviet Mediterranean squadron). American airborne forces in West Germany were placed on alert and ostentatiously moved to airports. The State Department sternly warned the Soviet Embassy of the likelihood of both Israeli and United States armed action unless the Soviet Union ordered its Syrian clients out of Jordan.[7]

Hussein's small but efficient air force began effective operations against the Syrian-Palestinian forces at Irbid on September 21. By the following day the situation in Amman had improved to the point that he could disengage ground troops and armor from the capital and despatch them to the north. Under this pressure, and doubtless on strong Soviet advice, the Syrians began to withdraw, and completed their evacuation of Jordanian territory on September 23.

---

[7]Kalb and Kalb, op. cit. pp. 197–209.

Thus, what President Nixon described as "the gravest threat to world peace since the Administration came to office," and comparable to the Cuban missile crisis of 1962, subsided without commitment of forces by the superpowers and without an open clash of will between them. The United States decision to treat the situation as a conflict between American and Soviet interests appears to have been based on a mechanistic analysis of the Middle East problem in terms of the single variable of power. The assumption that both the Palestinians and the Syrians were acting at the behest, and in the interest of, the Soviet Union in their attempt to overthrow the Jordanian regime was based on dubious evidence in both cases and ignored the long historical background of inter-Arab and Arab-Israel animosities, which had little or nothing to do with Soviet ambitions. It is true that, in the absence of diplomatic relations, the United States had no direct channel through which to place pressure on Syria; less direct avenues, including the possibility of winning the Soviet Union's cooperation in an effort to allay the crisis by political means, were not tried. The obvious American intention to resort to armed force aroused alarm in western Europe, and Britain made urgent diplomatic representations in Washington against it; the crisis underscored an increasing divergence within NATO with respect to the nature and handling of Middle Eastern problems. The American-Israeli exercise in joint planning for military action against Arabs, although it did not at the time become public knowledge,[8] had significant consequences. It resulted at once in a new spiral in the regional arms race. It greatly diminished the moral leverage the United States could exert on Israel toward the conciliatory actions that were a necessary condition of progress toward a negotiated settlement with the Arab states. In 1971 Secretary Rogers endeavored to induce Israel to accept and implement an interim arrangement with Egypt whereby Israeli forces would withdraw some distance from the Suez Canal, which would be cleared and reopened to traffic, as a first step toward full implementation of United Nations Resolution 242. Israel was unwilling to cooperate in the proposed scheme and, through Kissinger, secured Nixon's assurances that State Department pressure would cease and that deliveries of aircraft,

---

[8]Ibid., p. 204 ff.

which Rogers had intimated might be deferred, would proceed on schedule.[9] The Israeli Embassy in Washington made no secret of its favorable view of the President's campaign for reelection the following year. By 1972 more American military and economic assistance had been extended to Israel under the Nixon Administration than under all previous administrations combined. It was demonstrated to Israel's leaders that they could count on American arms and other support while preserving the freedom to act solely in accord with their concept of their country's interests.

King Hussein's actions had inflamed opinion in much of the Arab world. Both Libya and Kuwait suspended the subsidies agreed on at the Khartoum Conference (although Saudi payments continued). A truce between the King and PLO was imposed by the Arab League during a meeting at Cairo in September 1970. It soon became a dead letter. Hussein sought to assert mastery of his own house, and his army was even more determined than he in the aim of subduing the commandos. A major airlift of American arms and liberal United States financial aid permitted him to undertake a campaign, lasting until July 1971, by which Jordan was totally cleared of Palestine guerrillas. Over 2000 were captured and interned, while the remnants fled to Syria, some even to Israeli-held territory. By this time the fire-eating 'Atāsī-Jadīd-Zu'ayyin regime in Syria had been supplanted by a more moderate faction of the Ba'th under Hāfiz al-Asad who, as defense minister, had opposed the Syrian invasion of Jordan. The new government itself moved to restrain commando activity within Syria, confiscated arms shipments to them on arrival at Syrian ports, and even permitted Jordanian trucks to cross Syrian territory to transport weapons, destined for the Jordan Army, unloaded at Latakia.

The Palestinians emerged from the struggle weakened in military strength and further divided among themselves, but unquestionably an Arab nation on the level of the Syrians, the Egyptians, the Lebanese, and the rest, responsible for their own decisions, with their own national aims coinciding only partially with those of the Arab world at large. Aside from the Syrian effort, quickly abandoned, no Arab state came to their aid except by propaganda

---

[9]Ibid., p. 208.

or funds. The Arab League peace-making effort mediated between them and the Jordan government as between sovereign equals. Whatever credibility Hussein had previously possessed as authoritative spokesman for the Palestinians was gone forever. Treated for two decades as anonymous refugees, without personality, and an embarrassment to the international community's conscience, the Palestinian people could no longer be ignored. Their views and their consent were henceforth an essential element of any lasting, viable solution of the Arab-Israel issue, no matter how many years might be required for the great powers, the United Nations, the Arab governments, and Israel to accept and act on the fact. Meanwhile, anomic violence commended itself to them as the only available channel of communication with a deaf world.

Hussein's confrontation with the commandos (who had the general, if passive, sympathy of the two thirds of Jordan's population who were Palestinians) coincided with the growing use of international terrorism by various guerrilla formations outside the effective control of PLO and Fatah. These no doubt made a strategic mistake in throwing the weight of their military capability against the Jordanian—and later the Lebanese—regime instead of against the more formidable Israeli target. The error contributed to a sharp decrease in material support to the resistance movement from some Arab sources that had donated liberally in the immediate wake of the 1967 war. Fearing that their cause would be sacrificed in the search for an Arab-Israeli peace, some Palestinians sought to keep Arab and world opinion focused on it by hijacking airliners (five such incidents occurred on a single weekend in September 1970) and other wanton violence such as the murder of Israeli athletes at the 1972 Olympic games in Munich. These acts aroused some sympathy on the fringes of Arab and world opinion; on balance, however, they damaged the image of the Palestinians generally and diverted attention from their genuine grievances. They made it politically inexpedient for the United States to support United Nations resolutions condemning the terrorist raids freely conducted by the Israeli regular forces into the Arab states and were a major factor in the still-continuing American effort to create international institutions to combat terrorism and sabotage.

TOWARD RENEWED HOSTILITIES

The six years between the June War and the eruption of a fourth Arab-Israeli conflict were a period of rapid change in several Arab countries, in the relations among the Arab states, and in the international political setting. Preoccupied with the slow winding down of its involvement in Vietnam, with its initiatives to place relations with the major communist powers on a new, more stable footing, and later with domestic political crisis, the United States conducted normal exchanges with friendly Arab regimes while leaving the initiative toward restoration of official relations to the Arab states that had severed them. Administration spokesmen made clear from time to time America's faithfulness to the Rogers Plan and United Nations Security Council Resolution 242 as the proper basis for an Arab-Israel settlement; in the absence of movement toward that goal, ensuring Israeli military preponderance appeared to minimize the danger of renewed hostilities. While future energy supplies were of mounting concern and discussion, the debate did not directly relate fuel problems to American policies toward the Arab states; adhering to long-established procedures, the Administration left the question of access to Arab oil largely in the hands of the companies and countries concerned.

Revolutionary ferment in the Arab world continued, in the attempt to find Arab paths to the goals of independence, dignity, and justice. The military coups of 1969 in the Sudan and Libya show how closely the extremes of the political spectrum meet. In the Sudan the 'Abbūd junta (1958–1964), which had endeavored to conduct government without politics, was followed by the revival of parliamentary politics with rather little government worthy of the name. A disproportionate share of the energy and resources of both regimes was absorbed in the effort to assert central authority over the Sudan's three southern provinces whose population—Nilotic, Hamitic, and Bantu tribesmen, animists and Christians by faith—they sought to transform into Muslim Arabs. Thousands of southern Sudanese were converts and protégés of American (and other) missionaries, and their harsh repression strictly limited the willingness of an otherwise sympathetic United States government to assist the Sudan's economic development.

The Sudanese communist party, the largest and most efficient in Africa, flourished underground during the 'Abbūd era and emerged as a major political force after its overthrow. Eleven of its members were elected to parliament in the 1965 elections, but excluded by the conventional parties from participation in its proceedings. The communists were consequently eager allies in the coup led by Colonel (later General) Ja'far al-Numayrī in May 1969. The new junta represented a coalition among two branches of the communist party, Arab Socialists allied with Egypt's Arab Socialist Union, and a socialistic Sudanese Nationalist movement to which Numayrī himself belonged. The announced aim of the new regime was a politically united Sudan, its freedom from dependence on Western influences, and rapid social and economic development along socialist lines. It moved promptly and vigorously to nationalize the country's banks, insurance companies, and business firms (largely Western-owned), to reorient its trade toward the Soviet Union and other communist countries, and to align the Sudan with the radical Arab states. The most powerful conservative opposition element, the Ansar religious sect, was crushed by the massacre of its spiritual leader and several hundred of his adherents.

The communists saw their strong position in Numayrī's government as merely one step toward the assumption of exclusive power. They ignored the junta's order to disband their party and disregarded its policies. In the spring of 1971 Numayrī moved to dissolve the party's front organizations and its core structure. In July communist officers arrested the entire junta and proclaimed a new government, which was enthusiastically recognized and supported by the embassies in Khartoum of the communist states, but sharply denounced by Egypt and Libya. The coup succeeded only momentarily; army units loyal to Numayrī revolted and restored him to authority. The episode resulted in the decimation of the Sudanese communists and virtual destruction of their organization. Sudanese external policy swung away from close association with the communist states toward renewed cooperation with the West and closer association with Saudi Arabia and Kuwait, both of which were able and willing to assist in the Sudan's economic progress. Sudanese trade with the United States began to expand; full diplomatic relations were resumed in July 1972, but tragically compromised early the next year by the assassination of two American diplomats in Khartoum by Palestinian terrorists.

Numayrī's outstanding achievement has been the negotiation of an accord with the southern Sudanese leadership providing for broad autonomy in the south. The Regional Autonomy Agreement, signed in Addis Ababa in March 1972, gives the south its own legislature (but a strong voice also in the central government), its own official language (English), authority over its economic development, and guaranteed civil freedoms. The Anyanya, the southern guerrilla forces, were amalgamated with the Sudanese national army. The settlement represents a partial reorientation of the Sudan away from the Arab world and toward sub-Saharan Africa unpalatable to some Arab states and to many northern Sudanese. Numayrī, on the other hand, gained substantial prestige in Africa and the West and vastly enhanced prospects for foreign development assistance. The United States responded promptly to an appeal through the United Nations for assistance in the rehabilitation of nearly a million southern Sudanese displaced persons and refugees, and reinstituted its aid program suspended in 1967.

The right-wing coup of September 1969 in Libya that toppled King Idris instituted a military regime that fits no tidy category. Colonel Mu'ammar Qadhdhāfī, who led the usual Revolutionary Command Council, invoked an undefined "socialism" and, indeed, embarked on a radical restructuring of Libyan economy and society, while proclaiming Islam the basis of authority and the *sharī'a* the supreme law of the land. He conducted an Islamic "cultural revolution" reminiscent in style and illogic of its Chinese precedent, but quite different in content. Vociferously anticommunist, the regime nevertheless moved toward relations with the communist states, avoided by its predecessor. It placed itself in the vanguard of the oil-producing states in demanding a rising share of profits, increased participation and, finally, outright nationalization. In external affairs it became the most vocal and uncompromising proponent of the Arab struggle against Zionism and against the interests of the United States as Israel's principal backer. It moved immediately to loosen the close and cordial ties that the monarchy had maintained with America. On its demand a sizable Peace Corps contingent was withdrawn in October 1969 and the

Wheelus Air Base evacuated by the end of June 1970. During 1972 a series of (largely inoperative) bilateral Libyan-American agreements was formally terminated, and the size of United States diplomatic representation in Libya substantially reduced. In June 1973 the Qadhdhāfī regime carried out a politically motivated nationalization of an American oil concessionary, Nelson Bunker Hunt, against which the United States government protested unavailingly. Two months later 51% of the Occidental Oil Company's Libyan operation was taken over, on terms negotiated with the company, and similar measures were soon applied to the country's entire petroleum industry.

The Arabian Peninsula was not left untouched by the winds of change. In South Yemen the National Liberation Front, which replaced British rule in November 1967, promptly renamed the South Arabian Federation the People's Republic of Southern Yemen and, in 1970, still more emphatically the People's Democratic Republic of Yemen. Adopting "continuing revolution" methods, it has systematically and violently liquidated the traditional ruling and propertied classes and extended state control ever more pervasively throughout the economy and society. With material and technical aid from the Soviet Union, China, and Cuba, the regime has undertaken an ambitious program to subvert and radicalize the entire Peninsula. It is closely associated with a dissident movement that has smoldered for many years in Oman's province of Dhofar and with the Popular Front for the Liberation of the Occupied Arabian Gulf, aimed at the existing regimes in the Persian Gulf emirates. During the early 1970s it conducted a concerted campaign of terrorism and sabotage in the Yemen Arab Republic, punctuated by border clashes between the regular forces of the two states. The United States raised its consulate at Aden to embassy status upon South Yemen's independence; the mission was closed in October 1969, however, and official contact ended.

The Sultanate of Oman[10] emerged from its long isolation in July 1970 when Crown Prince Qābūs deposed his father, took the throne, instituted a policy of cultivating friendly relations with his Saudi and Gulf neighbors, applied for membership in the United Nations and the Arab League, and turned the country's modest but

---

[10]The new regime dropped the name "Muscat" from the country's traditional title.

growing oil revenues to the modernization and development of the realm. The United States which, for many decades had had only sporadic, if cordial, dealings with the Sultanate, responded to these changes by opening a resident embassy in Muscat in July 1972.

The last formal vestiges of European imperialism in Arab lands disappeared when Britain's special treaty relationships with the Persian Gulf states were terminated December 1, 1971. The British decision to withdraw all military forces from the area and to relinquish a political position of long standing was announced in 1968. There followed protracted negotiations among the rulers of the states involved looking toward a possible federation of states embracing them all. The discussions were complicated by a tangle of dynastic rivalries and animosities between Bahrain and Qatar and among the shaikhly families of the Trucial Coast, by ill-defined boundaries, by the vast disparity between the oil-rich statelets (Qatar, Abu Dhabi, Dubai and, to a lesser degree, Bahrain) and their poverty-stricken neighbors, by shadowy Iranian imperial claims and ambitions, by Saudi Arabia's drawing power and suspected territorial aspirations, and by the uncertain factor of a resurgent Oman. The obstacles to comprehensive union proved insurmountable. On December 2, 1971 the Trucial territories of Abu Dhabi, Dubai, Sharjah, 'Ajman, Umm al-Qaywain, and Fujairah proclaimed their independence as the United Arab Emirates, to which Ras al-Khaimah, the remaining Trucial Coast state, shortly adhered. Bahrain and Qatar went their separate ways as independent entities. The United States moved rapidly to open diplomatic relations with the newly independent governments and emphasized its interest by a visit to Bahrain by Secretary of State Rogers in July 1972, during which he publicly expressed American concern for the development of strong, stable governments in the area, cooperating constructively among themselves and free of disruptive outside interference.[11] The small Gulf states began their independent careers without major convulsion, pursuing moderate policies and cooperating closely with their large Saudi neighbor, the Arab League, and (for those blessed with oil wealth) OPEC.

---

[11] *United States Foreign Policy 1972* (Washington, D.C.: USGPO, Department of State Publication 8699, 1973), p. 387.

In Saudi Arabia change took the form of a searching reexamination of the regime's long-standing attitude that oil economics and management constituted a separate set of problems, unrelated to those of international politics. At some cost to his standing among Arab leaders, King Faisal had been consistently friendly to the United States. Considering communism a mortal danger to the Arabs, he had, in recent years, devoted a significant portion of his energies to mobilizing the Islamic world's political forces against radicalist subversion. He had acknowledged that his country had a moral obligation to see that the industrialized nations were not deprived of the energy they need. At the same time, he became more and more convinced that what he saw as the one-sided United States policy in support of Israel and its indifference to Arab interests and aspirations would eventually drive the entire Arab world into the communist camp and destroy the few Arab friends America had left, including his own regime. Faisal long refused to be swayed by arguments of militant Arab leaders that Arab oil resources should be used as an instrument in the pursuit of Arab national objectives. As late as September 1972 he put forward, through his Petroleum Minister Ahmad Zaki Yamani, the suggestion (which elicited no affirmative United States response) that, under a long-term arrangement, Saudi crude oil be given privileged access to the American market, while Saudi revenues would be invested in downstream oil operations in the United States. By the summer of 1973 the King's attitudes had evolved significantly. He had meanwhile become seriously preoccupied with the prudent conservation of his country's reserves, with the strictly finite level at which its revenue could be absorbed by the Saudi Arabian economy, and with the declining value of foreign currency balances (Saudi Arabia had already lost several hundred million dollars in currency devaluations). He now warned that Saudi oil production must be held to a level realistic in terms of the Saudi economy and, furthermore, that Saudi Arabia would find it difficult to continue cooperation in the petroleum field with the United States unless the latter moved toward a more balanced policy in the Middle East. The response of United States government spokesmen to this shift in posture was to declare, somewhat airily, that oil considerations would not affect American policy in the Middle East. American opinion was little moved; the sentiment was widespread that embargos and boycotts do not work, and that the Arab oil producers were as dependent on the United States as the latter was on them.

An era in the Arab world closed at the end of September 1970 with the death of Gamāl 'Abd al-Nasser. In his eighteen-year career the Egyptian leader had contributed mightily to the achievement of Arab freedom from foreign tutelage and to the assertion of Arab self-respect and dignity. His final years nevertheless were years of disillusion and frustration. The unity of Arab effort and purpose for which he had striven was as elusive as ever. Egypt was beholden, for its economic survival, to the traditional Arab monarchs he had sought to depose. The Palestinians, whose patrimony he had promised to restore, remained homeless. The Egyptian army, which was to have fulfilled that promise, had shown itself incapable of preventing the loss in war of a sizable chunk of the national territory and even of protecting the remainder, except by the demeaning presence of foreign advisors and auxiliaries in their thousands.

The heir apparent, inasmuch as he was Vice President, was Anwar al-Sādāt, long a friend and associate of Nasser but somewhat on the margin of the late President's tight inner circle of intelligence chiefs, political organizers, and military officers. This Egyptian "Mafia" allowed the succession to pass to Sādāt in the expectation that he would be easily controlled and that the reality of power would rest in their hands. The new President soon demonstrated that he intended to make and pursue his own policies, domestic and foreign, including the liberalization of commercial and industrial activity, relaxed restrictions on civil freedoms, strengthening Egypt's relations with the moderate Arab countries, and a cautious mending of fences with the West. Within three months the shift in posture was reflected in new IBRD loans to Egypt, the resumption of wheat and vegetable oil shipments from the United States, and restoration of Egyptian relations with West Germany. In May 1971 an ill-coordinated attempt was made by the aforementioned clique to depose Sādāt. He parried the plot with little difficulty, brought its authors to trial, imprisoned them for long terms, and purged their power bases—the intelligence services, the Arab Socialist Union, and the armed forces—of their sympathizers. The President's own position was nevertheless uncertain. Egypt was troubled by strikes, demonstrations, and other signs of unrest. Student riots erupted, demanding the resumption of war against Israel and action against American interests in the Middle East. Somewhat rashly, Sādāt publicly announced that 1971 would be the "year of decision" for the Israel question.

The Soviet leaders had obvious reason for concern at the trend of the new regime and became genuinely alarmed when the perpetrators of the abortive May coup, precisely those Egyptians with whom they had been accustomed to work, were imprisoned. President Podgorny traveled to Cairo in unseemly haste and succeeded in concluding with Sādāt a fifteen-year treaty of friendship and cooperation of which the secret articles promised continuing Soviet military support. Egyptian-Soviet relations came under considerable strain in July 1971, when Sādāt gave strong political and material support to Numayrī's action against the Sudanese communists. Once the danger from the regional communists receded, however, Sādāt began to drift toward Soviet points of view in his public pronouncements. The "year of decision" passed without movement toward the recovery of occupied Egyptian territory, and action became more and more urgent to rehabilitate Sādāt's sagging prestige. He pressed a somewhat reluctant Soviet Union for the supply of offensive weapons, including the latest-model MIGs and surface-to-surface missiles. The Soviets' assistance to India in her war with Pakistan during the winter of 1971 to 1972 provided a temporary excuse for refusal of a request they found embarrassing. They had not the slightest illusion that additional sophisticated arms to the Egyptian forces would tip the balance of military capability against Israel nor any desire to commit their own troops in support of an Egyptian attack. More particularly, the Soviets attached overriding importance to the maturing negotiations for a détente with the United States, which a Middle East war might compromise or wreck.

For the Arabs confronting Israel, détente thus implied a substantial abandonment by the Soviet Union of its support for their aspirations. It raised poignant problems for Sādāt, who had failed to translate his boastful talk into effective action to regain the Sinai. The presence on Egyptian soil of upward of 20,000 Russian military personnel, a threat to Sādāt's freedom of action and potentially to his tenure, whose relations with their Egyptian pupils were furthermore by no means harmonious, lost much of its justification. A month after the Moscow summit meeting of June 1972, when the signature of a long series of Soviet-American agreements appeared to mark a decisive reordering of relations between the superpowers, Sādāt brusquely ordered the repatriation of Soviet technicians operating Egyptian seaports and airfields, and most (not all) military advisors. Neither side had reason to push the crisis to an irreparable break. Egypt remained dependent on the Soviet Union for replacements and spare parts, any future increment of armament, and political support; the Soviets, whatever their disillusion with Sādāt, had invested too much wealth and prestige to abandon Egypt and, by keeping their hand in, could hope for happier relations with some future successor regime. Sādāt embarked on a tentative movement toward rapprochement with the United States in the hope of American action to induce Israel to begin relinquishing the occupied territories under some version of the Rogers Plan more favorable to Egypt. These exchanges reached a climax in March 1973 when Hafez Ismail, Sādāt's security advisor, visited Washington and conferred with President Nixon who, according to Egyptian accounts, told him the United States would exert its influence on Israel only if Egypt publicly undertook to make concessions going beyond the Rogers Plan; only a few days later a presidential decision was announced for the supply to Israel of forty-eight additional Phantoms. Sādāt, losing all hope of breaking the deadlock by political means, saw no alternative to the resort to armed action that he had so often threatened. In order to enhance the chances of military success, he instituted planning with Syria for a coordinated attack, and with King Faisal for the simultaneous imposition of an oil embargo to deter the United States from intervening in behalf of Israel. The decision was furthermore made known, along with urgent appeals for new arms, to the Soviet leadership. The latter, having succeeded in obtaining exceedingly attractive terms in their agreements with the United States on grain purchases, strategic arms limitations, and other matters, judged that détente was substantial enough to withstand the strain of a new round of war in the Middle East; during the spring and summer they resumed the flow of military supplies to Egypt and Syria including, for the first time, equipment of a clearly offensive instead of primarily defensive character.

Despite preoccupation with the burgeoning Watergate scandals the Arab military buildup did not go unnoticed in Washington; no particularly ominous conclusions were drawn from it, however. The senior American leaders were not entirely immune from the propensity, common among the Arabs, to be persuaded by their own rhetoric. The President and his Security Advisor had encouraged the public to believe that the era of confrontation had ended, that the linkages constructed with the Soviet Union would promote the evolution of Soviet society toward open, liberal, democratic institutions, and that Soviet-American frictions would henceforth be dealt with by discussion instead of muscle flexing. The United States and the Soviet Union had formally covenanted to consult with each other on situations likely to disturb their mutual relations; it was unthinkable that the Soviet Union, knowing that Arab states intended to go to war, should fail to inform the United States and to collaborate on measures to avert a crisis or to confine it within reasonable bounds. The American leadership judged that if the Middle East powder keg exploded, the spark would most likely take the form of an Israeli preemptive strike, and they had warned the Israeli government against any such initiative. On September 22 Dr. Henry Kissinger took the oath of office as Secretary of State, without relinquishing his national security functions at the White House. In early meetings with the press in his new capacity he expressed the President's concern and his own at the dangerous nature of the Middle East situation, and it was assumed that he planned some new initiative toward a settlement. In the context of the United States General Assembly's annual session, then beginning, he took special pains to meet with the representatives of the Arab states, the more moderate of which gave cautious indications that they would welcome a new American peace-making effort. News of the Egyptian and Syrian attack against Israeli forces in the occupied territories thus came as a rude surprise for which America was ill prepared.

CHAPTER IX

The October War and Beyond

T HE FOURTH ROUND OF FULL-SCALE ARAB-ISRAEL WAR AMPLY FULFILLED PRESIDENT NIXON'S PROPHESY that the Middle East powder keg would presently ignite if not defused and thereby endanger world peace. The conflict was, it may be noted, not among minor military powers. The number of tanks the Egyptians and Syrians committed—about 4500—was larger than that of the entire Western alliance in Europe; the scale of the Sinai tank battle was exceeded in history only in one major World War II engagement between Germany and Russia. Arab tank losses were in the range of 1800, while Israel lost more than 500 of her initial 1700. Somewhat less than half of Syria and Egypt's 1000 planes and more than 100 Israeli aircraft were destroyed. The widespread assumption that any Arab-Israel war would last only a few days was disproved; a ceasefire was not achieved until October 22, and it became truly effective only a week later. The war was fought at a higher technological level than before; sophisticated antitank and antiaircraft weapons in the hands of trained Arab soldiers sharply reduced the edge Israel had previously enjoyed through the superior mobility of her armor and effective control of the air over the battlefield. In contrast with 1956 and 1967, the Arab armies were not destroyed; they were outmaneuvered and defeated, but they remained in being as potentially operational military forces. As a consequence of the great powers' resupply operations, both sides emerged from the war with a military capability but little impaired. Arab high military strategy exhibited some serious faults. On the other hand, the stereotype of the Arab soldier as incapable of learning to use modern weapons effectively was discredited, along with that of Israeli invincibility. One significant lesson of the war was its demonstration that the Arabs were capable of planning and carrying out major, coordinated programs of military action. Another was the renewed confirmation that the United States and the Soviet Union perceived their respective interests to be so closely engaged in the Middle East that they would not permit an Arab-Israel war to be fought to a decisive conclusion among the contending parties.

On the morning of October 6 three Syrian armored divisions, with upward of 1000 tanks, advanced along a twenty-five-mile front against the lightly defended Israeli lines on the Golan heights, while paratroops seized Israeli observation posts on Mount Hermon, the strategic key to the area. After a day's fighting, the Syrian armor threatened to spill over into the heavily populated Galilee Plain. During the following two days, the Syrian attack lost its momentum; liaison failed with Moroccan and Druze forces holding Mount Hermon, which was lost. Hastily mobilized Israeli forces were concentrated against the Syrian advance, which was stalled by October 9. An Israeli counterattack drove the Syrians (with Jordanian and Iraqi troops that had joined the battle) in six days of fighting to a point near Sa'sa', twenty-two miles from Damascus, where a stalemate was reached.

Concurrently with the Syrian attack, Egyptian infantry crossed the Suez Canal in a well-executed operation, smashed the Bar Lev Line of Israeli fortifications, and dug in at a five-mile depth from the Canal. The Egyptian command was remarkably deliberate in bringing its armor across the Canal and renewing the advance, in part perhaps because of the spirited but localized counterattacks undertaken by the opposing Israeli forces and Egyptian reluctance to move beyond the shelter of the surface-to-air missile screen to the west of the Canal. Armored units began to cross the waterway only on October 11 and, when the offensive resumed on October 14, it faced the bulk of Israel's military might. Within two days the Israelis were in a position to undertake a counterattack. A wedge was driven between the Egyptian Second and Third armies, to the north and south respectively, and pushed to the banks of the Canal at the north end of the Great Bitter Lake. The Israelis exploited this success by establishing a bridgehead on the west bank, which was expanded to a length of twenty miles and a depth of twenty-five, threatening communication between Cairo and the city of Suez. By October 22, when a United Nations ceasefire appeal was accepted by both Egypt and Israel, the latter's forces had virtually surrounded the Egyptian Third Army. Both sides continued operations to improve their positions, in disregard of the ceasefire, and the conflict immediately developed into a super-power confrontation.

The war erupted at a moment when the accumulating Watergate revelations had already raised doubt that President Nixon could serve out his second term. Notwithstanding public reassessment of some aspects of détente with the Soviet Union, the Administration's accomplishments in external affairs were generally acknowledged to be its strongest asset; a major failure in foreign policy would further compromise its position. Preoccupied with his domestic troubles, the President gave only broad and intermittent guidance to his Secretary of State in the management of the Middle East crisis. The Washington Special Actions Group, composed of the Secretary, his Deputy Kenneth Rush, Assistant Secretary Joseph Sisco, Defense Secretary James R. Schlesinger, Admiral Thomas H. Moorer, Chairman of the Joint Chiefs of Staff, and CIA Director William E. Colby, met on October 6 and decided on initial emergency measures, including the despatch of Sixth Fleet units toward the disturbed area. Direction of events thereafter was principally a one-man show, at some expense to optimum coordination within the government establishment.

At the President's direction, Kissinger's initial efforts were aimed at preventing a full-scale war and at effecting an early ceasefire in cooperation with the Russians. He sent messages also to King Faisal and King Hussein, requesting their good offices; the former responded by urging the United States to secure Israel's withdrawal from Arab lands and the honoring of Palestinian rights. The Secretary's peace-keeping endeavor failed; the spirit of détente was insufficient to persuade the Soviets to press on Syria and Egypt the abandonment of a military action that was already showing gains. As it became clear that a full-scale war was in train, Kissinger determined that its outcome should be a situation in which, neither side having suffered a clear defeat, productive Arab-Israeli negotiations might be instituted. It would be demonstrated to the Arabs that they could not hope for a decisive victory with Russian arms and support and that they could realize their aspirations only with the assistance and mediation of the United States. Such a program entailed furnishing to Israel, whose losses were unexpectedly heavy during the first days of combat, arms in carefully measured quantities sufficient for her to regain the initiative but not to repeat the spectacular 1967 victory. This limited aim and tactic lacked appeal, for obvious and contrasting reasons, either to Israel or to American defense and oil company officials anxious to avoid provoking the Arab states, by any assistance to Israel, into interrupting the supply of oil to the American armed forces and the civilian economy. The Secretary's plan was vulnerable not only to domestic political pressures, but to Soviet action affecting the battlefield situation.

The Soviet leaders, notwithstanding the less than satisfactory state of their relations with Egypt and Syria, interposed no obstacle to their resort to war for the limited purpose of breaking the deadlock over the occupied areas and provided the bridging equipment and other war material needed to mount the attack. Encouraged by the initial Arab advances, they blocked America's early attempts toward a United Nations-imposed ceasefire. As early as October 10, they began a large-scale airlift and accelerated surface shipments to replace arms destroyed in battle, and markedly increased their naval force in the Mediterranean. They undertook an intensive political campaign to mobilize third world opinion in support of the Arab war effort. The Kremlin objective seems to have been to effect a ceasefire as soon as the Arab forces had won the maximum advantage from their surprise attack, and before Israel had time to mount an effective counteroffensive. At the end of the second day's operations, Brezhnev informed President Nixon that he was prepared to consider a ceasefire in the United Nations, expressing the hope that the fighting could be contained. By October 10 the Soviet Union was urging the immediate imposition of a ceasefire by the United Nations Security Council, a notion that outraged the Israelis, who were determined to force the Arabs back to their prewar positions.

On October 16 President Sādāt made his first formal public statement during the war. Although Israel had now seized the initiative, he exhibited full confidence in the battlefield situation. He declared Egypt's willingness to accept an immediate ceasefire, subject to Israeli withdrawal from the territories occupied in 1967, and furthermore to attend a United Nations-sponsored peace conference once the evacuation were accomplished. On the same day Premier Kosygin traveled to Cairo to discuss peace terms and reportedly proposed to Sādāt a settlement by which Egypt would consent to minor concessions from the 1967 truce lines, while the Soviet Union and the United States would guarantee and police the new, definitive Egypt-Israel borders. Sādāt rejected the notion of any sacrifice of Egyptian territory[1] and hesitated to suspend hostilities while Israeli forces were operating west of the Canal. He nevertheless reluctantly agreed to a ceasefire on condition it were enforced by the Soviet Union and the United States or, if need be, by the former alone.[2] The Russians appear to have realized sooner and more accurately than Sādāt the dangerous strategic implications of the Israeli operations, both east and west of the Canal. After the Premier's return to Moscow on October 19, an urgent review of the military situation led to the conclusion that the Egyptians were headed for disaster, and that the Soviet Union now needed the help of the United States in imposing an early ceasefire. Invoking the agreed Soviet-American procedures for the handling of crises, Brezhnev requested President Nixon to send Dr. Kissinger to Moscow for urgent consultations.

Sentiment in the American Congress, the press, and much of the public was thoroughly aroused from the outset in behalf of Israel as the victim of aggression, with little reflection that Israel was defending Arab land. The Administration took a certain political risk in the first days of the war in holding its assistance to Israel to a level unlikely to invite Arab retaliation. On Monday, October 8, the first working day after the outbreak of hostilities, the Senate adopted a resolution deploring the outbreak of war and calling on the Administration to seek a ceasefire and restoration of the October 6 truce lines. Pressure by individual senators and representatives on the White House for prompt and effective support of Israel intensified as details of the Soviet airlift to Syria and Egypt became known. Following strong representations by the Israeli Ambassador in Washington, Nixon approved in principle the re-

---

[1]Walter Laqueur, *Confrontation: The Middle East and World* Politics (New York: Bantam Books, 1974), p. 183.
[2]Marvin Kalb and Bernard Kalb, *Kissinger* (Boston: Little, Brown, 1974), p. 481.

placement of Israel's battle losses in planes, tanks, and other war-like material and agreed to furnish electronic devices to neutralize the surface-to-air missiles that were taking a heavy toll of Israel's aircraft. The Pentagon retreated only gradually from its reluctance to take action offensive to the Arabs. Initially, Israel was required to send its own cargo planes, with identifying markings effaced, to take delivery of equipment at military installations within the United States. On October 10, at Kissinger's urging, the Defense Department began to explore the feasibility of chartering civilian planes to transport cargoes to Israel; no company, it proved, was prepared to take the involved risk of Arab reprisals. On October 12 Defense Secretary Schlesinger, meeting with the Israeli Ambassador, stated that American military aircraft would fly equipment to the Azores, but that onward transportation would be an Israeli responsibility; he added that Phantom aircraft would be delivered only at the rate of one and one half per day, to an eventual maximum of fifteen. The Ambassador, who had for several days made frantic demands on Kissinger for an American match of the Soviet airlift, punctuated with more and more explicit threats to mobilize the Zionist lobby and its sympathizers in Congress and the press[3] against the Administration's aloof posture, appealed at once to the Secretary of State. The latter, by then having lost hope that the Russians, through respect for détente, would restrain the Arabs, and having moreover received intelligence reports of the alert of three Soviet airborne divisions, apparently for service in the Middle East, referred the matter to the President. Nixon, in a climactic meeting of his senior advisors on October 13, ordered an all-out airlift by American military aircraft direct to Israel, with a refueling stop in the Azores, and the first C-5 Galaxies were on the way before the end of the day. This enabled Israel to place its counteroffensive plans in full operation on October 15. On October 19 the President requested Congressional approval of $2.2 billion in military assistance to Israel, with discretion to provide it as grant aid. This move effectively disarmed domestic critics of the Administration's attitude toward the war. The Arab oil-pro-

---

[3]Senate Foreign Relations Committee, *Emergency Assistance to Israel and Cambodia* (Washington: USGPO, 1973), pp. 130–132; p. 162. See also Kalb and Kalb, op. cit., pp. 450–478.

ducing states, on the other hand, took it as a clear signal that United States partiality toward Israel remained unchanged, and they retorted by suspending shipments of petroleum to America.

The shift of tide on the battlefield brought the United States and the Soviet Union into agreement on the urgent desirability of a ceasefire and movement toward a more stable situation in the Middle East. In response to Brezhnev's invitation Kissinger flew to Moscow, arriving on the evening of October 20. The ensuing two days set something of a speed record in multilateral diplomacy. Kissinger and Brezhnev worked out the following brief and somewhat ambiguous formula, which was to become United Nations Security Council Resolution 338.

The Security Council
1. Calls upon all parties to the present fighting to cease all firing and terminate all military activity immediately, no later than 12 hours after the moment of the adoption of this decision, in the positions they now occupy;
2. Calls upon the parties concerned to start immediately after the cease-fire the implementation of Security Council resolution 242 (1967) in all of its parts;
3. Decides that, immediately and concurrently with the ceasefire, negotiations start between the parties concerned under appropriate auspices aimed at establishing a just and durable peace in the Middle East.[4]

Kissinger elicited, and assured the Kremlin of, the Israeli government's undertaking to respect a ceasefire in place, and similar acquiescence was forthcoming promptly from the Arab combatants. The hastily assembled United Nations Security Council adopted the joint text early on the morning of October 22.

The ceasefire failed to hold on the ground. On the crucial southern front the Egyptian Third Army continued its unsuccessful attempt to break the Israeli encirclement, while Israeli troops west of the Canal consolidated their bridgehead and completed their blockade of the city of Suez. The Kremlin leaders concluded that they had been duped by Kissinger for the purpose of ensuring a decisive Israeli victory, a supposition made plausible by the fact that Kissinger, on his return trip from Moscow, stopped in Tel Aviv for discussions with Prime Minister Meir. They at once initi-

---

[4]Senate Foreign Relations Committee, op. cit., p. 8.

ated military measures which, as interpreted by American intelligence services, indicated that the Soviet Union intended to intervene directly in the Middle East with as many as seven divisions of troops, under cover of missiles capable of firing nuclear warheads. On October 24 President Sādāt appealed both to the United States and to the Soviet Union to send troops to enforce the ceasefire; he began soliciting third world support for a United Nations resolution to that end. The United States declared its firm opposition to intervention in the area by any nuclear power. That evening Brezhnev addressed a stiffly worded message to Nixon condemning Israel's ceasefire violations and proposing the immediate despatch of Soviet and American troops to impose an end to hostilities, failing which the Soviet Union would consider taking "appropriate" action unilaterally, with the "gravest consequences" for Israel. On the recommendation of the National Security Council, the President ordered the American armed establishment, including nuclear strike forces, on virtually global alert, as an unmistakable warning that the United States would forcefully oppose Soviet unilateral intervention. His reply to Brezhnev insisted that the United Nations should provide peacekeeping forces, drawn from nonnuclear powers that were not permanent members of the Security Council. Faced with evidence of American determination and anxious, after all, to preserve the benefits of détente, the Soviets coordinated action with the United States toward the despatch of a United Nations peace-keeping force constituted according to the American view. This was rapidly accomplished, under United Nations Security Council Resolution 340, adopted on October 25, which furthermore specified a return to the positions occupied at the time the October 22 resolution took effect. The American alert, which had alarmed America's European allies as well as the American public, was rapidly relaxed, whereas the Soviet Union kept its forces in a state of readiness. The possibility of direct Russian intervention thus persisted, in some measure balancing the advantageous Israeli position on the ground.

Secretary Kissinger now had the elements of the negotiating situation toward which he had directed American policy, and he at once applied his talents toward a personal mediation among the Middle Eastern leaders concerned in order, first, to stabilize the precarious ceasefire, then to achieve progress on further steps in the direction of peace and, finally, to persuade the Arab states to lift their oil embargo against the United States. The Secretary's exercise in "shuttle" diplomacy over the succeeding months has been justly praised. In broad terms, it resulted in the following succession of accomplishments.

1. The restoration of full diplomatic relations between the United States and Egypt.
2. Direct conversations between Egyptian and Israeli officers on the modalities of implementing the ceasefire. While these discussions, begun on November 11 at kilometer marker 101 of the Cairo-Suez road, broke down, the face-to-face meeting was an innovation with important psychological impact.
3. The agreement of Israel, Egypt, and Jordan to attend a peace conference at Geneva under the chairmanship of the United Nations Secretary General, with the participation of the United States and the Soviet Union. The conference met for two days, on December 21 and 22. While it resulted in no decisive action, it established a mechanism that remains available for further direct Arab-Israeli discussions.
4. The negotiation of an Egypt-Israel agreement for disengagement of forces going well beyond the existing ceasefire in place. Signed separately by President Sādāt, Prime Minister Meir, and their military representatives at kilometer 101 on January 18, 1974, the arrangement provided for the withdrawal of Israeli forces from both sides of the Canal to a line about twenty miles east of the waterway; Egyptian and Israeli zones east of the Canal were demarcated, within which troops and arms were limited to specified levels; a buffer strip was set up between the two zones, to be occupied and patrolled by United Nations forces.
5. The conclusion of a disengagement arrangement between Israel and Syria, after three months of renewed hostilities on a reduced scale (February to May 1974). The agreement, signed at Geneva on May 29, marked Syria's first step toward accommodation with Israel and her first public acceptance of United Nations Resolution 242 as a basis for a future settlement.
6. In light of the progress made on the above, the Arab oil-producing states (except for Syria and Libya) lifted their restrictions on oil shipments to the United States on March 18. Saudi Arabia announced an increase of production of 1 million barrels per day, ear-marked for America.

These gains were accomplished in the context of, although not formally in exchange for, substantially enhanced American moral and material commitments to the Middle Eastern countries involved. Economic assistance was promised to Israel, Jordan, Egypt and, potentially, Syria. The United States undertook to help clear the Suez Canal so that it could be reopened to traffic. Atomic energy programs were offered to both Israel and Egypt. The Secretry agreed to seek Congressional authority to place American military assistance to Israel on a long-term basis instead of the normal year-to-year basis. He assured Israel of American political support in such action as it might take in retaliation against incursions by Palestinian militants. The series of negotiations and related understandings led the warring parties to prefer truce to war at one particular juncture in time. Disengagement solved none of the fundamental elements of the Arab-Israel dispute, but simply created conditions in which they could be addressed. As interpreter among the parties, the United States linked its own credibility to their good faith and subsequent actions, and its vital interests, notably the future supply of energy, became peculiarly dependent on its ability to stimulate early movement toward an enduring peace.

THE OIL EMBARGO AND THE WORLD ENERGY CRISIS

The October War dramatized a transformation in the global petroleum industry to which the conflict itself was not a direct contributing factor. The suspension of shipments from Arab producers to certain consuming countries removed all doubt of the Arabs' ability and will to employ oil to further their political interests. Momentous changes in the industry's structure were already in train with profound implications for the control of world energy resources, for the price at which oil would be available to consuming nations, and for international financial stability. The American leadership, which had attached to signs of the approaching war less importance than they merited, similarly discounted indications that the use of Arab oil for political purposes, long advocated and threatened by the more radical Arabs, would soon become a reality. With a complacency that seems feckless in retrospect, the United States ignored the fundamental shift in Saudi Arabian petroleum policy that had occurred by the summer of 1973,[5] notwithstanding King Faisal's frank and painstaking explanation of the kingdom's new attitude to American diplomats and to the international media of mass communication.

President Sādāt visited Saudi Arabia toward the end of August 1973. During his confidential talks with Faisal, it is probable that a general understanding was reached that Saudi Arabia would use the oil weapon against countries aiding Israel in the anticipated renewed hostilities. It is furthermore plausible that the King raised the subject with the Ruler of Kuwait, who paid Saudi Arabia a state visit the following week. The King nevertheless acted with great deliberation after the war's outbreak. Omar Saqqaf, his Minister of State for Foreign Affairs, then in the United States, joined other Arab diplomats in emphasizing the limited aims of the Arab states in the war and expressed hope that it would be brought to a prompt conclusion. The Arab oil producers acted only after the American airlift of arms to Israel was in full operation. On October 14, the day it was made public by the State Department, Kuwait called for a meeting of OAPEC which, in fact, convened two days later. On October 17 the Organization announced that the eleven participating countries would reduce exports by 5% each month to countries unfriendly to the Arab cause until the territories occupied in 1967 were evacuated and Arab rights respected. The next day Abu Dhabi halted oil exports entirely to the United States; Saudi Arabia announced a 10% reduction in production and warned that shipments to the United States would stop if its aid to Israeli forces continued. Libya placed an embargo on exports to the United States and other countries sympathetic to Israel. Saudi Arabia followed suit the next day, and the remaining Arab producers soon after.[6] Bahrain announced the cancellation of its agreement with the United States Navy for the use of its port facilities.[7]

The embargo (which applied to other countries as well, notably the Netherlands and Denmark) remained in effect for five months, until Secretary Kissinger's efforts toward a disengagement agree-

---

[5] See above, p. 240.
[6] Iraq, however, whose economy could ill afford the loss of revenue, quietly continued normal exports.
[7] This action was subsequently reconsidered.

ment between Israel and Egypt bore fruit. President Sādāt, who toured Arab capitals to explain and defend the agreement, is credited with effective encouragement of the oil-producing states to resume shipments. The Secretary's success in convincing the Arabs that the United States had moved toward a less partisan stance in the region was reflected in arrangements for considerably closer cooperation than before between the United States and Saudi Arabia. During a visit to Washington in June 1974 by the King's brother, Prince Fahd, it was agreed that joint committees would be formed to plan the expansion, diversification, and industrialization of Saudi Arabia's economy and the further development of its armed forces. If the procedures operate as anticipated, the Kingdom will have taken an important step toward socioeconomic modernization and toward rational use of the currency balances accumulating rapidly, largely as a result of its active participation in OPEC.

As noted in a previous chapter OPEC was founded for the purpose of joint action among oil-exporting countries against posted-price cuts by the major international companies. Although its efforts in this direction were fruitless for a decade, it was a prime mover in the establishment of patterns of cooperation and solidarity among the member states. It is the joint instrument by which they have revolutionized the structure of the world petroleum industry and the terms on which their oil is accessible to consumers.

The price at which petroleum enters the world market is an emotion-charged issue with many ramifications. For our present purpose it is pertinent to note that during the 1960s, when the United States, Japan, and Western Europe were achieving a remarkable degree of industrial expansion made possible partly by a copious and dependable supply of inexpensive energy, the manufactured products they sold to the oil exporters increased in price by about 50%. The price of crude oil from OPEC producers, given the ample supply and the anxiety of each to maximize its own revenues, remained remarkably stable at a level well below $2 per barrel until 1970. By then Libya had reached a position where accumulated revenues relieved its policy of dependence on current receipts. Its government was thus able, in May 1970, when Syria interrupted the flow of oil through Tapline, to make effective demands for sharply increased tax payments, ordering cutbacks in production as leverage. The disruption of supply to Western European markets brought a steep increase in the cost of tanker charters, which the companies operating in Libya took into account, together with their increased taxes and royalties, in posting a substantial rise in the price of Libyan crude. The Persian Gulf producers promptly demanded and received a proportionate increase, whereupon Libya, on the basis of the greater security and accessibility of its supply, demanded a further rise.

In this chaotic situation the major companies operating in the Persian Gulf area, already threatened by embargoes or nationalization in some producing countries, agreed to negotiate with OPEC a petroleum price policy based on collective bargaining with the governments. Agreements signed at Tehran in February 1971 provided for a standardized 55% income tax rate; a 33 cents per barrel rise in posted prices was to increase by additional annual increments of 5 cents; a further price escalation of 2.5% per year was introduced, to compensate for inflation of the currencies in which oil was traded. The companies were assured that the new price system would remain stable for a period of five years. These agreements constituted a revolution in the structure of the world oil industry. After a decade of modest growth, OPEC had become the catalyst whereby the major exporting countries acquired the ability to coordinate their actions and bring the combined weight of their sovereign authority to bear against the great international companies. It was demonstrated that, acting together, the members of OPEC could successfully assert control over the cost of oil moving in world trade.

In March 1971 discussions were resumed in Tripoli on a new price structure. The Libyan government, which conducted the negotiations, was in an exceptionally strong position in that a number of its concessionaries were independents with few alternative sources of crude. This, with the brilliant tactics of the Libyans and the solidarity of their OPEC colleagues, resulted in an agreement even more advantageous to the government than the Tehran accord. Application of the Tripoli Agreement's provisions to crude from Saudi Arabia and Iraq delivered to Mediterranean pipeline terminals was promptly demanded by those countries' governments and accepted by the companies concerned.[8]

The expectation that these agreements would remain operative through the promised five-year term was soon eroded. In August 1971 the Nixon Administration introduced economic measures that led to successive devaluations of the dollar and to a corresponding decrease in the real value both of the producers' revenues from current exports and of their dollar balances previously accumulated. OPEC-sponsored negotiations at Geneva produced a compensatory 8.49% increase in posted prices in 1972. As the dollar continued to decline into the following year, the Saudi Petroleum Minister pronounced the Tehran agreements "dead or dying." In September 1973 OPEC summoned the principal companies to further talks at Vienna. The meeting was adjourned following the outbreak of the October War. The disruption of the world oil market attendant on the conflict provided an opportunity for the producing states to improve their position through unilateral action. On November 30 Algeria raised the export price of its "sweet" crude from $4.80 to $9.25 per barrel, then the highest price for Middle Eastern oil. Iran announced on December 11 that bids in a recent auction of crude owned by its national company had reached $17.40. On December 22 the oil ministers of the Persian Gulf producers met and raised the tax-reference price of crude by about 10% above the previous level, to $11.65, effective January 1, 1974. This figure became the OPEC guideline throughout the year.

Iran and Venezuela, not the largest Arab producers, had taken the lead in the campaign for higher prices. Saudi Arabia's Oil Minister, in fact, stated in January 1974 that King Faisal feared the destructive impact of oil costs on the general world economy and intended to take steps toward reducing them; he made clear, at the same time, that Saudi Arabia would act only in concert with other Persian Gulf exporters. During 1974, because of the deepening

---

[8]A competent account of the transformation of the industry is Neil H. Jacoby, *Multinational Oil* (New York: Macmillan, 1974), passim. The *Chronology of the Libyan Oil Negotiations* compiled for the Senate Foreign Relations Committee (Washington: USGPO, 1974), is useful. An intriguing and detailed report on the Tripoli negotiations is given in "Agreement: Tripoli—Dramatic 33 Days," *Arab Oil Review,* March-April 1971, pp. 5–19.

global recession, increased costs, and consumption restraints in important countries, oil did not move at the established price. Kuwait, Abu Dhabi, and other governments failed to elicit bids for purchase of their equity oil at the tax-reference price , and the effective selling price stabilized at about 93%. On OPEC recommendation the governments nevertheless continued to improve their position by a 2% rise in royalties imposed on the operating companies. In December OPEC adapted its policy to market realities. It proposed a 38 cent rise for Saudi light crude (the "marker," or standard, from which the price of other grades is figured) from the level of $9.86 current during the last quarter of the year, while reducing from $10.83 to $10.46 the price at which the governments would sell their own crude. The new formula, which was to remain in effect for the first nine months of 1975, was expected to prevent the major companies from passing on higher costs to the consumer by placing a ceiling on the prices at which third parties would buy from the companies. It was furthermore calculated that the companies' profit margin would fall from $1 to somewhat over 20 cents per barrel.

The cumulative effect of these sweeping changes on the 1974 situation of the Arab oil-producing states is reflected in Table 3. Among them they possessed three fifths of the world's proven reserves. With a production rate of 8.4 million barrels a day Saudi Arabia passed the United States as the world's largest producer. Above all, Arab oil revenues soared to nearly $64 billion as a result of the fourfold price increase since mid-1973 in the realized price of their oil. Their accumulated surpluses at the end of the year were estimated to total $60 billion.

The spectacular increase in crude oil prices served as an accelerator for the definitive extension of control by the governments of the exporting countries over the oil-producing function. Through OPEC, they had in 1968 established the policy of assuming eventual ownership of the operating companies. Four years later OPEC was able to win the reluctant acquiescence of the major firms to this principle. An agreement signed at New York in October 1972 provided that the governments could purchase, at an "up-dated book value," an initial one-fourth participation in the companies, increasing by increments to 51% in 1982. The price revolution of the ensuing year removed any fiscal deterrent to shortening this

Table 3 Arab Oil in 1974[a]

	Estimated Production (thousands of barrels)		Estimated Revenue, 1974 (millions of dollars)	Proven reserves (billions of barrels)
	1973	1974		
Saudi Arabia[b]	2,735,137.5	3,062,700.0	28,207	144.60
Kuwait[b]	1,036,687.5	888,562.5	9,725	74.74
Iraq	763,162.5	675,270.0	6,015	32.36
Libya	784,395.0	582,750.0	7,505	26.20
Abu Dhabi	468,937.5	525,000.0	4,896	22.09
Algeria	383,655.0	382,500.0	4,125	6.67
Qatar	205,212.5	183,750.0	1,694	5.39
Oman	108,427.5	112,500.0	1,012	5.25
Egypt	102,397.5	90,000.0		
(of which Sinai[c]:)	41,250.0	33,750.0		
Dubai	82,852.0	90,000.0	800	2.56
Syria	38,602.5	45,000.0		7.50
Tunisia	29,085.0	23,000.0		0.94
Bahrain	24,500.0	24,000.0		0.36
Total Arab:	6,763,052.0	6,685,032.5	63,979	336.51
Total Mid-East:	9,202,402.5	9,200,235.0	84,207	398.19
World total	21,358,500.0	21,999,255.0		670.50

[a] Adapted from *Middle East Economic Digest*, Vol. 18:52 (December 27, 1974), p. 1589. Volume figures converted from metric tons to barrels at 7.5 barrels per ton.
[b] Includes share of Partitioned (former Neutral) Zone.
[c] Sinai occupied by Israel, which controlled production.

schedule. In 1973 Iran completed the total nationalization of its petroleum resources and facilities. By the end of 1974, 60% participation was a fact in the principal Arab producing countries (Kuwait, Saudi Arabia and Qatar). By mid-1975 it was clear that full ownership of the producing firms' assets in the Arab states was a question of months, not years. Henceforth the availability and destination of Arab oil, as well as its cost, depended upon the sovereign will of Arab governments.

The grave problems raised for the world economy by the new shape of the oil industry are still being explored. It has been estimated (without, however, taking full account of the current economic recession) that consuming countries might pay OPEC members (including the non-Arab participants) at least $600 billion between 1975 and 1979 if present oil prices remain stable, world economic expansion continues at a modest rate, major disruption of international political relations does not occur, and the importing states can find means of payment. The chief Arab producers, with their small populations, cannot conceivably absorb their oil revenues for purposes of current consumption, industrialization, and economic expansion. Even though the United States is not their principal market, about 60% of the oil they export is paid for in dollars; the disposition of vast "petrodollar" balances will be a major common concern between the Arab and American governments within the context of the global problem.

United States policy in the new situation has not crystallized. Resentment over the Arab embargo and fear that it might be renewed have enhanced an American tendency to view it as an adversary relationship between the consuming nations and OPEC, which is too often stereotyped as consisting simply of the Arab producers. American officials have attempted to "talk down" oil prices, uttered occasional provocative threats of military against oil-rich countries, and attempted to organize consumer governments for pressure to destroy OPEC solidarity and create a world oil market in which uncoordinated competition among exporters would result in drastic price declines. In some quarters there is realistic acknowledgment that new international institutions are needed to absorb oil revenue balances and channel them into productive uses. The IMF has instituted a special fund, capitalized in part by OPEC countries, for emergency assistance to less-developed importing countries. The United States has sponsored a proposal for a fund, to be formed in cooperation with the OECD countries, to serve as a "safety net" for embarrassed governments by extending credits or by guaranteeing bank loans. None of the multilateral schemes thus far advanced appears consciously designed to associate Arab and other producer governments as full partners in agencies to facilitate orderly adjustment to the new conditions. This is an important requisite, it would seem, for the development of the close collaboration that will certainly be needed between the United States and the Arab countries whose dollar balances will soon reach critical levels.

TOWARD THE FUTURE

During the June 1967 War Egypt and certain other Arab countries that broke diplomatic relations with the United States stopped short of severing intergovernment contact entirely. On Egyptian initiative the flag of Spain, the power protecting American interests in Egypt, was raised over the American Embassy in Cairo which, with a much-reduced staff, became the "American Interests Section of the Spanish Embassy," manned by United States Foreign Service officers. Similarly, Egyptian diplomats composed the UAR Interests Section of the Indian Embassy in Washington. This "soft break" permitted direct and authoritative, if technically informal, exchanges between the two estranged governments. By mutual consent the rank of this semiofficial representation was raised to the ministerial level well before the restoration of full diplomatic relations in 1974. With some Arab governments, including Iraq, a "hard" break in 1967 later became "soft" when American diplomats returned to their capitals as personnel of the American interests section of the protecting power's embassy.

The "radical" Arab states thus recognized that they had interests that could best be protected by some direct contact, however unconventional, with the American government. Some have suggested that the Arabs hoped, through such channels, to induce the United States, as the only power with appreciable influence in Israel, to ensure the evacuation of occupied Arab territory, and this was no doubt a consideration. It would, however, be wrong to reduce United States-Arab relations simply to terms of the Pales-

tine problem. In Egypt, after the formal break, American petroleum firms engaged in exploring and developing the country's
modest oil resources continued work as usual, free of the pressures
and harrassments common elsewhere. An Egyptian administrator
was appointed to head the American University at Cairo, but one
sympathetic to its continued operation on substantially the existing basis and to the maintenance of its academic standards. Other
cultural exchanges were maintained at a level remarkable in view
of the "war of attrition" atmosphere. Privately sponsored American medical missions in Yemen continued their work undisturbed.
Political evolution in both Yemen and the Sudan, in directions
determined by domestic concerns, created the desire for restoration of a balance in external relations; both took the initiative in
repairing the diplomatic breach with the United States. In the
absence of official contact Algeria entered into long-term contracts
with American companies for the sale of liquefied petroleum gas,
involving very substantial commitments of capital on both sides.
More recently, both Egypt and Iraq have intensively encouraged
American private enterprise to invest in their economies and to sell
in their markets.

The point to be stressed is that the Arab states, regardless of
political orientation, recognize that there are areas in the economic
and cultural fields in which continuing cooperation with the
United States is in their interest. The historical roots of this interaction, as this volume has shown, lie deep; they were planted
on the private initiative of American citizens and associations with
little government intervention, and they have survived profound
constitutional and political change in the Arab countries. Of the
three major American national interests in the Arab world, the
economic one, notably access to its energy resources, has until
quite recently been left primarily in the hands of private enterprise. With the transformation of the world petroleum industry in
the past few years this is no longer feasible. Direct government
policies and action are henceforth needed to ensure the cooperation with Arab and other oil producers necessary for the supply
of energy and the rational use of petrodollar balances on which
American prosperity and fiscal stability will depend at least for the
coming decade. Such cooperation will be possible to the extent
that the United States pursues its other major interests in the

Middle East in ways the Arabs perceive as just and as consonant with their own vital concerns.

The assumption that the Arab states lack the will, capability, and sophistication to protect their own independence from Soviet influence and communist subversion is no longer a productive basis for American defense policy, if indeed it ever was. As early as the Truman Administration the United States took the position that the Middle East, including the Arab countries, was territory in which the Soviet Union had no right to a presence: any Soviet penetration there constituted a threat to the Atlantic Alliance and the United States itself, which must be opposed. The notion that the Soviet Union, although itself adjacent to the area, had a legitimate interest in neighborly relations with its governments was repugnant to cold war doctrine. After the Suez War and the eclipse of Anglo-French influence, American strategy was much preoccupied with the idea that there was now a power "vacuum" in the Middle East that the United States must fill lest "international communism" flow into the void. Few analysts treated the "vacuum" expression as the metaphor it was, whose aptness needed to be checked against realities; instead, it was accepted *a priori,* and the policy deductions drawn were reflected in the Eisenhower Doctrine and successive Sixth Fleet interventions. The metaphor was a galling one to Arab leaders, implying as it did that they were incompetent to protect themselves or to manage their own affairs, but were forced to choose between Western and Eastern tutelage and clientship. The American effort to impose on Egypt its own conception of the appropriate level of Egyptian armament and its purpose opened to the Soviet Union its first major opportunity for close association with an Arab country. It has built on this foothold by the same methods the United States has used to protect and further its own interests in the area: by arming its clients, extending them technical and economic assistance, lending diplomatic support for their national aspirations, and providing them a security umbrella through the disposition of its armed forces. The symmetry extends to ideological justifications that have a somewhat dubious applicability to the Arab world. The Kremlin has devised a theory that "revolutionary democracies" engaged on noncapitalist paths will ultimately progress toward communism. It has invested substantial resources in, and committed its prestige to, the survival of Arab regimes that have persecuted local communists, repudiated the principle of class warfare, slid backward toward capitalist enterprise, and declined to follow Soviet counsel in their external affairs. The United States, in the name of liberal democracy, has backed traditional authoritarian regimes that, however anticommunist, appear to many Arabs to be obstacles to modernization, progress, and freedom.

The major thrust of Arab nationalism and of the policies of the principal Arab countries has been to achieve freedom from outside control from whatever source. If Arab actions have often been directed against Western strategic assets, it is precisely because the Arabs perceived that the immediate threat to their independence of action came from the West. The expulsion of Soviet advisors from Egypt in 1972, notwithstanding the high degree of Egyptian dependence on the Soviet Union, was only the most sensational indication that the Arabs are both able and determined to remain masters in their own house. We have been accustomed to seeing American and Soviet presences in the Arab world as a zero-sum game, where any increment of Russian activity represents a net loss to the West, while any Soviet setback constitutes an American triumph; such a simplistic view has led highly placed Americans to speak in terms of "expelling" the Russians from the Middle East. Many, but by no means all, Soviet activities are indeed directed specifically against Western interests in the Arab states. On the other hand, the Soviet Union has cooperated with Arab governments in industrial, agricultural, and communications projects that the West has been unable or unwilling to undertake and that are, in many cases, of positive value to the host countries' economy. Exclusive reliance on the United States and the West for development assistance would in all probability become a political irritant for many Arab countries. Encouragement of both the Soviet and the Arab governments to steer their joint activities into constructive channels would appear to be a more promising American policy than a sterile and ultimately futile attempt to eliminate all Soviet presence from the Arab world. The basic components of the American security interest in the Arab world— access to its oil and to its avenues of communication—are compatible with the independence to which the Arabs themselves are strongly attached. It is reassuring that the capability of the Arab states to maintain their freedom of action is growing. Inter-Arab ideological differences, a source of weakness, certainly persist. Since 1967, however, these have not precluded sustained cooperative effort, of which the effectiveness is enhanced by the vastly increased resources available to the oil-rich states.

Equally in need of reexamination is the notion that the Palestine issue is inherently related to global strategy and that Israel constitutes an asset to the NATO alliance as well as a defense of conservative, pro-West Arab regimes against the militant clients of the Soviet Union. This concept was, as we have seen, specifically formulated in 1967. The polarization effected by the United States' own choice served the tactical interests both of Israel and of the Soviet Union. It committed the United States to Israeli interests without reserving an effective American voice in defining those interests or the methods by which they were to be pursued. It tended to make Egypt and Syria dependent on the Soviet Union, permitting the latter to extend its influence over their policies; it resulted in the introduction into the area of a new, more sophisticated generation of weapons; it gave the Soviet Union the use of valuable military facilities; and it increased the political vulnerability of the moderate Arab regimes on friendly terms with the United States. It resulted, in 1970, in the commitment of Soviet military personnel to the defense of Egypt and in the use by the Soviet navy of logistic facilities in Syria and Egypt. It made it possible for the Israeli embassy in Washington, in collaboration with the Zionist lobby, to denounce, discredit, and eventually frustrate Secretary Rogers' peace-making endeavors. These having failed, it made inevitable the outbreak of the October 1973 War, of a scale and duration vastly enhanced by the American—and Soviet—contributions to the regional arms race.

The October War laid bare the fallacies and dangers in this conception of the Palestine problem. America's European allies made it unmistakably clear that in their view NATO military responsibilities did not extend to the Middle East; that their interests there were economic ones, to be safeguarded by political and diplomatic means; and that American intervention jeopardized those interests instead of protecting them. Arab preparations for the conflict were coordinated jointly for common ends between "progressive" states and Saudi Arabia, one of the conservative countries that, according to the doctrine, were supposedly in need of Israel as a shield against Arab radicalism.

While the War thus demonstrated the regional, political nature of the Arab-Israel problem, it showed at the same time its very real potential for bringing the United States and the Soviet Union into hazardous confrontation. Since the suspension of hostilities, both superpowers have rearmed their clients to an unprecedented level; in any resumption of armed action the possibility will increase that weapons of mass destruction, not thus far employed in the conflict, will be used against centers of civilian population. It is no disparagement of Secretary Kissinger's diplomatic effort in the months following the War to emphasize that it achieved the disengagement of the opposing forces, an essential step toward eventual settlement, but not peace itself. By January 1975, as this is written, it was obvious that the arrangement was inherently no more stable than previous truces and that without further movement toward an agreed settlement war would be resumed. There appear to be several factors to be taken into account in the further diplomatic effort necessary to avert renewed hostilities and their attendant dangers. An active Soviet role, first, is an essential to progress toward a broader settlement. There must be recognition that the Palestine Arabs are, in fact, a nation, and that recognition must be translated into some concrete realization of their aspiration to territorial sovereignty. Finally, acknowledging the unpleasant fact that there will be no solution that will appear satisfactory and just to all those directly involved, the United States should, in the last resort, be prepared to agree with other outside nations on the general lines of a practicable settlement and to refrain from support of either Arab or Israeli action which would tend to defeat such a settlement.

It should perhaps be emphasized that, contrary to much rhetoric in news media and other quarters, extinction of the state of Israel was not the objective either of the Soviet Union or of Israel's neighbors in the October War. Since 1969 Egypt and Jordan have acknowledged that the Zionist state is here to stay; they have consistently expressed willingness to renounce belligerency upon recovery of their national territory occupied in 1967. President Sādāt devoted considerable effort in 1973 to persuading Syria to accept the limited war aim of achieving some movement in this direction, and one feature of the 1974 Syria-Israel disengagement agreement was Syria's acceptance of United Nations Security Council Resolution 242 as the basis of an eventual settlement. As soon as the Soviet leadership judged that the Arab attack had spent itself, its endeavors were concentrated on securing a ceasefire leading to peace along lines of the applicable United Nations resolutions.

The Soviet Union supported the original United Nations partition resolution, which gave international sanction to Israel's sovereignty. None in the long series of United Nations actions toward composition between Israel and her Arab neighbors could have been taken without Soviet support or acquiescence. Under the United Nations Charter the Soviet Union is obligated to respect and defend the territorial integrity of Israel, just as the United States is bound in the same way with regard to the Arab states. It is true that since 1954 Soviet-Israeli relations, for reasons that need not be recited here, have ranged from moderately poor to very bad; but this does not mean that the Soviet Union seeks Israel's destruction. If one chooses to place the worst possible interpretation on Soviet motives, it could be assumed that the Soviet Union has a positive stake in the survival of Israel as an irritant in Arab-Western relations; without the Israeli presence Arab states would feel far less need for the military cooperation on which the Soviets have built their influence and in which they have invested substantial effort and funds.

There are thus reasons to suppose that the Soviet Union has an interest in promoting an Arab-Israeli settlement, provided it has an equitable share in bringing it about and incurs no unacceptable political loss in the process. More important, the Soviets have considerable ability to frustrate a settlement in which they have had no voice and in which their prestige is consequently not engaged. The Geneva framework established during Kissinger's disengagement negotiations whereby, under the symbolic chairmanship of the United Nations Secretary General, American and Soviet representatives are to assist the contending parties toward some bearable compromise, appears to offer the brightest hope of progress, although it was utilized only momentarily. The complex, contentious matters at issue must be addressed in some such international forum. Both Israel and the Arabs responded gratifyingly to the Secretary of State's personal mediation in establishing a truce; the long, frustrated effort of Ambassador Jarring should nevertheless suggest that there are limits to what a single intermediary, however skilled and imaginative, can accomplish. No single Arab state can make peace separately with Israel, not only because none is politically strong enough, but also because the necessary elements of a settlement cannot be reduced to distinct sets of bilateral issues. Navigation of the Tiran Strait, as one example, directly concerns three Arab countries as well as Israel, while the status of the Islamic shrines in Jerusalem concerns them all. An Arab consensus must consequently be created in support of any viable settlement, and this is likely to be reached only with the active encouragement of both superpowers. It cannot, moreover, come about without the collaboration of acknowledged spokesmen for the Palestinians.

Earlier in these pages we traced the evolution of the Arab Palestinians toward nationhood. The leaders of the Arab states, at a summit meeting at Rabat in October 1974, formally acknowledged this status. They declared the Palestine Liberation Organization's exclusive right to speak in the name of the Palestinians and asserted that a future Palestinian state will be under PLO administration. King Hussein himself reluctantly conceded the extinction of his claim to be the Palestinians' spokesman. A measure of international recognition was accorded to PLO in November 1974, when Yāsir 'Arafāt was accorded the opportunity to state the Palestinians' case before the United Nations General Assembly. The National Charter adopted by PLO in July 1968 unequivocally expresses its aim of liquidating the Zionist state by force of arms and establishing an Arab state comprising the entire area of the former Palestine mandate. These objectives and the concept of Zionism are so mutually exclusive that there appears to be no matter that could be usefully discussed between PLO and Israel. The latter's leadership has indeed rejected the notion of attending any conference in which PLO is a participant or of countenancing the formation of a PLO-controlled state on the West Bank. In some distant future Israelis and Palestinians may be brought together by the shared mystical attachment to the land of Palestine, by the common experience of a past as peoples without a home, feeling themselves—and treated by others—as separate and different, and subjects of discrimination and hardship. Policies and institutions are not necessarily immutable. Between the June and October wars some peaceful commercial exchange went forward between Israel and Jordan, and a modicum of opportunity in the Israeli economy was afforded some members of the captive Arab population in the occupied territories. Surely, to act on the assumption that responsibility for administering an independent Palestinian entity on the West Bank would prove a steadying, sobering influence on PLO or whatever alternative leadership might emerge is preferable to the defeatist view that mutual hostility is forever inevitable. Meanwhile, however, the lack of a dialogue save by bombs and bullets imperils regional and world peace so gravely and imminently that the great powers cannot prudently neglect an intermediary role in the search for an alternative to terrorism and war. For the United States this implies instituting some such meaningful exchange with the PLO leaders as the Soviet Union, after long hesitation, began in 1973.

The Arab and Israeli flexibility needed for an early and fruitful resumption of the Geneva Conference may not materialize. In this case it is important that the United States and the Soviet Union reach more specific understandings than the existing crisis-control arrangements to avoid being drawn once more into confrontation as a result of the resumption of Arab-Israel war. It should not be forgotten that in October 1973 it was Israeli violation of the ceasefire that set in motion the sequence of events culminating in the alert of American nuclear forces. The Soviet Union has furnished more than one indication of its readiness to collaborate with the United States to ensure that the Middle East situation does not get completely out of hand. In 1969 the Soviets sought a great-power agreement on an overall Arab-Israel settlement that the contending parties would be pressed to accept and carry out; since both powers continue to support United Nations Resolution 242, a meeting of minds on a detailed plan should be well within the realm of possibility. In October 1973 Brezhnev proposed that Soviet and American troops jointly enforce and police the United Nations ceasefire. The United States rejected and has continued to oppose the principle of an imposed settlement, which not surprisingly appeals to none of the disputing parties. If, however, the Arabs and Israelis cannot agree among themselves on peaceful arrangements, the United States and the Soviet Union have a higher and joint responsibility, as permanent members of the United Nations Security Council and for their own safety, to act to prevent the outbreak of another war. Both are formally committed to the security and territorial integrity of *all* states in the area. They have both, whether wisely or not is immaterial, committed their prestige to opposing sides in the dispute; neither can effectively control the acts of its protégés. The risk of a new confrontation between the great powers is thus continuing and is in part independent of their own acts. It is not suggested that American and Soviet troops should impose an agreed program. On the other hand, both the United States and the Soviet Union could undertake to gear economic, military, and political support of their clients to the carrying out of a plan drawn according to principles already endorsed as just by an overwhelming preponderance of world opinion, except insofar as departures from it were freely negotiated by the parties directly concerned. This approach would have several advantages. It would define for the contending parties the circumstances in which they could and could not depend on the support of their great-power protectors. It would relieve the latter of their dangerous commitment to underwrite decisions in which they have no decisive voice, thus localizing the conflict and reducing the likelihood of escalation to a nuclear confrontation between them. It would introduce a third alternative into a situation where there are presently only two: an unlikely negotiated peace among Arabs and Israelis, and the renewal of hostilities on an unpredictable scale.

In this context it should be feasible to extend to Israel the American security guarantee she has long sought, without irreparable damage to United States relations with the Arab states. America's moral commitment to Israel's existence and security is a legitimate one, not inherently incompatible with what the consensus of the world community, expressed in resolutions on the United Nations books, has established as the only practicable framework for peace in the Middle East. The commitment is as yet undefined, however. The Arabs have had plausible ground for viewing it as open ended, and as promising American support for any action Israel decides on to further her own interests; the long-term American support now being proposed for the Israeli defense establishment can hardly be reassuring to them. A public undertaking by the United States to ensure Israel's defense only within specified, internationally sanctioned borders would help to allay Arab uncertainty and suspicion regarding American intentions; it should encourage Israel to move toward the accommodations without which no stable situation in the Near East will come about.

Such an approach would avoid reinstituting a polarization that did great harm to the American image among the Arabs. Not the least significant accomplishment of Secretary Kissinger's diplomacy has been the restoration of a measure of trust in America among key Arab leaders and confidence in United States understanding and respect for vital Arab interests. This is an asset to be anxiously nurtured for the welfare of all Americans. Within a very brief span of years the Arab states have gained control of enormous economic and financial resources of which the disposition will have profound impact on the prosperity of much of the world and will force the United States into increasing involvement, on some terms, with the Arab countries. The new Arab power can be used either for destructive purposes or in ways that will enhance the welfare of all. The manner of its use will be decided by Arabs, to advance aims they perceive as important to themselves. The Arabs are, and are determined to remain, members of the unaligned third world; they cannot be expected to commit themselves to either constellation of world powers or to follow outside advice without searching question. In its own interest the United States must identify and extend the areas in which mutual cooperation can be demonstrated to the Arabs to serve their own legitimate and constructive ends as well as ours. This book has drawn attention to some of the past events and persisting attitudes on both sides that have made the encounter between American and Arab an uneasy one on the political plane. Patterns and habits of cultural and economic interchange have nevertheless survived, which permits us to hope that there is wisdom and understanding enough on both sides to foster the further growth of mutual confidence and cooperative endeavor.

Epilogue

DURING THE PAST SEVERAL MONTHS THE UNITED STATES HAS SOUGHT SOLUTIONS for its energy and petrodollar problems through numerous avenues. From the standpoint of American-Arab relations an essential element has seemed missing from these efforts: a concern for fostering a basis for cooperation between the United States and the Arabs and for associating the Arab governments in the institutions that will be needed for the effective recycling of petrodollar balances in the interest of the world's economic recovery. Instead, an adversary atmosphere has been allowed to develop in which the American public is encouraged to regard Arab-American differences as irreconcilable and to conclude that the United States can safely ignore Arab interests and aspirations or can impose solutions on its own terms by armed force. Regrettably, such an atmosphere deters the development within the American public of the understanding of the Arab world and its political realities on which sound national policy must ultimately rest.

The principal thrust of American action has been directed toward the destruction of OPEC and its ability to maintain world oil prices at a high level. This emphasis, among other things, tends to encourage the misconception that America's economic difficulties are chiefly due to the inflated price of Arab oil whereas, as noted in this book, measures taken by the United States to deal with already existing problems were the catalyst for the first major OPEC price increases.

The Congress, in reaction to the Arab oil embargo of October 1973, included in the Trade Act of 1974 a clause denying trade preferences to any member of OPEC or a party to any agreement designed to withhold vital commodities from international trade or increase their price to unreasonable levels. In a foreign policy speech in April 1975 President Ford objected to this provision because it punished friends of the United States who had not participated in the embargo (Ecuador, Venezuela, Nigeria, and Indonesia) and "seriously complicated our new dialogue with our friends." Broadly sponsored legislation introduced in Congress in March was designed explicitly to "break" OPEC by establishing a government purchasing agency that would accept sealed bids from oil suppliers and sell the oil to domestic refiners and marketers. Prominent oil economists have proposed that the federal government instead set an import quota and sell "quota tickets" to importers by sealed, competitive bid. Either proposal, it was claimed, would induce a price war among the producers leading to drastic reductions in price. United States participation in the April 1975 Paris conference of oil producing and importing countries was openly designed to mobilize consuming nations' pressure against OPEC solidarity.

The eventual efficacity of these efforts against OPEC is very dubious. It is true that in mid-1975 producing capacity is far above world demand, and that some oil-exporting countries feel the pinch of falling revenues. This is not a phenomenon without precedent, however; in similar situations in the past the major international companies that then served as the "cartel" were able to adjust production and distribution without sharp fluctuations in the price of crude. The OPEC countries have achieved wealth and power largely through the coordination of their policies, and they are highly unlikely to abandon this successful strategy in order to take individual action to exploit momentary market opportunities. Furthermore, OPEC's members are not commercial firms but sovereign states. As such they have, and acknowledge, a responsibility to husband their oil in the interest of future generations. Although some are lavishly endowed with reserves, their petroleum is a finite, wasting resource that cannot be replaced when exhausted. Maximization of short-term profits by increasing production against declining prices is not prudent national policy; common action to secure maximum benefit from each barrel exported is.

American frustration over the Arab oil embargo and the OPEC price increases has given rise to a still-continuing public discussion of the possibility of seizing OPEC oilfields by force. The debate was stimulated by a remark by Secretary Kissinger at the end of 1974 in response to a journalist's observation that some businessmen regarded military action as, in the long run, the only "answer" to OPEC prices. This would be, the Secretary said,

A very dangerous course. We should have learned from Vietnam that it is easier to get into a war than to get out of it. I am not saying that there's no circumstances where we would not (sic) use force. But it is one thing to use it in the case of a dispute over price, it's another where there is some actual strangulation of the industrialized world.

He added this observation regarding the possibility of Soviet intervention against such American military action:

I don't think this is a good thing to speculate about. Any president who would resort to military action in the Middle East without worrying what the Soviets would do would have to be reckless. The question is to what extent he would let himself be deterred by it. But you cannot say you would not consider what the Soviets would do. I want to make clear, however, that the use of force would be considered only in the gravest emergency.[1]

Although Kissinger's remarks could scarcely be construed as endorsing the notion of armed action, they did not exclude it as a remote option, and they received the President's prompt, public concurrence. Many commentators were consequently encouraged to interpret the Secretary's words as a serious threat and to present the idea as a feasible and desirable policy. Knowledge of the Arab world's political realities has been singularly absent from most of the discussion, as one experienced student of the area, mentioned

---

[1]"Kissinger on Oil, Food, and Trade," *Business Week,* No. 2363 (January 13, 1975), p. 69.

earlier in these pages,[2] has noted in colorful terms.[3] The ongoing discussion calls disturbingly into question the depth of commitment, on the part of some leaders of American opinion, to the principles of peaceful settlement of international disputes and the respect for the territory and sovereignty of all nations. More dangerously, it promotes the escapist dream that there are easy, final solutions that the United States can impose without regard for the concerns of other peoples, and that the American public, which is ultimately responsible for the nation's policies, therefore need not bother to understand or adapt to them. The American leadership of the 1950s, so sharply criticized in one chapter of this book, nevertheless realized that history had already overtaken the era of imperialism in the Arab world. The American experience in southeast Asia since that time should leave no doubt that force is not an adequate, facile surrogate for soundly informed policy in our relations with weaker nations.

The goal of self-sufficiency in energy that the present Administration has set for the nation is certainly unexceptionable in principle. The enormous complexities involved in attaining it are

[2]See above, p. 54.

[3]Professor Carleton S. Coon, letter to the editor of *The Christian Science Monitor* published January 29, 1975:

What is all this media-chatter about sabre-rattling over the Muslim oilfields? Have the newscasters and cartoonists ever been to Saudi Arabia? Do they think it would be like taking Honduras or Gambia? If they do they know neither their history nor the essence of religions. It would be another Holy War, a Jihad between the Muslims from Mauritania to Mindanao, from Turkestan to Tanzania, and the other peoples of the book. The lands once held in uneasy fiefdom by Britain, France, Italy, Spain, and Portugal would have to be ruled by the war-weary, inchoate might of the United States. Marx might chuckle in his grave; Mao in his bed.

Of course we would win, but what? A new world of colonialism, and holding an empty bag.

Who taught the Arabs modern fighting? Who has educated their generations since the arrival of the first sail-borne missionaries? The British. The Americans. The French.

Since the memory of man, the Arabs and the Phoenicians before them have been trading by land and by sea. A bargain costs less than a battle. Not ransom must anyone pay, but the price of a blowless, bickering bargain, and if needed, with all the histrionics of boothkeepers in bazaars.

Let us paint religion out of the picture. Let us use our common sense.

reflected in the difficulty the executive and legislative branches are having in formulating an agreed program. Thus far the executive has sought to reduce imports of OPEC (i.e., Arab) oil by progressive increases in import duties; the volume of imports has in fact fallen, both because of this measure and because of the general decline in economic activity. The approach has some unfortunate side effects. It tends to reduce the total supply of energy, an essential for economic recovery. By increasing the cost of energy it aggravates inflationary pressures that will intensify with recovery. It accepts a petroleum strategy of "drain America first," disquieting at a time when the proportion of "dry holes" resulting from exploratory drilling in the United States is rising sharply. A major motive in the self-sufficiency program is obviously to free American policy from the necessity to adapt to vital national concerns of the Arab states. Ironically, this necessity will persist even if the United States achieves the ability to do without a single barrel of Arab oil.

Reacting to the threat of military action, certain Arab countries transferred fairly substantial sums on deposit in American institutions to European banks, intensifying downward pressure on the value of the dollar. It is important to understand that the petrodollars in Arab, and other OPEC, hands are eventual claims on the American economy and that, since much Arab oil is sold to third countries for dollars, such balances will continue to accumulate even if the United States does not itself purchase Arab oil. Although projections of the level they may reach during the next five years have been revised downward from the figures cited earlier in this book,[4] they remain quite substantial. The Arab governments have thus far, in view of the uneasy political atmosphere between them and the United States, shown extreme caution in investing their dollar surpluses in America, limiting their placements largely to short-term government securities and bank deposits. Longer-term investment has been mainly by wealthy

---

[4]In April 1975 the World Bank estimated that the accumulated reserves of OPEC nations might reach $460 billion by 1980, on the assumption that oil prices will rise proportionately with world inflation. On other assumptions, far lower projections were made by the Brookings Institution and the Morgan Guaranty Trust Company. The latter anticipated that OPEC balances would reach a maximum of $250 billion in 1978 and decline thereafter. (*New York Times,* March 30, 1975)

private Arab individuals. If petrodollar balances are not to wreak continuing damage, whether deliberate or not, on America's fiscal health, a significant portion of them must be productively invested in the United States. Playing on popular prejudices and ignorance, some have warned of an Arab financial "invasion" and takeover of American industry. Such apprehensions ignore the decisive historical role of foreign investment in the growth and prosperity of our economy. The real danger, as recently noted by one financial authority, is not that the Arabs may invest in the United States, but that they may not.[5]

The United States cannot, therefore, ignore the Arab states and simply support Israel as the only significant American interest in the Middle East. The fact that our economic welfare and our security are linked to an Arab world often unstable, unpredictable, and unresponsive to our counsel constitutes a thorny problem for national policy. Events both encouraging and disappointing over the past months reflect the area's continuing effervescence. King Faisal, a staunch if not uncritical friend of the United States, was felled by an assassin's bullet; his successors promise to remain faithful to his policies, but must build their own position of influence among the Arab states. The American effort in March to build on the 1973 disengagement agreement toward a more formal bilateral peace between Egypt and Israel was shattered against the unyielding core of the Palestine issue. The Ba'th government in Iraq at last succeeded in mastering the prolonged Kurdish rebellion and in ending the long-smoldering border war with Iran. Warfare between Palestinian Arabs and Lebanese Phalangists paralyzed civic life in Beirut and produced Lebanon's first, if evanescent, military government.

Abrupt change is the present condition of Arab political life. The massive influx of wealth and the industrial revolution it is making possible will inevitably stimulate social transformations. Readers of this book, it is hoped, will have gained some insight into the sources of past change and the reasons for the direction it has taken. The United States has, by its attitudes and actions, had a measure of influence over the quality of change, sometimes with results disconcertingly different from those intended. Aware-

---

[5]Julian M. Snyder, in *New York Times*, March 30, 1975.

ness of the manner in which our interaction with the Arabs has developed over a period of two centuries is essential to a constructive outcome of an encounter from which neither America nor the Arab states can withdraw.

Austin, May 1975

Bibliographical Essay

MANY OF THE DOCUMENTARY AND SECONDARY SOURCES ON WHICH WE HAVE RELIED are indicated in the footnotes. The pertinent literature is, of course, enormous; a listing even of all the important materials would require a fair-sized volume. A brief, systematic statement may assist the reader not specialized in Middle Eastern affairs in identifying some of the more informative works on each of the major topics treated in the text.

THE ARAB STATES

In descriptive and geographical works the Arab world is treated only exceptionally as a unit. The eastern Arab states are usually taken as part of a "Middle East" variously delimited. Sound introductory data, now outdated in some respects, are contained in William B. Fisher, *The Middle East: A Physical, Social and Regional Geography* (London: Methuen, 6th ed., 1971). For reliable basic information on both the Arab East and the Maghreb, *The Middle East and North Africa: Survey and Directory,* issued annually (London: Europa) is a valuable country-by-country reference for historical, economic, educational, and political data.

The standard general history of the Arabs up to the present century is Phillip K. Hitti, *History of the Arabs* (New York: St. Martin's, 8th ed., 1964), published also in an abbreviated version by the same publisher (5th ed., 1969). A concise overview by an eminent British scholar is Bernard Lewis' *The Arabs in History* (New York: Harper Torchbooks, 2d ed., 1967).

For the indispensable political background on the individual countries many monographs are readily accessible. For Saudi Arabia, R. Bayly Winder's *Saudi Arabia in the Nineteenth Century* (New York: St. Martin's, 1965) is a good point of departure, to be followed by H. St. John Philby's *Saudi Arabia* (New York: Praeger, 1955); David Howarth's biography of the contemporary Kingdom's founder, *The Desert King: The Life of Ibn Saud* (London: Mayflower, 1968); and Gerald de Gaury's adulatory but well-researched biography of the present monarch, *Faisal, King of Saudi Arabia* (New York: Praeger, 1967). Eric Macro, *Yemen and the Western World* (New York: Praeger, 1967) deals primarily with the country's external relations and is usefully supplemented by Manfred W. Wenner, *Modern Yemen, 1918–1966* (Baltimore: Johns Hopkins, 1967), which is the best concise contemporary history of Yemen presently available. Robert Geran Landen's *Oman Since 1856: Disruptive Modernization in a Traditional Arab Society* (Princeton, N.J.: Princeton University Press, 1967) is a scholarly, authoritative study of the country's political, economic, and social past. Among the few comprehensive works on the Persian Gulf states, Husain M. al Baharna, *The Legal Status of the Arabian Gulf States* (New York: Oceana, 1969) and B. C. Busch, *Britain and the Persian Gulf, 1894–1914* (Berkeley and Los Angeles: University of California Press, 1967) are useful for the preindependence era.

The standard work on Iraq is Majid Khadduri, *Independent Iraq* (New York: Oxford, 1961), an authoritative account firmly grounded in primary sources and interviews with key political figures, together with its sequel, *Republican Iraq: A Study of Iraqi Politics since the Revolution of 1958* (New York: Oxford, 1969). Also basic and reliable, with a somewhat different time frame, is Stephen H. Longrigg, *Iraq, 1900–1950, A Political, Social and Economic History* (London: Oxford, 1950).

Longrigg's *Syria and Lebanon under French Mandate* (London: Oxford, 1958) is meticulous, detailed, authoritative, and rather heavy going. The student might begin with the older but well-informed "political essay" of Albert Hourani, *Syria and Lebanon* (London: Oxford, 3d impression, 1954), and A. L. Tibawi's *Modern History of Syria Including Lebanon and Palestine* (New York: St. Martin's, 1970). For internal political developments at a critical juncture, Itamar Rabinovich, *Syria Under the Ba'th 1963–66* (Jerusalem: Israel Universities Press, 1972) is highly recommended. A valuable study of Lebanese politics is Michael C. Hudson, *The*

Precarious Republic: Political Modernization in Lebanon (New York: Random House, 1968).

Among the useful background works on Jordan are the *Memoirs of King Abdullah*, the country's first ruler (Washington: American Council of Learned Societies, 1954); P. J. Vatikiotis, *Politics and the Military in Jordan: A Study of the Arab Legion 1921–1957* (New York: Praeger, 1967), and *A Soldier with the Arabs* (New York: Harper, 1957), by the Legion's long-time commander, Sir John Bagot Glubb. Peter Snow's *Hussein* (London: Barrier & Jenkins, 1972) is a sympathetic biography of the present King, whose own writings are important for the understanding of his problems and policies: *Uneasy Lies the Head* (London: Heinemann, 1962) and *My "War" with Israel* (New York: William Morrow, 1969).

The entire period of British involvement with Egypt is treated in John A. Marlowe, *A History of Modern Egypt and Anglo-Egyptian Relations, 1800–1956* (Hamden, Conn.: Archon, 1968). Focused more closely on internal pre-World War I developments is Robert L. Tignor, *Modernization and British Colonial Rule in Egypt, 1882–1914* (Princeton, N.J.: Princeton University Press, 1966). For the ensuing period two works are worth noting: Mahmud Z. Zayid, *Egypt's Struggle for Independence* (Beirut: Khayat's, 1965), and Farhat J. Ziadeh, *Lawyers, the Rule of Law and Liberalism in Modern Egypt* (Stanford, Calif.: Hoover Institution, 1968). Of interest also is a work by an American member of the mixed courts in Egypt, later Secretary of the Egyptian International Law Society: Jasper Y. Brinton, *The Mixed Courts of Egypt* (New Haven, Conn.: Yale University Press, rev. ed., 1968). Reasons for the scant attention paid to Egypt by American policymakers before World War I are examined in L. C. Wright, *United States Policy Toward Egypt 1830–1914* (New York: Exposition Press, 1969). For the Muslim Brotherhood, a political movement with broad regional significance, the standard work is Richard P. Mitchell, *The Society of Muslim Brothers* (London: Oxford, 1969). The origins of the Egyptian revolution are searchingly explored in Nadav Safran, *Egypt in Search of Political Community* (Cambridge, Harvard University Press, 1961). The Nasser era, beginning in 1952, is the subject of a whole library of books of widely varying quality. Any listing must include Robert Stephens, *Nasser: a Political Biography* (London: The Penguin Press, 1971); also of value are Keith Wheelock, *Nasser's New Egypt* (New

York: Praeger, 1960), Charles D. Cremeans, *The Arabs and the World: Nasser's Arab Nationalist Policy* (New York: Praeger, 1963), and Charles Issawi, *Egypt in Revolution: An Economic Analysis* (New York: Oxford, 1963).

Libya has received less scholarly attention. John Wright's *Libya* (New York: Praeger, 1969) surveys the country's history from ancient to modern times; Majid Khadduri, in *Modern Libya: a Study in Political Development* (Baltimore: Johns Hopkins, 1963) is concerned with the postindependence period (i.e. after 1952).

The standard work on the history of North Africa is in French: Charles-André Julien, *Histoire de l'Afrique du Nord: Tunisie—Algérie—Maroc. De la Conquête arabe à 1830* (Paris: Payot, 2d ed., 1956, 2 vols.).[1] A valuable study of the interwar Maghreb by a distinguished French scholar is Jacques Berque, *French North Africa: The Maghreb between Two World Wars* (New York: Praeger, 1967). Highly recommended is Elbaki Hermassi, *Leadership and National Development in North Africa—A Comparative Study* (Berkeley and Los Angeles: University of California Press, 1972). Competent monographs are D. L. Ling, *Tunisia: From Protectorate to Republic* (Bloomington, Ind.: Indiana University Press, 1967), J. P. Halstead, *Rebirth of a Nation: The Origins and Rise of Moroccan Nationalism* (Cambridge, Mass.: Harvard University Press, 1967), and William B. Quandt, *Revolution and Political Leadership: Algeria 1954–1968* (Cambridge, Mass.: M.I.T. Press, 1969).

The pioneering work on the rise of Arab nationalism is George Antonius, *The Arab Awakening* (first published 1938; reprinted in 1955 by Khayat's, Beirut), which is reliable for the circumstances of the Arab Revolt and valuable for the inclusion of key documents, including the Hussein-MacMahon correspondence. Later research correcting and supplementing Antonius is found in Zeine N. Zeine, *The Emergence of Arab Nationalism—With A Background of Arab-Turkish Relations in the Near East* (Beirut: Khayat's, 1966). For the evolution of ideas in Arab society during the crucial period the indispensable work is Albert Hourani, *Arabic Thought in the Liberal Age 1798–1939* (London: Oxford, reprinted with corrections 1967). William L. Cleveland has contributed a valuable study

---

[1]The second volume is available in English translation as *History of North Africa* (New York: Praeger, 1970).

of a key theoretician in *The Making of an Arab Nationalist: Ottomanism and Arabism in the Life and Thought of Sati'al-Husri* (Princeton, N.J.: Princeton University Press, 1971). Some perceptive insights may be gained from Hans E. Tütsch, *Facets of Arab Nationalism* (Detroit: Wayne State University Press, 1965).

For an introduction to Arab radicalism and neutralism the following may be recommended: Sami A. Hanna and George H. Gardner, *Arab Socialism—A Documentary Survey* (Leiden: E. J. Brill, 1969), Jaan Pennar, *The U.S.S.R. and the Arabs—The Ideological Dimension* (London: C. Hurst, 1973), Fayez A. Sayegh, *The Dynamics of Neutralism in the Arab World: A Symposium* (San Francisco: Chandler, 1964), and David Kimche, *The Afro-Asian Movement: Ideology and Foreign Policy of the Third World* (Jerusalem: Israel Universities Press, 1973). Among numerous works dealing with militarism in Arab politics, two deserve special mention: J. C. Hurewitz, *Middle East Politics: The Military Dimension* (New York: Praeger, 1969) and Eliezer Be'eri, *Army Officers in Arab Politics and Society* (New York: Praeger, 1969); the latter, while well documented and informative, needs to be read with the author's bitter hostility in mind.

Perhaps the best way to approach the important subject of inter-Arab relations is through Robert W. Macdonald's scholarly study *The League of Arab States—A Study in the Dynamics of Regional Organization* (Princeton, N.J.: Princeton University Press, 1965). The pivotal issue of Syria in Arab politics is illuminated in two valuable works: Patrick Seale, *The Struggle for Syria—A Study of Post-War Arab Politics 1945–1958* (London: Oxford, 1965) and Malcolm Kerr, *The Arab Cold War 1958–1967* (New York: Oxford, 2d ed., 1967).

EARLY UNITED STATES-ARAB CONTACTS AND DEVELOPMENT OF AMERICAN INTERESTS

For United States relations with the Barbary states an early work remains quite useful: Charles Oscar Paullin, *Diplomatic Negotiations of American Naval Officers 1778–1883* (Baltimore: Johns Hopkins, 1912). The events are placed in a broader context in James A. Field, Jr., *America and the Mediterranean World 1776–1882* (Princeton, N.J.: Princeton University Press, 1969), and further details are furnished in Luella J. Hall, *The United States and Morocco 1776–1956* (Metuchen, N.J.: The Scarecrow Press, 1971).

A wide-ranging and highly readable account of the early American contacts with the Middle East is given by David H. Finnie, *Pioneers East: The Early American Experience in the Middle East* (Cambridge, Mass.: Harvard University Press, 1967). Recent studies of missionary endeavor have been able to draw on the archives of the American Board for Foreign Missions. The resulting works have added new insights and corrected some previous misapprehensions. Particularly worthy of mention are Abdul Latif Tibawi, *American Interests in Syria 1800–1901: A Study of Educational, Literary and Religious Work* (Oxford: Clarendon Press, 1966), Robert L. Daniel, *American Philanthropy in the Near East 1820–1960* (Athens, O.: Ohio University Press, 1970) and Joseph L. Grabill, *Protestant Diplomacy and the Near East: Missionary Influence on American Policy 1810–1927* (Minneapolis: University of Minnesota Press, 1971). An interesting lunatic-fringe episode in the Protestant millenarian movement is recounted by Harold Davis, "The Jaffa Colonists from Downeast," *American Quarterly,* Vol. III, No. 4 (Winter 1951), pp. 344–356.

The service of American army officers in the Egyptian forces is the subject of two books: Pierre Crabitès, *Americans in the Egyptian Army* (London: George Routledge & Sons, 1938) and William B. Hesseltine and Hazel C. Wolf, *The Blue and Gray on the Nile* (Chicago: University of Chicago Press, 1961), which is based on broader research and gives a more sympathetic appraisal of the officers' accomplishments for the Khedive.

Reference to the beginnings of American archaeological enterprise in the Arab countries are interspersed in several of the books already mentioned. Outstanding, with specific reference to Egypt, is the engaging study by John Albert Wilson, himself a distinguished Egyptologist, *Signs and Wonders upon Pharaoh: A History of American Egyptology* (Chicago: University of Chicago Press, 1964). William Foxwell Albright's *Archaeology of Palestine and the Bible* (New York: Fleming H. Revell, rev. ed., 1935) remains informative.

For the later development of United States interests in the region, up to the eve of World War II, John A. De Novo's *American Interests and Policies in the Middle East 1900–1939* (Minneapolis:

University of Minnesota Press, 1963) is indispensable. A concise contemporary analysis of the bases of American concern with the area is George Lenczowski, ed., *United States Interests in the Middle East* (Washington: American Enterprise Institute for Foreign Policy Research, 1968).

For the decline of the Ottoman Empire and its implications in international politics, Matthew Smith Anderson's *The Eastern Question, 1774–1923* (London: Macmillan, 1966) has superseded Sir John Marriott's classic. Two able studies of the disposition of Turkey at the Paris Conference are recommended: Harry N. Howard, *The Partition of Turkey: A Diplomatic History 1913–1923* (Norman, Okla.: University of Oklahoma Press, 1931) and Laurence Evans, *United States Policy and the Partition of Turkey 1914–1924* (Baltimore: Johns Hopkins, 1963), which focuses more directly on the American role, with particular reference to the developing interest in Arab oil. Howard's *The King-Crane Commission* (Beirut: Khayat's, 1963) gives the only full-dress treatment of a particularly important, if finally thwarted, American initiative in the context of the peace settlement. Leonard Stein's magisterial *The Balfour Declaration* (New York: Simon & Schuster, 1961) is the basic study of the historic pronouncement. More wide-ranging, covering a much longer time span, and less sympathetic to Zionism, is Desmond Stewart's well-written *Middle East: Temple of Janus* (Garden City, N.Y.: Doubleday, 1971). On the development of Zionism in America Samuel Halperin, *The Political World of American Zionism* (Detroit: Wayne State University Press, 1961) is an interesting supplement to the broader works of Ben Halpern, *The Idea of the Jewish State* (Cambridge, Mass.: Harvard U. Press, 1961) and Frank E. Manuel, *The Realities of American Palestine Relations* (Washington: Public Affairs Press, 1949), which focuses more specifically on United States policy. Particularly interesting for its sociological insight is Yonathan Shapiro's *Leadership of the American Zionist Organization 1897–1930* (Urbana, Ill.: University of Illinois Press, 1970.)

AMERICA AND ARAB OIL

There are two standard works on the origins and development of the Middle East petroleum industry. Stephen H. Longrigg, *Oil in the Middle East: Its Discovery and Development* (London: Oxford, 1954) is completely authoritative and completely sympathetic to the participating companies. Benjamin Schwadran, *The Middle East, Oil, and the Great Powers* (New York: Halsted, 3d rev. ed., 1973; first published 1955) is a comprehensive survey, with particular attention to policies of the countries involved, unsparing of criticism either of the companies or the governments concerned. In *Oil and State in the Middle East* (Ithaca, N.Y.: Cornell University Press, 1960) George Lenczowski examines social, political, and economic problems arising from the impact of the industry on the producing countries during the early stage of the revolution in concession terms. Edith Penrose, *The Growth of Firms, Middle East Oil and Other Essays* (London: Frank Cass, 1971) includes several perceptive articles on strictly economic aspects of the industry before its recent transformation. Two works are indispensable background for the energy crisis of the early 1970s: George W. Stocking, *Middle East Oil: A Study in Political and Economic Controversy* (Nashville, Tenn.: Vanderbilt University Press, 1970) brilliantly synthesizes the economic and political determinants of petroleum events, with particular attention to the IPC-Iraq dispute; Sam H. Schurr et al., *Middle Eastern Oil and the Western World: Prospects and Problems* (New York: American Elsevier, 1971) is a valuable description of the state of the industry at the time of its publication, with a clear delineation of the role of OPEC. These should be read in conjunction with M. A. Adelman, *The World Petroleum Market* (Baltimore: Johns Hopkins, 1972) for contrasting conclusions reached when analysis is based on conventional economic factors. In 1972 the Subcommittee on Foreign Economic Policy of the U.S. House of Representatives Committee on Foreign Affairs heard testimony from industrial, academic, and government specialists on the oil crisis; the record of its hearings furnishes a broad spectrum of informed opinion (*Foreign Policy Implications of the Energy Crisis,* USGPO, 1972). The Ninety-third Congress, for obvious reasons, concentrated even closer attention on the question of Middle Eastern oil. Committee prints of particular value include *Oil Negotiations, OPEC and the Stability of Supply* and *The United States Oil Shortage and the Arab-Israeli Conflict* (both published by USGPO in 1973 for the House Foreign Affairs Committee); and *Chronology of the Libyan Oil Negotiations, 1970–1971,*

Energy and Foreign Policy, and *The International Petroleum Cartel, the Iranian Consortium and U.S. National Security* (USGPO, for the Senate Foreign Relations Committee, all 1974). The full implications of the energy crisis and the use of oil by the Arab producers as a political instrument have been explored only in a preliminary way, and the reader is thus far dependent for enlightenment on the periodical literature; attention is invited to articles by various specialists in the quarterly *Foreign Affairs,* beginning in 1972.

THE ARABS AND AMERICAN DEFENSE

The first stirrings of United States concern with the Middle East as a factor in the national security are reflected in President Truman's *Memoirs* (New York: Doubleday, 1956) and writings of two of his key cabinet officials: Walter Millis, ed., *The Forrestal Diaries* (New York: Viking, 1951) and Dean Acheson, *Present at the Creation: My Years in the State Department* (New York: W. W. Norton, 1969). The motives behind the American attempts during the 1950s to organize the region's defense are set forth in President Eisenhower's memoirs, *Waging Peace 1956–1961* (Garden City, N.Y.: Doubleday, 1965) and in several biographies of his Secretary of State, among which may be noted Richard Goold-Adams, *John Foster Dulles—A Reappraisal* (New York: Appleton-Century-Crofts, 1962), and the more recent, blisteringly critical *The Devil and John Foster Dulles* of Townsend Hoopes (Boston: Little, Brown, 1973). The most extended analysis of the problem as it was conceived at this period in history is John C. Campbell's *Defense of the Middle East: Problems of American Policy* (New York: Praeger, rev. ed., 1961). A more popular statement is Harry B. Ellis, *Challenge in the Middle East: Communist Influence and American Policy* (New York: Ronald Press, 1960). The Soviet penetration to which the United States was reacting is delineated in Walter Laqueur, *The Struggle for the Middle East* (London: Macmillan, 1969).

THE ARAB-ISRAEL DISPUTE

Completely dispassionate works on the Palestine problem are written only in heaven. Among the infinite number of earthly books Fred J. Khouri, *The Arab-Israeli Dilemma* (Syracuse, N.Y.:

Syracuse University Press, 1968) is as good as any general study through the June War. The Arab case on the basic points at issue is cogently stated by an international lawyer, Henry Cattan, *Palestine, the Arabs and Israel: The Search for Justice* (London: Longmans, Green, 1969). Several aspects of the problem have received special attention. For the question of the Jordan waters Kathryn B. Dogherty's *Jordan Waters Conflict* (New York: Carnegie, 1965) may be recommended as well as Samir N. Saliba, *The Jordan River Dispute* (The Hague: Martinus Nijhoff, 1968), and Edward Rizk, *The River Jordan* (New York: Arab Information Center, 1964), which states the official Arab League position. On the emotionally "loaded" problem of Jerusalem, Evan M. Wilson's *Jerusalem, Key to Peace* (Washington: Middle East Institute, 1970) is a calmly reasoned analysis by an experienced American diplomat. Hisham Sharabi, *Palestine Guerillas: Their Credibility and Effectiveness* (Washington: Georgetown University, 1970) is a brief description of Palestinian activism, while a full-length, valuable study of Palestine nationhood is William B. Quandt, Fuad Jabber, and Ann Mosely Lesch, *The Politics of Palestinian Nationalism* (Berkeley and Los Angeles: University of California Press, 1973).

The Suez War of 1956 is treated in perspective in Hugh Thomas, *The Suez Affair* (New York: Harper & Row, 1967), and Erskine Childers, *The Road to Suez* (London: MacGibbon and Kee, 1962). The apologia of a key figure in the affair, the British Prime Minister, appears in Sir Anthony Eden, *Full Circle* (London: Cassel, 1960), which must be read together with Anthony Nutting, *No End of a Lesson* (New York: Clarkson N. Potter, 1967).

The June War of 1967 has generated a copious literature. Among the many accounts may be mentioned Kennett Love, *Suez: The Twice-Fought War* (New York: McGraw-Hill, 1969), J. Bowyer Bell, *The Long War: Israel and the Arabs since 1946* (Englewood Cliffs, N.J.: Prentice-Hall, 1969), and Walter Laqueur, *The Road to Jerusalem: The Origins of the Arab-Israeli Conflict 1967* (New York: Macmillan, 1968). For United Nations actions during the crisis Arthur Lall, *The UN and the Middle East Crisis, 1967* (New York: Columbia University Press) is particularly useful and well documented. For Arab views of the war see Ibrahim Abu-Lughod, ed., *The Arab-Israeli Confrontation of June 1967: An Arab Perspective* (Evanston, Ill.: Northwestern University Press, 1970).

Thus far only one book-length treatment of the October 1973 War has appeared; Walter Laqueur's *Confrontation: The Middle East and World Politics* (New York: Bantam Books, 1974) shows signs of haste in preparation, but places the events in a global context.

UNITED STATES POLICY

Basic documents on United States relations with the Arab states are included in the standard series of government publications: *American Foreign Policy: Basic Documents 1950–1955* (*Current Documents* after 1956, annually through 1967), *Foreign Relations of the United States,* and the invaluable weekly State Department *Bulletin.* The Council on Foreign Relations annual *The United States in World Affairs* and *Documents on American Foreign Relations* are useful supplements. Several State Department compilations of materials related specifically to the Middle East are indispensable: *The Suez Problem, July 26–September 22, 1956: A Documentary Publication* (Washington: USGPO, 1956), *United States Policy in the Middle East, September 1956–June 1957: Documents* (USGPO, 1957) and, for the June War, *United States Policy in the Near East Crisis* (USGPO, State Department Publication 8269, 1967).

Highly recommended are several recent Congressional committee prints. *The United States Oil Shortage and the Arab-Israeli Conflict* (USGPO, 1973) is the report to the House Foreign Affairs Committee on a study mission to the Middle East conducted by Representative Leo J. Ryan. Two records of hearings on United States policy on the Arab-Israel problem are particularly valuable for presenting the analytical views of academic and other Middle East specialists: Senate Committee on Foreign Relations, *Emergency Military Assistance for Israel and Cambodia* (USGPO, 1973), and House Foreign Affairs Committee, *The Impact of the October Middle East War* (USGPO, 1973).

Two volumes by authors directly involved in United States-Arab relations in official capacities during the 1960s are indispensable: *The American Approach to the Arab World,* by John S. Badeau, former American Ambassador to the United Arab Republic (New York: Harper and Row, 1968), and *The United States and the Arab World* (Cambridge, Mass.: Harvard University Press, rev. ed., 1969), by William R. Polk, who was a member of the State Department's Policy Planning Staff. A number of misconceptions concerning the United States role in the creation of Israel are challenged in Joseph B. Schechtman, *The United States and the Jewish State Movement. The Crucial Decade: 1939–1949* (New York: Herzl Press, 1966), and John Snetsinger, *Truman, the Jewish Vote and the Creation of Israel* (Stanford, Calif.: Hoover Institution, 1974).

The herd instinct being notably strong among writers on the Middle East, much useful material on the Arab States and United States relations with them is contained in compendia by numerous authors. Among the most enlightening may be mentioned Georgiana G. Stevens, ed., *The United States and the Middle East* (Englewood Cliffs, N.J.: Prentice Hall, 1964), J. C. Hurewitz, ed., *Soviet-American Rivalry in the Middle East* (New York: Praeger, 1969), and Willard A. Beling, ed., *The Middle East: Quest for an American Policy* (Albany, N.Y.: State University of New York, 1973).

Index

'Abbūd, Ibrāhīm, 235
Abdül 'Azīz (Ottoman Sultan), 96
Abdül Ḥamīd II, 96
Abdullah ibn Hussein, Amir of Trans-
   jordan 39, King of Jordan, 121, 122,
   130
'Abdullah, Sīdī Muḥammad ibn, Sultan
   of Morocco, 2, 5
'Abduh, Shaikh Muḥammad, 100, 101
Abū Dhabī, 239, 255
Acheson, Dean G., 84, 85, 133
Adams, John, 4
Aden, 49, 180, 188, 238
al-Afghānī, Jamāl al-Dīn, 99-100
Aflaq, Michel, 173, 199
Afro-Asian Solidarity movement, 168-
   169
al-'Ahd, 34, 39
Aḥmad bin Yaḥyā, Imam of Yemen,
   180, 181, 184 fn.
Algeria, Algiers, 3, 5-6, 8, 53, 92, 140,
   175, 195, 208, 213, 263
Allen, George, 139
Allenby, Sir Edmund (Gen.), 30, 35
'Amir, 'Abd al-Ḥakīm, 181
Anderson, Rufus, 16
Arab League, 110, 117, 130-131, 194,
   227, 230, 239
Arab Solidarity Pact, 151
Arab World (defined), viii-xii
'Arafāt, Yāsir, 228-229
Archaeology, 22-24, 47-48
'Arif, 'Abd al-Salām, 199
Armenians, 38, 46, 96

al-Asad, Ḥafiz, 199, 233
Aswan High Dam, 139-140, 142-143
al-'Atāsī, Nūr al-Dīn, 199, 213, 230,
   233
Attlee, Clement, 109

al-Badr, Muhammad, 180, 185
Baghdad Pact (CENTO), 137-138, 167
Bahrain, 64-65, 239, 255
Bainbridge, William (Capt.), 7
Balfour Declaration, 32, 36, 44-45,
   U.S. attitude, 45-46
Bandung Conference (1955), 167, 168
Barbary States, 2-8
Barclay, Thomas, 5, 6
Ba'th Party, 151-152, 152-153, 173-
   174, 199
Begin, Menahim, 207
Belgrade Conference of Nonaligned
   Nations (1961), 167
Ben Bella, Aḥmad, 169, 175, 195
Ben Gurion, David, 109, 123
Berbers, xi, 2
Bevin, Ernest, 110
al-Bizrī, 'Afīf (Gen.), 152
Bliss, Daniel, 18
Bliss, Howard A., 35
Boumedienne, Houari, 213
Brandeis, Louis D., 43, 45
Breasted, James H., 23
Brezhnev, Leonid, 249, 251, 252, 270
Bunche, Ralph, 119, 193
Bunker, Ellsworth, 185
al-Bustānī, Buṭrus, 19

293